Packed with astute observation and insightfully dr[illegible] on sociological theory, *Religion and Change in Australia* pro[illegible] anal-ysis of the state of religion in modern Australia. [illegible] peoples' religion changed since European invas[illegible] influence current Australian politics? Did H[illegible] crease in witchcraft? Whatever your quest[illegible] plex concepts both readable and entertair[illegible]

Marion Ma[illegible] *Sciences,* [illegible] *, Australia*

This much-needed volume is a *tour de* [illegible] to become a classic source for information and underst[illegible] the evolution of religion in Australia. It is thoroughly grounded [illegible] evant sociological theory and also full of detailed descriptive material that contributes to the theoretical analyses the authors present. The volume is a must-read for anyone interested in Australia's religious history, but also should be viewed as an important commentary on the evolution of religion in all Western societies.

James T. Richardson, *Professor Emeritus of Sociology & Judicial Studies, University of Nevada, Reno, USA*

Religion and Change in Australia

This timely book offers a panoramic overview of the enduring significance of religion in late modern Australian society. Applying sociological perspectives and contemporary theories of religion in society, it challenges conventional assumptions around the extent of secularisation in Australia and instead argues that religious institutions, groups, and individuals have proved remarkably adaptable to social change and continue to play a major role in Australian life. In doing so, it explores how religion intersects with a wide range of other contemporary issues, including politics, race, migration, gender, and new media.

Religion and Change in Australia explores Australia's unique history regarding religion. Christianity was originally imported as a tool of social control to keep convicts, settlers, and Australian Aboriginal peoples in check. This had a profound impact on the social memory of the nation, and lingering resentment towards the "excessive" presence of religion continues to be felt today. Freedom of religion was enshrined in Section 116 of the Australian Constitution in 1901. Nevertheless, the White Australia policy effectively prevented adherents of non-Christian faiths from migrating to Australia and the nation remained overwhelmingly Christian. However, after WWII, Australia, in common with other Western societies, appears to have become increasingly secularised, as religious observance declined dramatically.

However, *Religion and Change in Australia* employs a range of social theories to challenge this secularist view and argues that Australia is a post-secular society. The 2016 census revealed that over half of the population still identify as Christian. In politics, the socially conservative religious right has come to exert considerable influence on the ruling Liberal-National Coalition, particularly under John Howard and Scott Morrison. New technologies, such as the Internet and social media, have provided new avenues for religious expression and proselytisation, whilst so-called "megachurches" have been built to cater to their increasing congregations. The adoption of multiculturalism and increased immigration from Asia has led to a religiously pluralist society, though this has often been controversial. In particular, the position of Islam in Australia has been the subject of fierce debate, and Islamophobic attitudes remain common. Atheism, non-belief, and alternative spiritualities have also become increasingly widespread, especially amongst the young.

Religion and Change in Australia analyses these developments to offer new perspectives on religion and its continued relevance within Australian society. This book is therefore a vital resource for students, academics, and general readers seeking to understand contemporary debates surrounding religion and secularisation in Australia.

Adam Possamai is Professor of Sociology and Deputy Dean at the School of Social Sciences, Western Sydney University, Australia. He is the author and editor of more than a dozen academic books, 5 novels, and close to 100 refereed articles and book chapters. He is a past president of the International Sociological Association's Committee 22 on the Sociology of Religion and of the Australian Association for the Study of Religion. He has been a visiting professor at the City University of New York and the École des Hautes Études en Sciences Sociales in Paris. His latest books are the *Sage Encyclopedia of the Sociology of Religion* (edited with Anthony Blasi, Sage, 2020), *The Social Scientific Study of Exorcism in Christianity* (edited with Giuseppe Giordan, Springer, 2020), *The i-zation of Society, Religion, and Neoliberal Post-Secularism* (Palgrave Macmillan, 2018), *Sociology of Exorcism in Late Modernity* (with Giuseppe Giordan, Palgrave Macmillan, 2018), and the short stories collection *Perles Noires* (Rivière Blanche, 2021).

David Tittensor is a Lecturer in Studies of Religion in the School of Humanities and Social Sciences at Deakin University, Melbourne, Australia. His research interests are Muslim movements, Turkish politics and society, and religion and development with a focus on Islam. He is the author of *The House of Service: The Gülen Movement and Islam's Third Way* (Oxford University Press, 2014), co-editor (with Matthew Clarke) of *Islam and Development: Exploring the Invisible Aid Economy* (Routledge, 2014), co-editor (with Fethi Mansouri) of *The Politics of Women and Migration in the Global South* (Palgrave, 2017), and series editor for *Muslims in Global Societies* (Springer).

Religion and Change in Australia

Adam Possamai and David Tittensor

Routledge
Taylor & Francis Group
LONDON AND NEW YORK

Cover image: Top left and middle right: by street artist Adnate; middle left: © David Tittensor; top right and bottom left: Mark Stevens, courtesty of the City of Sydney Archives; bottom right: © RS Crew.

First published 2022
by Routledge
4 Park Square, Milton Park, Abingdon, Oxon OX14 4RN

and by Routledge
605 Third Avenue, New York, NY 10158

Routledge is an imprint of the Taylor & Francis Group, an Informa business

British Library Cataloguing-in-Publication Data
A catalogue record for this book is available from the British Library

Library of Congress Cataloging-in-Publication Data
Names: Possamai, Adam, author. | Tittensor, David, author.
Title: Religion and change in Australia / Adam Possamai and David Tittensor.
Description: Abingdon, Oxon; New York: Routledge, 2022. |
Includes bibliographical references and index. |
Identifiers: LCCN 2021037733 (print) | LCCN 2021037734 (ebook) |
ISBN 9781760295837 (hardback) | ISBN 9781032186030 (paperback) |
ISBN 9781003255338 (ebook)
Subjects: LCSH: Australia—Religion. | Religion and sociology—Australia.
Classification: LCC BL2610 .P68 2022 (print) | LCC BL2610 (ebook) |
DDC 200.994—dc23
LC record available at https://lccn.loc.gov/2021037733
LC ebook record available at https://lccn.loc.gov/2021037734

ISBN: 9781760295837 (hbk)
ISBN: 9781032186030 (pbk)
ISBN: 9781003255338 (ebk)

DOI: 10.4324/9781003255338

Typeset in Bembo
by codeMantra

We would like to thank the Religion and Society Research Strand and the School of Social Sciences at Western Sydney University for their support for this book. We would also like to thank Lisa Lewis who provided some assistance with this manuscript and Awais Piracha who designed the maps in Chapter 5.

Contents

Figures

Tables

Acknowledgements

Three chapters of this book contain reworked and updated sections of various earlier publications. These are listed below. We would like to thank their publishers.

Chapter 2 contains reworked and updated material from sections of:

Possamai, A. 2007. 'Secularisation' and 'Religion' as Zombie Categories? *The Australian Religion Studies Review 20*(2): 233–242.

Possamai, A. 2017. Post-Secularism in Multiple Modernities. *Journal of Sociology 53*(4): 822–835.

Chapter 6 contains reworked and updated material from sections of:

Cox, J. and Possamai A. 2016. Religion, Cultural Hybridity and Chains of Memory. In J. Cox and A. Possamai eds. *Religion and Non-Religion among Australian Aboriginal People.* Ashgate, Aldershot, pp. 179–204.

Onnudottir, H., Possamai, A. and Turner, B. 2013. *Religious Change and Indigenous Peoples: The Making of Religious Identities.* Aldershot: Ashgate.

Chapter 12 contains reworked and updated material from sections of:

Possamai, A. 2008. Australia's 'Shy' De-secularisation Process. In Imtoual, A. and Spaler, B. eds. *Religion, Spirituality & Social Science.* Bristol: Policy Press, pp. 23–35.

Possamai, A. 2018. *The i-zation of Society, Religion, and Neoliberal Post-Secularism.* Basingstoke: Palgrave McMillan.

Possamai, A. and Possamai-Inesedy, A. 2021. Freedom for and from religions in Australia. Beyond Post-Secularism? *Social Compass 68*(3): 359-374

1 Introduction

Australia has a unique history when it comes to dealing with religion. It started with the arrival of Indigenous peoples at least 45,000–50,000 years ago when the now dusty landscape was a fertile lake system, making them the oldest living communities in the world (Griffiths et al., 2017). Much later, with the first fleet in Sydney in the 18th century, Christianity was imported as a tool of social control to keep convicts and other peoples in check. This had such a strong impact on the social memory of this country that resentment towards the "excessive" presence of religion is still felt today. At the same time, the religion of Australian Aboriginal peoples was seen as so elementary, and it was assumed that it would not survive the civilising process that the country was going through. The Indigenous peoples were hunter-gatherers, and as they were not harvesting, their religion, contrary to that of the Maori in New Zealand for example, was seen as so inferior that the land was regarded as uninhabited. Further, while colonial expansion generally had a devastating effect on the local populations, Australia was among the worst hit. It was the only territory in the Commonwealth to be considered *terra nullius*; that is, the land was deemed to belong to no one. This approach was underpinned by a social Darwinist understanding of religion. If only the religion of the Australian Aboriginal peoples had been given more credence at the time, not only would their history had been different, but also the whole conception about the so-called disappearance of religion, that is secularisation, could have taken a radical turn (see Chapter 6).

Yet, while the pre-white settlement of this country was disregarded, tension between Catholics, Anglicans, and other Protestant groups was so problematic at the time Australia became a nation that it led to a specific type of secularism in 1901. Secularism can mean different things in different contexts. The hard line supports the complete disappearance of religion from both the public and the private spheres. A softer

DOI: 10.4324/9781003255338-1

line only expects religion not to be part of the public sphere. With the latter view on secularism, it means that religion can still be practised, but that it should remain a private matter, something to speak about within the family, and certainly not in parliament. In the Australian setting, it took a specific meaning, that of minimising conflicts between Christian subgroups. Australia was at the time of federalism a Christian country, but even if the Anglicans were the most numerous, they were not dominant. Indeed, by the middle of the 19th century, the Anglican Church was brought into the fold and subject to disestablishment along with the others. For example, when the British Prime Minister Gladstone took a personal interest in the endowing of Australian bishoprics in Australia in 1846, he received a pragmatic response from the Colonial Undersecretary Lord Lyttleton:

> I do not not know what is the principle of the existing New South Wales Church Extension Law. There are two Established Churches in Gt. Britain. Their claims, therefore rest upon a clear foundation. But why one kind of dissent should be preferred to another–a Roman Catholic to a Baptist–or a Methodist to an Independent seems, in theory, unintelligible. The simple fact is that the Four most numerous and powerful Christian societies have divided the whole endowment among them, not because they had a better right than others, but because it was the method of obtaining the greatest amount of general satisfaction, with the least alloy of particular discontent.
>
> (as cited in Carey, 1996: 10)

In other words, the colonial period and the policy of secular egalitarianism developed amongst administrators were supportive of all the Christian denominations and precluded the formation of a state church (see Chapter 3).

Subsequently, the desire for politicians from the various states of Australia, who were getting together to form a new nation, was not to create a church state (that is, having a religion closely linked to a nation, e.g. Anglicans in the UK or Catholics today in Poland). However, if people today called themselves Christians without referring to any denomination, the case was quite different in those times. Catholics were loyal to the Pope, Anglicans to the Queen of England, Methodist and Presbyterian to English and Scottish puritanism, and Lutheranism to Germany. No one could speak on behalf of all Christians.

Race also formed a crucial part of early settler colonial identity. Christians of that time were seen as white people, and people from other faiths were generally perceived to be non-white. Indeed, upon Federation, the very first act of the parliament was the introduction of the White Australia policy via the *Immigration Restriction Act* of 1901, which created major barriers to any further immigration for those adhering to a different faith, such as Islam, Hinduism, and Buddhism. Migrants already settled, such as the Afghan cameleers and the Chinese gold diggers, could remain, but no more could migrate (see Curthoys, 2003; Scriver, 2004). However, since WWII, the religious landscape has changed as we are today less Christian than at the time of Federation, but we are still impacted by these early events. Australia has kept a strong Christian social memory – a point we will come back to later in the book (see Chapter 5).

The social history of religion in the US was quite different. Many religious groups left Europe to find freedom in a new land. Protestants, such as the Huguenots from Catholic France, or Catholic Irish from Anglican UK, were seeking a place to believe without fear of persecution. In this case, freedom was for religion. In Continental Europe, pushed by the excess of various religious governments against other religions (e.g. the massacre of Saint Barthelemy in 14th-century Paris where Catholics from the ultra-Conservative wing of the *Ligue* went down the streets to kill anyone dressed in black, as this was the uniform of the French Protestants), many thinkers (e.g. Voltaire) and atheist groups were contesting various damaging superstitions, and the abuse of power (e.g. Inquisition and burning of so-called witches), freedom, as it was understood, was more from religion than for religion.

In Australia, however, we are faced with a hybrid case. We have both a freedom for and from religion. Before the advent of multiculturalism, many religious groups left Europe for Australia to seek a land of freedom where they could practise their faith without fear of retribution, but as long as they were Christian. But along these lines, religion, as mentioned above, was used to control the population. This came from England at a time when industrialisation was gaining momentum and was creating new social inequalities. As new machines were created to harvest in rural areas, people had problems in finding a job. Through a rural exodus, they moved to the cities to find work in the newly created factories, but not everyone was successful. Some of these unfortunate men and women resorted to crime, sometimes serious, and other times petty, and many were put into overcrowded gaols. As the social sciences were developing to help government to control populations (e.g. Bentham's panopticon), religion was asked to become involved to "civilise" these new criminals. If they could pray and believe in God in an orderly way, they would not commit crimes but become docile.

This thinking followed the convicts from these overcrowded gaols as they were coming to Australia. If the religious landscape of England was built on the mixed mythologies of paganism and Christianity with King Arthur, on the crusade of Richard the Lionheart to bring Christianity to Jerusalem, on Henry the Eighth separating from the Vatican and its Italian bankers, on Cromwell bringing Christian puritanism in power, and so on and so forth, in Australia, it was imported to control and civilise its population.

Indeed, since the first white settlements there is a distrust in the Australian social memory when it comes to religion having any authority. This is part of the Australian spirit, wherein one has a disdain for any form of elitism and authoritarianism that could force working-class people to go against their will. In this history, religions, especially Christians before WWII, were welcome as long as they were not trying to dominate the country. Today, there is still a welcoming of religion, and it includes non-Christian ones, but none of them should be able to lead the country. As religions are free to settle, people are free from being controlled by them. However, with the proposed contemporary Religious Discrimination Bill, the way we understand religion in Australia between freedom of religion and freedom from religion may be subject to change (see Chapter 12).

Given this, it is often believed that religion disappeared at one stage in the history of our societies but reappeared at the end of the 20th century. However, religion never drifted away, it simply altered. Religion is a lived experience, and life experiences change as society and culture change. Today, we live in multifaith societies where less and less people attend religious ceremonies, but these might nevertheless still believe in something, even if not always based in theology. The time when people felt obliged to attend a religious service because of a sense of obligation or duty has largely passed. Rather, in the current age, people attend such ceremonies only if it is of interest to them. As a result of this decline of bricks-and-mortar religion, religious figures are resorting to new media platforms to spread their message and create virtual communities. More and more religious leaders and spokespeople are actively engaged in public discourses to send their messages. In particular, religious community leaders have taken to social media with gusto, microblogging sermons and live streaming events to allow people to engage in digital "collective effervescence." In doing so, many have become what has been dubbed "pastor-preneurs" through their carefully curated personas on Twitter and Instagram, wherein the line between religious leader and celebrity has been blurred (see Burroughs, 2013; Cheong, 2016; see also Chapter 10). This does not mean that more people are religious, but that religious people are more vocal than they were in the past. This is reflected in the current proportion of politicians in the Australian federal parliament who have a Christian confession, which cuts against the ever-increasing secularisation of the wider polity (see Chapter 11).

This disjuncture can sometimes create difficulties. For many people, religious issues can be lost in translation when the attendant vocabulary used in the public sphere is received by those who are not versed in scripture. For Davie (2017), this leads to a poor standard of public debate, as there is a lack of constructive engagement.

As with other social and cultural aspects of life, religion is in a constant state of flux, and the case of Australia is no exception. Religious institutions, groups, and individuals either adapt themselves to changes in our society or react to them. As religions are part and parcel of consumer culture, many spiritual activities have moved – as Mara Einstein (2007) has argued in her work on the branding of religion – from pews to pixels. Social media has given a new pathway for religion to be expressed and to grow. We now have religious groups that design apps for mobile devices to help Muslims pray on time and in the correct direction, Spell Books for witches to record their ritual experiences, a confession booth to help Catholics deal with their sins, and digitalised Bibles. The latter can be used by churchgoers to check if the reading of the priest is correct by following the speeches using keywords on the device, to help busy people to read the important verses before a Bible class after work and before picking up the kids, or by atheists who want to prove to some evangelicals their misreading of the holy book (Possamai, 2018).

Alongside these technological and cultural changes, the population in Australia is increasing and suburbs are expanding. Religious groups follow these developments with new religious buildings, often in industrial parks; emblematic of this development is the purchase of the iconic music venue Festival Hall in the city of Melbourne by Hillsong Church for $23 million (Boseley, 2020). Religion has also become more vocal in the public sphere to the point that we speak about Australia as a post-secular society, that is, a society in which the religious and non-religious are engaged with each other outside of the private sphere. However, the question that confronts us is how post-secular is Australia? For example, while interfaith issues are publicly celebrated, same-sex marriage (see Chapters 11 and 12) and the application of *Shari'a* are difficult topics of discussion (see below and Chapter 5). People, when speaking about such matters, often fail to engage in the type of communicative action (one based on building constructive dialogue) that the German philosopher Habermas (1984) argues to be necessary for a successful post-secular society (see Chapter 12).

Given this tension, this book takes the temperature of the times with regard to religion and society in Australia. It not only brings to the reader understanding of both classical and new social theories on religion, but also proposes new angles to grasp current changes. Further, although the book covers up-to-date current research on census data, it also presents new findings on, for example, contemporary religion and Indigenous Australians.

Davie (2017: 94) argues that policymakers should be more religiously literate to be able to take on board the sensibilities of religious people, and likewise those with a religious interest should be "policy" literate to be able to be heard and understood. This book aims to help people engage in such public debates and understand what religion is today. It is focused in Australia and is designed for readers to follow social and cultural issues created by, or impacted on, religious groups. It is a social scientific book aimed at a wider audience. It is written with not only the Generation Z in mind who tend to have lower levels of religious literacy (see Halafoff et al., 2020), but also the older generations who would want to fill some gaps in their years of knowledge, be it gained from a university or from general interest.

Is religion still important in Australia?

In a demographic study, the Pew Research Centre (2017) analysed the future of world religions by working on population growth projections through to 2060. One of the key findings was that the world is not likely to be less religious. Taking into account that the world's total population is expected to rise to 9.6 billion, even if the number of atheists, agnostics, and other people who do not affiliate with a religion will likely grow in some countries in the northern hemisphere, its proportion will decline (from 16.0% in 2015 to 12.5% in 2060). The global Buddhist population will remain roughly the same size in terms of numbers but will lower in terms of percentage (from 6.9% in 2015 to 4.8% in 2060), the Hindu population will drop marginally (from 15.1% in 2015 to 14.5% in 2060), while the Jewish population will remain the same at 0.2%. The Christians will have a marginal increase from 31.2% to 31.8%, while the Muslim global population will grow steadily and will edge close to parity with Christianity (from 24.1% in 2015 to 31.1% in 2060). It is thus estimated that the numbers of Muslims in the world will roughly equate that of Christians in 40 years from now. To maintain parity in a growing world population, the number of Christians will increase, but mainly in sub-Sahara Africa where four out of every ten Christians will live. India will remain a Hindu majority, but the increase of its Muslim population will be so significant that, in this projection, it will become the country with the largest Muslim population, surpassing Indonesia. But what of Australia? In line with these global estimations from 2015, current predictions have shown a decline of Christians from 67.3% in 2010 to 47% in 2050, and an increase of those professing no religion from 24.2% to 40.4% and of Islam from 2.4% to 4.9% (Pew-Templeton, 2016; see also Chapter 5 for a more detailed analysis). In other words, the growth of religion will happen around Australia but not within. However, as we will explore in Chapters 11 and 12, this does not mean that they are not active in the public sphere and influential.

While the above focused on population growth, the Pew Research Centre (2018) released another report on the age gap in religion around the world. This can provide further understanding of the Australian case. They found that overall in the world, 88% of their sample of more than 100 countries were affiliated with a religion, and 54% claim that religion is very important to them. In Australia, only 57% of people are affiliated with a religion and only 18% claim that this is very important. Among the Australian adults younger than 40 years of age, only 43% claim to be affiliated with a religion, and the number goes up for the adults older than 40 years, to 66%. As with many secularised countries in the world, religion is less important for the younger generations in Australia (see Chapter 5). Again, religion is growing in the world, but not in Australia, and it seems to be something of a concern to the older generation.

However, having someone state that religion is not important does not mean that there is no interest. What of people who say they are spiritual but not religious? By spiritual, they might mean that though they are not connected to a specific group, they think that there is something out there that makes sense to them, but at the same time would rather not have to deal with an authority. They are also interested in some eclectic beliefs (e.g. mixing meditation, astrology, Sufi music, and Christian prayers), which would be difficult to deal with for some religious professionals who want to keep their scriptures untouched by anything not included in their credo.

Of course, interpretation of what people say when they are religious depends on what they understand to be a religion. Is it their religion only? Is it a specific credo? Is it a set of beliefs (e.g. in God) that can be shared by distinct religious groups (e.g. Abrahamic groups)? In sociology, we refer to this as the substantive understanding of religion; that is, what people say religion is. In our multifaith world, it is impossible to encapsulate all beliefs into a clear and universal definition because not all religions have a god, a hell, or include the notion of sin (Possamai, 2009). In another approach, sociologists use a functionalist understanding of religion; that is, what it does for people or groups. Karl Marx (1818–1883) had a negative view in the 19th century and thought that religion in Europe was used by the upper classes to control and take advantage of the working class. Later, the famous French scholar Durkheim (1858–1917) claimed in the 19th century that religions helped to keep a community together through the sharing and transmission of values and morals (see Chapter 6). He thought of this as a positive thing, but observed that less and less people were attending churches and that religious people were clearly losing their authority in the political sphere. Science was developing, cities were growing, and education became more democratic – all reasons that were speculated to lead to secularisation. Subsequently, he wrote about a substitute: civil religion.

This "non-religious" religion makes reference to all the values and morals promoted by the nation that help people feel part of the same community. Think about Australian Day and the flags and symbols that are promoted by people who celebrate the anniversary of the arrival of the First Fleet. It is also a contested day by Indigenous peoples and their supporters who consider this day to be Invasion Day. Civil religion in Australia is also present with the veneration of the ANZACs, which is almost a sacral entity. Those who celebrate it in Australia venerate symbols associated with the nation, and the spirit of sacrifice to the nation as lived by soldiers during war. It is also celebrated alongside the gambling game of two-up and drinking alcohol. Fallon (2017) finds in her survey that in contrast to people celebrating this in public, some are more passive, and while they desire to interact with the ANZAC mythos, they do this in a quieter and more solemn commemoration. On the other hand, some of her respondents are in conflict with the androcentric and predominantly white history of WWI, which often omits women, Indigenous Australians, and Australian immigrants. They contest this nationalistic pride while still acknowledging the sacrifice of these soldiers at a time of war. However, it is important to note that this contestation has it limits. Reflective of this was the vitriol with which Yassmin Abdel Magied was subjected to when she was seen to have besmirched the honour of those that had fallen, when she wrote a private Facebook post on ANZAC Day that stated "LEST. WE. FORGET. (Manus, Nauru, Syria, Palestine …)." Yassmin, a Sudanese refugee who had come to Australia at the age of 18 months, who also happens to be a Muslim woman, was attacked by both politicians and the media – an attack that ultimately caused her to lose her job at the ABC and relocate to the UK (Fyfe, 2017; Gilmore, 2017). In this sense, just like how not all people are engaged in religion, not everyone is involved in civil religion. However, this substitute civil religion does not involve any supernatural elements and does not deal with the afterlife (see Chapter 3).

Secularisation and civil religion notwithstanding, religion in Australia will not disappear. Rather, it still has many intensities and aspects that we will cover in this book. For the time being, it suffices to state that the issue is complex and diverse. As a reader, you might have a preconceived idea, and we are not here to challenge you. You might also have a knowledge gap and may be expecting us to provide you with all the answers. Unfortunately, we cannot, even if we wish we could. This book will broaden your understanding of religion and will generate in you more questions than answers. Further, just to make this clear, this book is not about making religious people more or less religious, nor about making those without faith religious or trying to promote atheism. This book only seeks to present the current social reality of religion in Australia, and includes, in terms of social cohesion, the success and failures of this country. However, instead of social cohesion, we would rather use the term "deep equality" (Beaman, 2017). It is understood here as an alternative to social cohesion, (a term seen as problematic in Australia (see Ezzy et al., 2020), as the former is more focused on the day-to-day interaction rather than on policies and legislation. The social policies that pursue social cohesion can sometimes aim at the status quo and protect existing structure and privilege certain groups, rather than aim at social change leading to more full engagement with diversity. "Deep equality" is about respect, a recognition of similarity, and an acceptance of difference in one's community.

Freedom of religion versus freedom of speech

One such area that poses a challenge to this "deep equality" is the pursuit of freedom of speech in relation to one's faith. Can we say anything we want about religion? Of course, yes. Can we say it in whatever way? No, of course not. We touched on the difference between freedom of religion and freedom from religion above, but we also have freedom of speech. But how do we understand speech? Can we say anything without caring about offending people? Freedom of speech is crucial and is the basis of democracy. We should indeed be able to contest certain religious approaches that we find in the Bible, such as comments against homosexuals, but not to the point where one denigrates the religion. Similarly, people should also be able to discuss child abuse by religious professionals without being attacked for being anti-religious. Discussions about taxes and why religions should stop avoiding paying them if they do not do charity work should also be part of a constructive dialogue (we will come back to this with Habermas' notion of communicative action in Chapter 2). However, the way we speak about religion should not be free. Indeed, social media allow people behind their keyboard to make hurtful comments. As an example, Hussain and Possamai (2013) found in their research on *Shari'a* that there were many hurtful comments made against Islam in general. *Shari'a*, however, is a misunderstood concept. There has been much political consternation about the potential practice and implementation of *Shari'a* in Western liberal democracies (see Berger, 2013; Possamai et al., 2015). This anxiety has been driven by the perception that any official recognition or accommodation of *Shari'a* within secular legal systems poses a threat to liberal democratic values, the separation of church and state, and the rule of law. However, as Abdullah Saeed (2006: 43) notes:

> Shari'a represents the divine guidance contained in the revelation communicated to the Prophet through the Qur'an and further illuminated in his sayings and deeds (Sunna). In the context of Islamic law, shari'a refers to the totality of this guidance contained in the Qur'an and Sunna and generally expressed in their commands and prohibitions.

As we will further explore in Chapter 5, the practice of Islam and the *Shari'a* are hence inextricable from one another and feature in the everyday life of Muslims, cutting across social, cultural, legal, and economic practices (Possamai et al., 2013). It is a lived experience for Muslims, and they marry using *Shari'a* law the same way, for example, that Catholics get married following canon law.

Further, as Muslims in Australia are not interested in using corporal punishment (see Dagistanli et al., 2018), Christians are not interested either in returning to the time of the Inquisition. But people feel it is also difficult to say anything about Islam for fear of retribution. The recent attack on *Charlie Hebdo* is a case in point. The point of this magazine, amongst others, was to comment with a satirical spirit of contest on anything and defend freedom of speech. This spirit grew out of this freedom from religion outlined above. Religious institutions in France were not necessarily acting for the good of the people and were hiding behind the legitimacy of their religion and godly message. Humour was used to discredit the dominant religion (and of course other non-religious politicians). But humour there had a purpose against the powerful. However, in this example, some cartoons were offensive to Muslims (and even non-Muslims) because of the way they depicted their Prophet Muhammad. Freedom of speech is again crucial in our world, but as Davie (2017: 64) notes, there is a difference between the right to offend and the moral duty not to, and there is also a responsibility to use free speech to help debate constructively, raise social and cultural issues, but not to attack minority groups that are struggling in their social mobility and/or well-being.

Todd (2015), in his assessment of the situation in France after the *Charlie Hebdo* attacks, stresses the decrease in France's influence in the world, the vacuum left by the collapse of communism (see Michel, 2011), and the increase in inequalities tied to globalisation. This void creates a sense of anomie, and for Todd (2015), religion tends to express an aspiration towards equality. This is the reason that we have young people returning to their religion of origin, Islam, and even Catholics or secular people converting to Islam, and also, at the same time, rising Islamophobia (see Chapter 5). An increasing number of people are using Islam as a scapegoat in a "society that no longer knows what to do with its lack of belief and no longer knows whether it has faith in equality or inequality" (Todd, 2015: 188–189). These challenges are also currently at play in Australia, with the Muslim community feeling unfairly targeted in the post-9/11 era (Tittensor et al., 2020).

Given these types of challenges, this book is written to help the reader understand many of the social and cultural issues with regard to religion in Australia. Alongside this, it also seeks to provide some grounding in understanding religion and equip the non-religious educated reader to build constructive debates. These can be difficult and controversial, but they should not be offensive for the sake of it, even if one feels justified in the name of his or her religion, or in the name of atheism.

Structure of the book

In Chapter 2, "Contemporary theories of religion in society," we introduce some key concepts and theories that provide general analytical scaffold for many of the discussions that follow. It describes how the world and our perception of religion has changed over time and how we need new tools of analysis to make sense of our social environment. While the birth of the social sciences on religion was focused on the disappearance of religion (i.e. the secularisation thesis), the situation today is very different and in need of new understandings. This chapter therefore unpacks the concepts of "post-secularism" and "multiple modernities" and then argues that while Australia has many similarities with other Western countries, it is also different, especially with regard to its position towards religion. This lays the foundation of this book in terms of understanding Australia's specific approach to religion.

The following two chapters cover the history of religion in Australia before (Chapter 3, "A short history of religion in Australia before WWII") and after WWII (Chapter 4, "Post-WWII migration to Australia: from being Christian to religiously plural"). The post-war years have greatly changed the religious landscape of Australia after being for two centuries almost a mono-religious Christian country. Non-Christian religions and new religious movements have indeed come to Australia to increase its diversity. Further, in our multicultural society, the non-religious are also growing. This is addressed in Chapter 5, "Australia as a Christian, a post-Christian, and a non-religious country," by analysing the most recent census results and by claiming that, today, Australia is paradoxically at the same time, Christian, post-Christian, and non-religious. By post-Christianity, we make reference to a situation in which Christianity is no longer the dominant religion and has become one religion among other non-Christian ones. This chapter also covers current topics dealing with Christianity (the new Christianity), post-Christianity (Islamophobia), and the non-religion among Generation Z.

Chapter 6, "Australian Aboriginal peoples and contemporary religion," further unpacks some census data to explore the contemporary religious composition of Australian Aboriginal peoples to argue that they are as diverse in terms of religion as the whole country. It also comes back to the theory of secularism, which Chapter 2 has critiqued, to present a missed opportunity in the history of social theory. Indeed, if the writings of a missionary had been given more attention than the works of self-styled anthropologist in the late 19th century in Central Australia, our whole perspective on religion in society could have been quite different.

Following this chapter and its discovery that an Indigenous person in Australia is more likely to claim to be from a non-religious background than a non-Indigenous person, Chapter 7, "Non-belief: 'religious nones', atheists and the spiritual but not religious", concentrates on what it means to be an atheist or a non-religious person in Australia. It uncovers an array of perspectives as to what it means to be non-religious, a category often used by spiritual people to define themselves in the census.

Chapter 8, "Alternative spiritualities, ecology, and individualism", focuses on the more individualised religions and discusses the notion of spirituality. This includes an exploration of the interest in ecology. While this has been a slow development and is far from being a revolution (as some have claimed), there has been a growing interest in spirituality in recent times. The tendency towards eclecticism is strong for those drawn to spiritualities outside of religion to the point that we now face a new variation, one that incorporates popular culture in its paradigm, namely hyper-real religions.

Another point of difference amongst both the religious and the spiritual and the way they engage with their beliefs is gender. Given this difference, often referred to as the "gender gap", Chapter 9, "Feminised religion and the patriarchy", focuses on this dimension among the Abrahamic faiths and underlines the persistent patriarchal structure of religions in Australia despite all social and cultural advancements towards gender equity outside of religious institutions. It also uses the Pentecostal Hillsong Church as a case study to highlight that even as it adapts itself to a changing world, is deeply engaged with new technology (see Chapter 10), and has a high level of female involvement, it still remains patriarchal.

Indeed, Hillsong's adaptive capacity highlights that religions rarely withdraw from society. Rather, they often adjust with the spirit of the times. This is the case when using social media as explored in Chapter 10, "Religion and new media". While some religious groups are savvier than others in taking their faith outside of their brick-and-mortar structures, they are all using new technologies to send their message. Religion is no longer limited by traditional print and film technologies. Now with the advent of the Web 2.0 and social media platforms, their content can be accessed by anyone via a smart device in real time. This chapter uses Pentecostalism in Australia as a case study of this phenomenon.

Overarching all these religious changes in Australia is the federal government, which, in recent times, has overseen an ever-increasing intersection between religion and politics. Driving this change is a solid religious minority in both major parties that are seemingly at odds with an increasing secularised polity. In particular, these cohorts have been active in bringing back Christian values to the political sphere, while still promoting multiculturalism. This has been profoundly marked with the freedom of religion debate in which we have observed a recent shift, from a push to practise freely one's religion to one allowing religious groups to discriminate against other while bypassing human rights. Chapter 11, "Politics and religion: the use and abuse of faith", explores the recent shift in politics in Australia towards this neo-Christian push in a post-Christian country.

Chapter 12, "Conclusion: Australia as a post-secular society?", brings together the many elements explored in this book to understand the religious specificities of this country and is the conclusion to this book. It analyses the de-secularisation process at three levels – the macro, the meso, and the micro – to argue that while Australia is multicultural, multi-faith, spiritual, and non-religious at the micro level, the further we move to the macro level, the more it is Christian. It highlights that the legalisation of same-sex marriage in 2017 has been a catalyst for Australia at the macro level to become less post-secularist.

References

Beaman, L.G. 2017. *Deep equality in an era of religious diversity*. Oxford: Oxford University Press.

Berger, M. 2013. *Applying shari'a in the West: facts, fears and the future of Islamic rules on family relations in the West*. Leiden University Press.

Boseley, M. 2020. From faith no more to faith healing: melbourne's festival hall sold to Hillsong Church. *The Guardian*. https://www.theguardian.com/world/2020/oct/26/from-faith-no-more-to-faith-healing-melbournes-festival-hall-sold-to-hillsong-church (25.05.2021)

Burroughs, B. 2013. 'And I'm a (Social Media) Mormon: digital ritual, techno-faith, and religious transmedia. *Qwerty-Open and Interdisciplinary Journal of Technology, Culture and Education*, *8*(2): 71–81.

Carey, H.M. 1996. *Believing in Australia: a cultural history of religions*. Sydney: Allen & Unwin.

Cheong, P.H. 2016. Religious authority and social media branding in a culture of religious celebrification. In Hoover, S. ed. *The media and religious authority*. Pennsylvania State Unviersity Press, pp. 81–104.

Curthoys, A. 2003. Liberalism and exclusionism: a prehistory of the white Australia policy. In Jayasuriya, L., Walker, D. and Gothard, J. eds. *Legacies of White Australia: race, culture and nation*. Crawley: University of Western Australia Press, pp. 8–32.

Dagistanli, S., Possamai, A., Turner, B., Voyce, M. and Roose, J. 2018. The limits of multiculturalism in Australia?: The Shari'a flogging case of R v. Raad, Fayed, Cifci and Coskun. *The Sociological Review, 66*(6): 1258–1275.

Davie, G. 2017. *Religion in public life: levelling the ground.* London: Theos.

Einstein, M. 2007. *Brands of faith: marketing religion in a commercial age.* New York: Routledge.

Ezzy, D., Bouma, G., Barton, G., Halafoff, A., Banham, R., Jackson, R. and Beaman, L. 2020. Religious diversity in Australia: rethinking social cohesion. *Religions, 11*(2) https://doi.org/10.3390/rel11020092

Fallon, B. 2017. Anzac civil religion? A survey of the Australian public on their interaction with Anzac. *Journal for the Academic Study of Religion, 30*(2): 144–164.

Fyfe, M. 2017. Yassmin Abdel-Magieb on becoming 'Australia's most publicly hated Muslim.' *SMH Good Weekend, 18.* https://www.smh.com.au/lifestyle/yassmin-abdelmagied-on-becoming-australias-most-publicly-hated-muslim-20170816-gxxb7d.html

Gilmore, J. 2017. Hysteria over Yassmin Abdel-Magied's Anzac Day post cannot be separated from racism. *Sydney Morning Herald.* https://www.smh.com.au/lifestyle/hysteria-over-yassmin-abdelmagieds-anzac-day-post-cannot-be-separated-from-racism-20170427-gvtjdj.html

Griffiths, B., Russell, L. and Roberts, R. 2017. Friday essay: when did Australia's human history begin? *The Conversation.* https://theconversation.com/friday-essay-when-did-australias-human-history-begin-87251

Habermas, J. 1984. *The theory of communicative action.* Boston, MA: Beacon Press.

Halafoff, A., Singleton, A., Bouma, G. and Rasmussen, M.L. 2020. Religious literacy of Australia's Gen Z teens: diversity and social inclusion. *Journal of Beliefs & Values, 41*(2): 195–213.

Hussain, J. and Possamai, A. 2013. A down under approach and reaction to Shari'a: an impasse towards post-secularism? In Berger, M. ed. *Applying Sharia in the West: facts, fears and figures of Islamic rules on family relations in the West.* Leiden: Leiden University Press, pp. 65–78.

Michel, P. 2011. Concerning the current recomposition of religion and of politics. In Barbalet, J., Possamai, A. and Turner, B. eds. *Religion and the state: a comparative sociology.* New York: Anthem Press, pp. 265–276.

Pew Research Center. 2017. The changing global religious landscape. *Democraphic Projections.* https://www.pewforum.org/2017/04/05/the-changing-global-religious-landscape/

Pew Research Center. 2018. *The age gap in religion around the world.* https://www.pewforum.org/2018/06/13/the-age-gap-in-religion-around-the-world/

Pew-Templeton. 2016. *Global religious futures.* http://www.globalreligiousfutures.org/countries/australia/religious_demography#/?affiliations_religion_id=0&affiliations_year=2050 (25.01.2021)

Possamai, A. 2009. *Sociology of religion for generations X and Y.* London: Equinox.

Possamai, A. 2018. *The i-zation of society, religion, and neoliberal post-secularism*. Bassingstoke: Palgrave Macmillan.

Possamai, A., Richardson, J.T. and Turner, B.S. eds. 2015. *The sociology of shari'a: case studies from around the world*. New York: Springer.

Possamai, A., Turner, B.S., Roose, J., Dagistanli, S. and Voyce, M. 2013. Defining the conversation about Shari'a: representations in Australian newspapers. *Current Sociology, 61*(5–6): 626–645.

Saeed, A. 2006. *Islamic thought: An introduction*. London: Routledge.

Scriver, P. 2004. Mosques, ghantowns and cameleers in the settlement history of colonial Australia. *Fabrications, 13*(2): 19–41.

Tittensor, D., Hoffstaedter, G. and Possamai, A. 2020. Hyper-securitisation and belonging: understanding the plight of young Muslims in Melbourne, Australia. *Journal of Muslim Minority Affairs, 40*(3): 480–496.

Todd, E. 2015. *Who is Charlie? Xenophobia and the new middle class*. Cambridge: Polity.

2 Contemporary theories of religion in society

Introduction

The focus of this chapter is on social theories of religions by contemporary scholars who can help us to shed light on current changes. In doing so, we are updating some of the concepts that have developed in the social sciences, as the world has changed and we are still working at conceptualising, if not simply visualising, these alterations. This chapter first describes some problems and especially what are called zombie categories. It then brings these undead concepts back to life and adapts them to our current social context. Many social concepts on religion have been created by groundbreaking sociologists such as Emile Durkheim (1858–1917) and Max Weber (1864–1920) who were of course a product of their time and place. Their concepts emerged from an era that was going through rapid industrial changes, intense rural exodus, and colonial expansion. They thought that religion was going to disappear and that, as this Eurocentric thinking and capitalist development expanded, it would wither away from the rest of the world. However, Europe today is the main exception with regard to the growth of religion around the world (see Berger et al., 2008). Thus, this chapter addresses the move from theories of secularisation to post-secularism, especially within the context of multiple modernities.

Further to this, many social theories of the 19th and 20th centuries did not always treat religion adequately. Therefore, we aim to understand the changes that took place in Australia with regard to religion at the micro, meso, and macro levels (this will be explicitly addressed in Chapter 12). In doing so, we are not aiming to peddle a theological or an anti-theological position in disguise, as raised by the famous theologian John Milbank (2008) in his critique of secular social theories.

DOI: 10.4324/9781003255338-2

Rather, we look to revise these theories in order to make sense of religion today in Australia without favouring either a religious or a secular worldview.

Zombie categories

The German social philosopher and sociologist Ulrich Beck (1944–2015) was concerned about the rapid changes in our society. Being an astute observer, he admitted that the tools that social scientists developed to understand the world needed revisions, if not complete change. The concepts that are key to the social sciences were developed in the late 19th and 20th centuries to reflect the position of the world – a globe divided into nation states in which societies were developing through their own agenda. For example, the French thinker Emile Durkheim (1858–1917), an atheist and son of a rabbi, was a product of the Third Republic, a society that was building itself as a more developed democratic social entity away from the aristocratic rule of a king and away from its second emperor, Napoleon III. Similarly, according to Barbalet (2008), Weber's key work *The Protestant Ethic and the Spirit of Capitalism* was not so much an analysis of the development of modernity, but more about the concerns of his time regarding the political education of Germany's middle class. This political education had been conservative over too many years and he wanted a model and/or a call to develop the nation into a strong one. Through his work, Weber hoped to wake up this German middle class and make them stand up for their desire to build a stronger nation.

In contrast, Beck (2002, and Sznaider 2006) was concerned with the 21st century and the classical concepts at hand were created in a totally different context. This is why he refers to the need for social scientists to move to a "methodological cosmopolitanism" as opposed to the "methodological nationalism" that we have all used and are still using as cultural and social scientists. By "methodological nationalism," Beck makes reference to social scientists who adopt categories of practice as categories of analysis within a national framework. As Beck and Sznaider (2006: 4) highlight: "The decisive point is that national organizations as a structuring principle of societal and political action can no longer serve as the orienting reference point for the social scientific observer." By "methodological cosmopolitanism"; Beck makes reference to a still to be constructed new theoretical and methodological paradigm that would work with new concepts and methods applicable to the transnational aspect of our societies. Indeed, realities inside and outside the nation state are rapidly changing, and we need to get rid of what he calls the "zombie categories"; these are the living dead categories within a national framework that we still use in research and are no longer applicable in a cosmopolitan society.

For example, in this global economy, Habermas (2001) claims that classical Keynesian economics within national borders can no longer work. This was a type of economy that developed strongly in the Western world after WWII that included a more robust safety net and a stronger welfare state. It slowly disappeared with the advent of neoliberal economies in the 1980s, which are driven by powerful multinational corporations, and which escape the control of regulatory states. This has many consequences, one being the erosion of the welfare state. He therefore proposes to work on a postnational constellation, in which the focus is on the construction of supranational institutions to meet the demands of the global economy (as the nation state no longer has the capacity it used to have).

Another good example of a zombie category, which is central to this book, is the concept of "secularisation." This concept was dominant in the late 19th century until the end of the 20th century as it was cemented in the work of earlier theorists, including Durkheim, Weber, Marx (1818–1883), Freud (1856–1939), Berger (1929–2017), and Luckman (1927–2016), who saw religion slowly disappearing from the world due to the advancement of scientific knowledge and industrial discoveries. This led to the theory of secularisation that argues religion is disappearing from society. But it never really did. The social sciences were so influenced by the prediction of these scholars that they took for granted that religions would disappear (Martin, 2005). This also had some political implications. For example, after WWII, the then secular government of Australia did not consider that both the refugees and subsequent waves of migrants brought in to bolster the labour force could become more religious than when they were in their home country (see Chapter 4).

Certainly, less and less people were attending churches and religious ceremonies. Yet, somehow religion was still present in people's lives. From the hard-line secularisation thesis that predicted that religion would vanish, sociologists moved to another perspective, that of the privatisation of religion. This perspective believes that religion still exists in modern life but has shifted to the private sphere, and is no longer involved in politics and governance. However, social theories are products of their context, and this is not universally true. Davie (2004) has also pointed out that the concept of secularism did not seem to work well outside of a European framework (including Australia). As modernity is not a uniform idea and espouses different views on what makes societies modern, it is only in Europe that the connection between secularisation and modernisation is relatively strong. As Davie (2004: 83) concludes in her article: "the conceptual tools that emerge from the European case may not be appropriate elsewhere. We need instead to search for new approaches and new understandings in order to understand fully the nature of religion in the modern world – both within and outside Europe." Thus, there is no doubt that by moving to a post-Christian/post-Western understanding of secularisation, sociology of religion will be able to step closer to Beck's "methodological cosmopolitanism."

One of the new approaches that is required to understand Australia today, taking into account its social memory, is our understanding of social change which is context-dependent. With the First Fleet came colonialism, with Federation came modernity, and with post-WWII industrialisation came multiculturalism, globalisation, and late modernity. But what of today? Are we still in late modernity or somewhere else? If we are in a new phase of change, what is it? The leading social theorist Beck (2016) struggles to answer these questions with regard to the world as he finds no concept or theory capable of making sense of the world that is different today compared to how it was at the end of the 20th century. He writes about the metamorphosis of the world rather than its transformation or its evolution. We are currently changing, but it is not clear into what. Following his comment about zombie categories, he emphasises the need for social scientists to think afresh to better understand the radical changes that the globe is being exposed to. As Beck argues (2016: 6), our "fixed stars, fixed certainties, are not fixed any more." To answer these questions with regard to religion in the Australian context, the concepts of post-secularisation and multiple modernities will be of help.

Post-secularism

Casanova (1994) identified four main catalysts in Iran, Poland, Latin America, and the USA that effectively shifted religion from the private to the public sphere. When developing countries in the world were modernising and getting rid of religion in their governments, the 1979 Iranian Revolution was a surprise to the Western world. Iran had become a secular country after WWII and a disfranchised and religious middle class wanted change in their society. Ayatollah

Khomeini, a highly ranked Shi'ite cleric in exile in France, came back to Iran to take power and turn the country into a theocracy. If Iran followed the Western style of development before it was contested, in Poland the link was with the communist bloc – another form of social and industrial advancement that had even less place for religion than the Western countries. A form of contestation against the communist regime led by Solidarity, a Catholic party, managed to change the regime. This was heavily supported by the then Pope John Paul II, himself Polish and against communism. These anti-Marxist sentiments were also used against an order from within Catholicism, liberation theology. This was a strong group in Latin America fighting in the political sphere against the corruption of many of its political leaders. They were close to the message of Jesus Christ and wanted to politically (rather than simply theologically) end poverty. Because of their fight for equality, they were portrayed as aligned with communism. Liberation theology still exists but no longer has the impact that it had before, and neo-Pentecostalism is today emerging as more popular in this region of the world (Cooper, 2015). The second half of the 20th century also saw the growth of an active religious movement in the US, the Christian right. Led by Paul Weyrich, it had strong involvement in politics, and the impact of its activities are still felt today (see Posner, 2020).

These developments demonstrated not only that religion could make a comeback in "secularized" countries but, perhaps more importantly, that it was capable of taking over the government. However, they were taken as isolated exceptions for many who still believed that secularisation was going to take over the whole world. It was not until the 9/11 terrorist attacks today (Torpey, 2010), with their devastating assault at the heart of Western culture and capitalism, that people were no longer able to ignore the "new" facts of the last quarter of the 20th century. The Twin Towers of New York were destroyed by two hijacked civil planes which flew into both buildings, killing thousands of people. This event changed the world as it became more securitised and more Islamophobic.

Religion is not only back, it has been reincarnated, and far from rejecting modernisation, it has adopted its creed of progress and emancipation in its many forms. Authors, such as Habermas, who has previously been defenders of the secularisation thesis, could no longer ignore this new reality. In dealing with these new issues, Habermas (2002, 2006; Habermas and Ratzinger, 2006) refers to the concept of post-secularism in association with the process of the deprivatisation of religion and the current dialogue about the management of the presence of religious groups in the public sphere.

As Calhoun notes, while reflecting on Habermas, religion is also seen as having the potential to provide new moral insights for the political sphere (Calhoun, 2011a, 2011b):

> Habermas wants to find a way to incorporate insights historically bound up with faith (and religious traditions) into the genealogy of public reason. He clearly sees faith as a source of hope, both in the sense of Kant's practical postulate that God must exist and in the sense that it can help to overcome the narrowness of a scientific rationalism always at risk of bias in favour of instrumental over communicative reason.
>
> (Calhoun, 2011b: 84)

It could thus be inferred that a way forward for working on the process of civilisation is to allow religious people, among a multitude of other social actors, to be part of a revised Enlightenment project. We can still strive towards the development of reason and progress, but seek reason that is not purely instrumental, and progress that is not purely material and quantitative. Religion and spirituality, among other factors, could help us deploy a more humane type of reason and allow for progress towards more equitable and value-oriented outcomes that promote human rights, human solidarity, justice, and spirituality and that oppose religious extremism and empty secularism. Of course, in suggesting such a fusion between faith and reason in a new civilisational project that would fit with our multicultural and multifaith world, we should be mindful that some religious groups make exclusivist truth claims, use violent means, and are intolerant towards others. These, including militant atheism, are not conducive to this new project of post-secularism.

With globalisation and migration movements, we are living in a culture of pluralism which redefines the role of religion (Giordan and Pace, 2012). This proves to be a challenge for religious institutions, which used to have the monopoly of faith in monocultural societies. Habermas (2006: 4) underlines that in plural settings, the challenge is to draw the "delimitations between a positive liberty to practise a religion of one's own and the negative liberty to remain spared from the religious practice of the others." In other words, how do we work with post-secular societies' religious tolerance in ways that celebrate religious diversity but does not foreclose upon the freedom to be an atheist? Part of the solution for Habermas is to have neutral and secular governments that can ensure that communities of various beliefs are able to coexist on an equal basis. His post-secular project is based upon the notion that the state is neutral and objective, yet we know from studies in sociology how the state usually and instrumentally serves certain groups over others (see Barbalet et al., 2011, and Chapter 11).

Following the theological point made by Roger Trigg (2007), if the voices of these religious people are silenced in the public sphere, they will be tempted to use other means to impact on society, such as lobbying, a practice that is being used successfully by the religious right in the US. Trigg (2007) contests Habermas' idea that reason should be the only language used in the public sphere. He does not agree that religious knowledge can be useful only if it is translated into the language of reason. He advocates for a metaphysical or religious grounding for the discussion, assuming that human knowledge is not self-sufficient. Whatever the veracity of Trigg's perspective, the public sphere only allows religious groups that are able to speak a language of "secular" reason. This, as Craig Calhoun (2011b) argues, is a process set by secularists, which limits the presence of religion in the public sphere and prevents them from understanding religious discourse; by creating a basis for equal inclusion based on reason, it provokes what he calls an "ironic exclusion." This is a privilege usurped by the secular middle class in many Western countries, and, in the US, by white elites at the expense of the more religious African Americans, Latinos, and migrant groups.

Along this line of inquiry, Taylor's (2007) *A Secular Age* makes reference to what he calls the "immanent frame" to describe the current context, or social imaginary, in which religion and secularism are included. It is a space today that is more open to religion but still secular. Rather than asking for religions to give up their own vocabulary (e.g. by quoting verses from the Bible) and use instead the allegedly neutral language of reason in the public sphere, the Catholic philosopher proposes that religious groups should mobilise their religious language to provide a voice against the discontent of late modernity. Both the secular and the religious would find a higher level of reflexivity if they were able to use their own social imaginary in the public sphere and enter into a relationship of tolerance and recognition. In this sense, Taylor wishes to increase the equality between religion and secularism, rather than have secularism dominate the public sphere.

When we come back in Chapter 12 to Australia being a post-secular society, we will argue that until recently this was indeed the case. Through its multicultural approach, the government has been aiming at supporting the diversity of faith, sometimes with difficulty. However, in recent years, and especially in the aftermath of the legalisation of same sex-marriage, a shift in discourse has taken place, especially with regard to the debate on religious freedom. As Chapter 12 shows, there has been a shift in understanding religious freedom as the freedom for all faiths to practise their rituals and beliefs freely (within the confines of Australian law) to the freedom *of* religious groups to express their view, even derogatory ones, on minority groups (e.g. LGBTQI, pagans, and Muslims) without the fear of censure. This, as it will be shown, signals the fact that Australia might be moving to a phase beyond post-secularism.

Secularisation and de-secularisation in multiple modernities

While it cannot be ignored that there were strong anticlerical attacks by philosophers (e.g. Machiavelli and Voltaire) prior to the French Revolution, it is mainly the advent of modernity that heralded the ideology of secularism. This new outlook advocated that religion, and not just its leaders, had to disappear once and for all, or at the very least be relegated to the private sphere. Also, with modernity came colonisation, and with colonisation came globalisation, and with globalisation came different modernities. Indeed, the modernity created in Europe and the US, which was exported and expanded upon around the world, was received in various ways. If some countries were eradicating religion from their public sphere to fit this mould (e.g. Mustafa Kemal Atatürk's Turkey), others were trying to keep religion, but within this modernist ethos (e.g. Malaysia).

A key tool to make sense of these changes is the work of Eisenstadt (2000: 2). He coined the term "multiple modernities" and describes this paradigm in cultural terms:

> The idea of multiple modernities presumes that the best way to understand the contemporary world—indeed to explain the history of modernity—is to see it as a story of continual constitution and reconstitution of a multiplicity of cultural programs. These ongoing reconstructions of multiple institutional and ideological patterns are carried forward by specific social actors in close

> connection with social, political, and intellectual activists, and also by social movements pursuing different programs of modernity, holding very different views of what makes societies modern.

It is a concept that attempts to undermine the hegemony of Western modernity and reflects cultural diversity and multiplicity. Unlike post-modernity, which is opposed to modernity as a meta-narrative, the multiple modernities thesis is in disagreement only with the Western domination at the roots of the project of modernity. As such, it does not reject modernity (Lee, 2006). In this sense, the theory of multiple modernities acknowledges specific expressions of culture and traditions and is reflective of a pluralist view of the world.

Berger, Davie, and Fokas (2008) find that the universal features of modernity pertain to science and technology, and the way they are institutionalised leads to different social and cultural outcomes. In a version that regards religion as not part of the same mould, there could be alternate forms of modernity in which religion can be included, but "the forms of religion may be as diverse as the forms of modernity" (Davie, 2013: 109).

As an example, *In Rethinking Secularization*, Casanova (2006) traces how the development of modernity in Europe was informed by secularism. The trajectory was to move away from religion towards the emancipation of reason, which would, in turn, lead to progress. In contrast, in the US, "there was 'collusion' between religion and the secular differentiated spheres" (Casanova, 2006: 11). This is explained by the fact that when the US modernised, it did not have to go through a European process of secular differentiation, which involved conflict with the established church. For example, the French Enlightenment was anticlerical and openly anti-Christian, whereas the American Enlightenment was not.

That said, one should not ignore that, bare a few exceptions, a specific type of modernity has collapsed and is no longer part of this multitude, namely, communism, which is a modern regime of a special type, as Eisenstadt (2003: 926) has noted. In this unipolar environment, the First World has been able to develop its neoliberal ideology globally, which allows various regions to be modern, but this is only as long as the market is free. With the theory of multiple modernities, there is a tendency to express cultural diversity in our globalised world, but through this illusion of equality, it often fails to address asymmetries of power (Thomassen, 2010).

Eisenstadt (2003: 934) has sought to balance this view. He claimed that the market ideology is indeed winning over the world, but that different types of political economy (e.g. how to deal with the market, state regulation and intervention, and welfare structure) will manifest across regions and reflect varied types of modernity. However, the importance of the place of religion in the public sphere can change from region to region, and time to time. This accords with Martin's observations about processes of secularisation and de-secularisation. The fundamental argument of his work is that secularisation is not a clear-cut process that happens homogenously in all countries. Indeed, as he argues in relation to Christianity:

> ...instead of regarding secularization as a once-for-all unilateral process, one might rather think in terms of successive Christianizations followed or accompanied by recoils. Each Christianization is a salient of faith driven into the secular from a different angle, each pays a characteristic cost which affects the character of the recoil, and each undergoes a partial collapse....
>
> (2005: 3)

If at one time period, in a specific place in the world, religion is strong, the same cannot be stated in another space and time. This can also be stated with regard to secularism. It can be militant at one place and time (e.g. France's laïcité) or low key for recognised religions somewhere else (e.g. Indonesia's Pancasila). The one modern trajectory that saw religion disappearing is a failed one. Rather than secularism and religion being antagonistic, we should see them as speaking to each other differently at various time periods and countries around the world.

Returning to the debate on multiple modernities and pluralism, the link with post-secularism becomes clear in the work of Rosati and Stoeckl. As they state:

> A truly postsecular society is a multi-religious society, where so to speak 'indigenous traditions nowadays live side by side with diasporic religious communities'...a postsecular society has to be understood as one in which a plurality of individual and collective religious belief and practices enrich and strengthen pluralism in general. A postsecular society is a society full of religious differences and particularities.
>
> (2012: 5)

Thus, the multiple modernities thesis gives support to post-secularism as a philosophical debate that discusses the place of religion in the public sphere. However, post-secularism is still dominated by secularism (the language of reason is dominant and not all religions are part of the public sphere), and as such is a type of low-key secularism, or even a type of secularism that is in elective affinity with neoliberalism (Possamai, 2018). As there are multiple types of modernity, there will be multiple types of secularism, and post-secularism is one of them. This type of secularism thus reflects a specific type of modernity that takes on board the voice of certain religious groups in the public sphere.

Australia's modernity

The issue now is to understand what type of modernity Australia has become. It is certainly a developed country, which has invested many of its resources in scientific knowledge. It strives to continue its development and be among the top Organisation for Economic Co-operation and Development (OECD) countries. But what of religion? The position of religion in Australia's project of modernity might be specific.

Contrasting Australia and France, for example, religion in the latter cannot have a place in the public sphere. In public institutions such as schools, students cannot wear any type of religious clothing such as a hijab or yarmulke. These are publicly funded by the French government, which would not tolerate its public money to be used in support of religious groups. In Australia, we do not have this issue in public schools. There are religious schools that are private and are partly funded by the federal government. Further, each sitting of the Federal Parliament starts with the Lord's Prayer, and there has been in recent times a resurgence of religious conservativism in politics, which affects both policies and laws (see Chapter 11). France has a very specific type of secularism, the *laïcité*, which drives its relationship with Islam. While the current government perceives Islam as being in a crisis stage (especially after the beheading of Samuel Paty in October 2020, a French high school teacher who showed a caricature of the Prophet Muhammad to his class), French secularism is also struggling (Kuru, 2020). Australia has a more multicultural approach to religion, even if there has been some recent backlash (Tittensor et al., 2020).

Comparing Australia and France with regard to multiculturalism, Bouma (2016) highlights the difference between the terrorist event of Charlie Hebdo and the perceived terrorist event of the Sydney Lindt Café siege. Australia's event has not resulted in sustained anti-Muslim action, and the resultant #illridewithyou movement demonstrated public support of diversity in religion. In this sense, contrary to France, religion is part of the Australian modern project. Compared to another country such as Malaysia, a fast-developing country prone to a project of modernity as well, religion is more present there in the public sphere than in Australia. This Muslim majority country allows, for example, *Shari'a* courts to run alongside official courts, and also the native legal system called *adat* (custom) (Shamsul, 2015).

When people move to Australia, they can have a different perception of the level of religiosity. If someone comes from a francophone country, they will see Australia as more religious than their country. On the other hand, a person from the US will see Australia as more secular than theirs. This can be a matter of perspective. But what about when it comes to how the modern project of Australia includes religion? Again, this can be a matter of perspective. A person, who does not see religion as having a place in the public sphere, will find that religion is not part of modernity. Another person who is in favour of the separation of church and state might still think that religion is included in Australia's project of modernity. But we have been making reference to religion in general. What about different types of religion? Is Christianity more a part of the public sphere than, let's say, Islam? Although the large majority of people in Australia are not racist, there are, however, still strong elements of Islamophobia that supports a religious monopoly of Christianity in the public sphere (see Chapter 5).

Here the concept of a chain of memory is of interest, as no contemporary setting can emerge from a social vacuum. Danièle Hervieu-Léger (2000) derives this concept from pre-WWII work on "collective" or "social memory" developed by the sociologist Maurice Halbwachs (1950), which was further unpacked by, for example, the art historian Aby Warburg (Assmann and Czaplicka, 1995). In her work focusing on France, Hervieu-Léger makes reference to modernity as oppositional to traditional societies. The latter are epitomised as "societies of memory," in which cultural heritage could be reproduced from one generation to the next. Institutional religions were thriving in this context and were able to retain their established positions. Societies in modernity, on the other hand, are for Hervieu-Léger societies of change and have greatly impacted institutional religions. These are now faced with difficulties in passing on their traditional teachings, that is, in continuing their chains of memory. Religion, it could be argued, has lost its memory. According to Grace Davie's (2000) research on the secularisation effect on modern Europe, the chain of religious memory does not simply keep going or gets broken. Alternatively, it can also mutate. More recently, Burchardt (2020) has adapted this concept into what he calls "religious heritage assemblage." He studied religion in the public sphere of Catalonia and of Quebec as a comparative analysis to understand the heterogeneous discourses, sites, and practices where religion is "articulated, authorized and institutionalized" (2020: 3). This "heritage religion," or diffused religion as theorised by Cipriani (2017), is part of the cultural heritage of these two locations and is under constant negotiation.

More specific to Australia, we will observe through the following chapters that Christianity and Australian Aboriginal religions are both heritage and contemporary religions that are part of the Australian social memory, but their chain of memory has been declining, while a new chain of memory based on non-Christian religions and no religion are being built. Australia, we will see, is at a cross-roads among all these chains of memory, sometimes in conflict, but most often in parallel.

Conclusions

This chapter presented a survey of useful social theories to understand the place of religion in Australian society. These are meant to help us understand the place of religion in a society and takes into account recent changes. The rest of the book deals with other concepts to explain what is religion today, how it has changed, and what is its future. Theories are always an approximation of reality as they tend to deal with idealised explanations of the phenomena in question, and as a result are truth-like at best. In other words, theories will always have limitations. But it is important to acknowledge their strength. They can help visualise reality, often hidden or unknown, and even lead to profound changes in the way we operate. Can we imagine a world today without the impact of Marx's theories on capitalism or Freud's views on the subconscious? Yet, as we have shown, theories can also have negative impacts. Secularisation, although proven to be incorrect, has misdirected our understandings of the change and place of religion in society. Indeed, so much so that Gauthier (2020) recently took the bold approach of refusing to engage with the theories of secularisation, almost as a concept no longer relevant in today's social analyses. As we will see in Chapter 6, there was a chance in Australia during the 19th century to radically change social theory in Europe, but this opportunity was missed.

The next chapter explores a short history of religion in Australia, mainly "white," to situate not only what has happened in this country but the social memory it has built, one based on considering this country as Christian. We will come back and focus on Australian Aboriginal peoples in Chapter 6.

References

Assmann, J. and Czaplicka, J. 1995. Collective memory and cultural identity. *New German Critique 65*(Spring–Summer): 125–133.

Barbalet, J.M. 2008. *Weber, passion and profits: 'the Protestant ethic and the spirit of capitalism' in context.* Melbourne: Cambridge University Press.

Barbalet, J., Possamai, A. and S Turner, B. (Eds.) 2011. *Religion and the state: A comparative sociology.* London: Anthem Press.

Beck, U. 2002. The cosmopolitan society and its enemies. *Theory, Culture & Society, 19*(1–2): 17–44.

Beck, U. 2016. *Metamorphosis of the world.* London: Sage.

Beck, U. and Sznaider, N. 2006. Unpacking cosmopolitanism for the social sciences: a research agenda. *The British Journal of Sociology, 57*(1): 1–23.

Bouma, G. 2016. The role of demographic and socio-cultural factors in Australia's successful multicultural society: how Australia is not Europe. *Journal of Sociology, 52*(4): 759–771.

Burchardt, M. 2020. *Regulating difference. Religious diversity and nationhood in the secular west.* New Brunswick: Rutgers University Press.

Berger, P., Davie, G. and Fokas, E. 2008. *Religious America, Secular Europe: a theme and variations.* Ashgate.

Calhoun, C. 2011a. Afterword: religion's many powers. In Mendieta, E. and Vanantwerpen, J. eds. *The power of religion in the public sphere.* New York: Columbia University Press, pp. 118–134.

Calhoun, C. 2011b. Secularism, citizenship, and the public sphere. In Calhoun, C., Juergensmeyer, M. and Vanantwerpen, J. eds. *Rethinking secularism.* New York: Oxford University Press, pp. 75–91.

Casanova, J. 1994. *Public religions in the modern world.* Chicago: University of Chicago Press.

Casanova, J. 2006. Rethinking secularization: a global comparative perspective. *The Hedgehog Review,* 8(1–2): 7–22.

Cipriani, R. 2017. *Diffused religion. Beyond secularization.* Cham, Switzerland: Palgrave Macmillan.

Cooper, T. 2015. Liberation theology in Latin America: dead or alive. In Brunn, S. ed. *The changing world religion map: sacred places, identities, practices and politics.* Dordrecht: Springer, pp. 1955–1969.

Davie, G. 2000. *Religion in modern Europe: a memory mutates.* Oxford: Oxford University Press.

Davie, G. 2004. New approaches in the sociology of religion: a western perspective. *Social Compass, 51*(1): 73–84.
Davie, G. 2013. *The sociology of religion: a critical agenda*. London: Sage.
Eisenstadt, S. N. 2000. Multiple modernities. *Daedalus,* 129(1): 1–29.
Eisenstadt, S.N. ed., 2003. *Comparative civilizations and multiple modernities* (Vol. 1). Leiden: Brill.
Gauthier, F. 2020. *Religion, modernity, globalisation: nation-state to market.* London: Routledge.
Giordan, G. and Pace, E., 2012. *Mapping religion and spirituality in a postsecular world.* Leiden: Brill.
Habermas, J. 2001. *The postnational constellation: political essays.* Cambridge: Polity.
Habermas, J. 2002. *Religion and rationality: essays on reason, god, and modernity.* Cambridge, MA: MIT Press.
Habermas, J. 2006. Religion in the public sphere. *European Journal of Philosophy, 14*(1): 1–25.
Habermas, J. and Ratzinger, J. 2006. The dialectics of secularization. *On reason and religion*. San Francisco: Ignatius.
Halbwachs, M. 1950. *La mémoire collective.* Paris: Presses Universitaires de France.
Hervieu-Léger, D. 2000. *Religion as a chain of memory.* New Brunswick, NJ: Rutgers University.
Kuru, A. 2020. Beheading in France could Bolster President's claim that Islam is in "Crisis" – but so is French secularism. *The Conversation*, October 21. https://theconversation.com/beheading-in-france-could-bolster-presidents-claim-that-islam-is-in-crisis-but-so-is-french-secularism-148070 [22/10/2020].
Lee, R. L. 2006. Reinventing modernity: reflexive modernization vs liquid modernity vs multiple modernities. *European Journal of Social Theory, 9*(3): 355–368.
Martin, D. 2005. *On secularization. Towards a revised general theory.* Aldershot: Ashgate.
Milbank, J. 2008. *Theology and social theory: beyond secular reason.* Oxford: Blackwell.
Posner, S. 2020. *Unholy: why white evangelicals worship at the Altar of Donald Trump.* New York: Random House.
Possamai, A. 2018. *The i-zation of society, religion, and neoliberal post-secularism.* Bassingstoke: Palgrave Macmillan.
Rosati, M. and Stoeckl, K. 2012. *Multiple modernities and postsecular societies (global connections).* Aldershot: Ashgate Publishing Group.
Shamsul, A.B. 2015. 'One state, three legal systems: social cohesion in a multi-ethnic and multi-religious Malaysia'. In Possamai, A., Richardson, J. and Turner, B. eds. *The sociology of Shari'a: case studies from around the world.* Cham, Heidelberg, New York, Dordrecht, London: Springer, pp. 17–30.

Taylor, C. 2007. *A secular age*. Cambridge, MA & London: Belknap Press of Harvard University Press.

Thomassen, B. 2010. Anthropology, multiple modernities and the axial age debate. *Anthropological Theory, 10*(4): 321–342.

Tittensor, D., Hoffstaedter, G. and Possamai, A. 2020. Hyper-securitisation and belonging: understanding the Plight of Young Muslims in Melbourne, Australia. *Journal of Muslim Minority Affairs, 40*(3): 480–496.

Torpey, J. 2010. A (post-) secular age?: Religion and the two exceptionalisms. *Social Research: An International Quarterly,* 77(1): 269–296.

Trigg, R. 2007. *Religion in public life: must faith be privatized?*. Oxford: Oxford University Press.

3 A short history of religion in Australia before WWII

Introduction

Australia is a former British penal colony where the Anglican Church was part of a more general system of social control. With growing Irish migration in the late 19th century, there was increasing competition between Anglicanism and Roman Catholicism, but colonial Australia was obviously not the multifaith society of today. The religious homogeneity of Christianity in early Australia began to change significantly after WWII, as post-war migration and conversion to new religious movements transformed the cultural, religious, and ethnic profiles of Australian society. While the next chapter focuses on the changes after WWII, this chapter takes a long view of Australia's religious history by incorporating an overview of precolonial and colonial times. This includes Australian Aboriginal religion, the hidden history of Islam (e.g. the interaction between the Makassar and Indigenous peoples in the Northern Territory before the 18th century), the import of Christianity, the endorsement of an Australian specific type of secularism through Federation, and the birth of ANZAC as a civil religion.

Australian Aboriginal religions

Australian Aboriginal peoples are very diverse and cannot be homogenised. Although there are today differences between urban and rural Indigenous peoples, there were already differences before colonialism between those from the north, centre, and south, between those on the mainland and those on an island, and between those close to freshwater and those on the shores of the sea (see Naden and Havea, 2014). However, at the core of this diversity, there is a strong link among Australian Aboriginal peoples to practices of ecology and land care, and a strong approach to the land which is perceived as connected to religion and law (Pattenden, 2014).

DOI: 10.4324/9781003255338-3

They were nomadic hunters and gatherers and have been in Australia for at least 45,000 to 50,000 years, with recent research suggesting the figure could be as far back as 65,000 years (Griffiths et al., 2017). They originally came from Asia (either through Timor or through New Guinea) at a time when the sea levels were lower and there were land bridges between Asia and Australia, and also between Tasmania and the Australian mainland. Around 20,000 years ago they had settled as far apart as Arnhem Land in the north and Tasmania in the south. By the time of white settlement, they occupied the entire continent and were adapted to a range of climates, being tropical or arid. There have been various estimations as to their numbers ranging from 300,000 to more than 1,000,000. More than 200 different Aboriginal languages were spoken among some 500 distinct groups. Today, there are hardly 100 languages still spoken, with many of them regarded as endangered. These are distinct languages, and not simply dialects. For example, a Pintubi speaker from central Australia would not understand a Pitjantjatjara speaker from the western desert region. As a result, these various groups did not have a sense of being part of an Australia-wide pan-Aboriginal nation. Therefore, it is more appropriate to speak about many Aboriginal Australian cultures, and religions should also be considered in the plural (Charlesworth, 1997).

The earliest European account of their belief system was the view that they had no religion at all. This was because they were understood to have no gods or concepts of an afterlife. Their religion is, however, earth-bound as the land generates their social and spiritual connections through totemic, mythological, and kinship bonds (Carey, 1996: 35). The closest to a European understanding of religion at that time was the Aranda word "Altjira" that has been initially translated as Dreaming or Dreamtime to explain their beliefs. This, as we will explore more fully in Chapter 6, has since been contested. There, we will come back to Indigenous religions in Australia more extensively.

British colonialism

British colonialism famously defined Australia as an empty territory and rejected property rights for Australian Aboriginal peoples who, being defined as nomadic, had no specific claims to land. The fact that Australia was seen as *terra nullius* appears to be a unique case in the history of the British imperial expansion in the 19th century (McLachlan, 1988: 378). With the first fleet and the establishment of a penal settlement, Anglicans arrived in 1788 in New South Wales. While Anglican ministers provided chaplaincy services and established the first schools, the Church of England did not become a state religion, as the declaration in 1818 in this new colony stated that church and state had to be separated and independent. While Irish Catholics, Scottish Presbyterians, and Jews were members of the crew and/or among convicts, the first Presbyterian service was only held in 1794 and the first Catholic priest arrived in 1800. Later, Methodists settled in 1812 and had their first minister in 1815. The first synagogue was established in Sydney in 1828–1830 (Bouma, 1996). Subsequently, the first census in New South Wales in 1828 had 36,484 respondents who were classified in only four groups: Protestant, Roman Catholic, Jewish, and "Mohammedan and pagan," the latter consisting of just 19 people (Carey, 1996).

Mol (1985) compared the landing in 1620 America by religious pilgrims who followed many religious observances with Australia in 1788. In the latter, to mark the landing at Sydney Cove on 26 January 1788, the flag was raised, the appropriate military rites were carried out, and the chaplain took no part in the proceedings. There was little religious ceremony or motivation among the convicts and officers. For Mol, this is symbolic of the fact that religion has since been on the periphery. This also led to an aversion to authority, as religion was used mainly as a form of social discipline, through a type of "military-chaplaincy" (Bouma, 1988). This, as we will continue to argue in forthcoming chapters, has been a basis for the development of Australia as a specific type of modernity in which religion is not central, but also never completely removed. In America, on the other hand, the Pilgrim Fathers landed at New Plymouth in 1620 and celebrated with Christian prayer and Bible readings. There was no flag or military ceremony.

Moreover, the Christianity that was brought to Australia was not traditional, but was one that had been reworked by the Reformation, Counter-Reformation, and Enlightenment. If sometimes Australia is seen as irreligious, it is because it could not have been religious in the traditional European sense (Mansfield, 1989). On top of this, no religion could have claimed to be a national church, which is one that worked very closely with the government and was symbolic of the nation (e.g. Anglicanism in England or Catholicism in Italy). All religions were in fact denominations, which are large religious groups that could have some impact on public life, but could never achieve dominance. Moreover, many different philosophical traditions have had an impact on the formative experiences of the colonial time. For example, Hudson (2016) highlights the strong presence of utilitarianism, especially through the influence of Benthamites on penology and educational reform. Even though Jeremy Bentham was irreligious, many followers of his philosophy were still believers, who were nonetheless persuaded to leave religion out of public affairs.

While non-Indigenous Australia was dominated by the Anglican, Protestant, and Catholic communities until the mid-19th century, the Gold Rush in 1850 in Victoria and New South Wales, and in the 1890s in Western Australia, changed some demographics. Between 1851 and 1861, the Australian population tripled from 440,000 to 1.15 million people and changed the religious landscape (Carey, 1996: 82). For example, Chinese migrants looking for gold also brought with them Confucianism, Taoism, and Buddhism. In the 1870s, Singhalese Buddhists came to work in sugar plantations in Northern Queensland. During that time, Hindus and the "Ghans" (a mix of Muslims and Hindus; see Deen, 2011 and below) also came to work as indentured labourers and camel drivers. Thus, Bouma and Halafoff (2017) claim that before the White Australia policy of 1901, Australia was already quite diverse, culturally and religiously.

Indeed, by the 1880s, Christianity was subject to a challenge by a growing secularist movement, especially from the free thinkers in the then most populous and cosmopolitan colony, Victoria (Thompson, 2002: 21). Some of these secularists pointed out that Australia was an irreligious society because of its anticlericalism and its godless convict past. However, this does not mean that Australia became more secularised. Hudson (2016) highlights how Christianity has been a key element of Australian society, even if for many religious colonists Enlightenment could be part of their belief system. As they attempted to build Australia, some of them did not see this as separated from building the Kingdom of God. Here, the key point for Hudson (2016: 1) is that unbelief (i.e. an inability to positively accept religious tenets) in Australia was not common at all. What was more mainstream was disbelief (i.e. the conviction that various religious tenets are false and irrational, but not all of them), as many Australians could be critical of organised religion, but were not necessarily against the sacred realm.

During the period of colonial expansion, many missionary organisations developed and aimed at changing not only the religion of Australian Aboriginal peoples but also their culture, which was deemed to be "unacceptable." Christianity was seen in Australia as superior to all other religions (Loos, 1992: 96). The clergy had as one of its prejudices that the nomadic lifestyle of Australian Indigenous peoples could not fit with the Christian gospel (Thompson, 2002: 5). As fertile land was taken by pastoralists during the 1840s, few areas were left for

Australian Aboriginal peoples to continue their nomadic lifestyle, and so some moved to Christian missions and received support when conforming to the colonial religion (Thompson, 2002: 30).

Further to this, the relationships between Christian and Aboriginal belief systems were not always or necessarily mutually exclusive. For example, Diane Austin-Broos (2010) provides a subtle interpretation of the problems of the translation of keywords between the Arrernte language and the Christian gospels in the Lutheran mission at Hermannsburg, which had been originally established in 1877. She argues that translation initially relied on metaphorical uses of Arrernte language to describe the Christian world, and that, over time, these metaphors became part of the lived experience of the everyday life of Australian Aboriginal peoples, which, in turn, eventually came to name new experiences and objects, as the life of the Arrernte people changed with sedentarisation.

The process of "turning from" to "turning to" in the conversion experience also involved an ontological shift corresponding to the radical experience of settlement. Contrary to the Protestant definition of the ideal-typical conversion, Austin-Broos (2010: 15) argues that "conversion is not a singular event but rather a worked-at process that is both intellectual and practical." It is during that time period that the locally famous Moses Tjalkabota Uraiakuraia (1869–1954), a proud Western Arrernte man, embraced Christianity and took the name Moses. Not only was he a "man of high degree" but also a Christian evangelist known in his time as the "black Messenger" (Latz, 2014). If in modern Australia the majority of Western Arrernte people identify as Lutherans, Arrernte beliefs remain nevertheless creative. There is indeed an adaptation of Christianity to their own sense of time and tradition. For example, this syncretism takes place when people claim that the mark of Jesus' footprint (*impartye Jesuake*) on the bed of the Finke River confirms their belief that Jesus was present in the Dreaming times long before the missionaries arrived (Cohen, 2016).

Around the same time, Reverend Charles Strong created the now defunct Australian Church. He came to Melbourne in 1875 to become a minister of a Presbyterian Church, but he was later threatened with a heresy trial. He was interested in the scientific study of religion, which he wanted to speak to theology, and form what he saw as a natural theology grounded within a scientific and psychological approach. His questions about religion were also dealing with comparative religion and the development of a new science at the time, sociology. After he resigned from the Presbyterian Church, many of his congregation joined him in his newly created Australian Church. Among those who attended his services was Alfred Deakin (Hudson, 2016: 111–118), a future prime minister. Strong wanted a new church which would be democratic and progressive. To do this, he moved away from old-world theologies and sectarianism and thus called it the Australian Church (Saunders, 1995).

Australia was also the host of various esoteric groups, such as Spiritualism and the Theosophic Society (Drury and Tillett, 1980), two worldwide religious movements of the late 19th century and early 20th century. The birth of modern spiritualism started with the Fox sisters (Leah 1813–1890; Margaretta 1833–1893; and Catherine 1837–1892) who discovered a way of communicating with the spirit of a dead person through mysterious raps and knocks. They began their career as spirit mediums through newspaper journalism and in public and toured throughout America. Their manifestations created an intense interest and controversy, and this was the starting point of the modern Spiritualist movement. In Australia, this group was first established in Ballarat in the late 1850s during the Gold Rush.

Helena Petrovna Blavatsky (1831–1891) and Henry Steel Olcott (1832–1907) created the Theosophical Society in New York in 1875. It was initially established as a centre dedicated to studying paranormal phenomena. Blavatsky wrote her first book *Isis Unveiled* (1877), wherein feminine power is assessed through the myth of Isis. Through this myth, the Theosophical Society wanted to restore power to feminine religion. When Blavatsky and Olcott came to India where they were welcomed by some non-orthodox Hindus, they founded in Adyar (Madras) the world centre of the Theosophical Society. Later, Blavatsky came back to America and wrote what would become the manifesto of the Theosophical Society: *The Secret Doctrine*. She developed a new cosmogony and cosmology based on seven planes of reality. This group would also become well established in Australia, thanks to the work of one of its world leaders, Charles Webster Leadbeater (1854–1934), who lived for 20 years (from 1914) in Sydney. He was important in the esoteric and occult milieu as one of their greatest clairvoyants, but was seen by many as an outsider, as a charlatan, and as an immoral corruptor of the youth.

Another esoteric group was Anthroposophy, based on the spiritual teachings of Rudolf Steiner (1861–1925). A former member of the Theosophical Society, he created a movement in 1913 which was more Christian and reintegrated the ideas of the Rosicrucians in his doctrine. Walter Burley Griffin (1876–1937), who designed Canberra, was influenced by some ideas from this movement (Hudson, 2016: 37). While Alfred Deakin was involved in the Australian Church (see above), he also held a belief in spirits and developed some interest in the Theosophical Society and Spiritualism (Bongiorno, 2006). We will come back to some of these latter groups in Chapter 8 when we cover contemporary spiritualities.

Hidden history of Islam

The seafaring Makassar arrived in Australia before the British, harvesting the waters of north-western Australia for *trepang* (sea slug) as far back as the early 1700s. While there is some academic debate surrounding the exact nature of the impact of the Makassar on the Australian Aboriginal population, there is ample evidence of a cultural impact. Anthropologists have recorded oral histories which provide accounts of trading activities, and there are Makassar cultural influences in Yolngu[1] song and dance. For example, Ian McIntosh (1996) offers a fine account of "Islamic references in *Yolngu* mythology and ritual" as evidenced by how the Yolngu have adapted aspects of Islam, via the Makassar, into their traditions. Makassar seamen were officially barred from entering Australian waters in 1907, when the value of the resources of these waters became apparent to the government (McIntosh, 1996).

While Makassar activities were confined to the Arnhem Land coast in what is now Australia's Northern Territory, the Afghan influence was more widespread. The Afghan influence upon Aboriginal Australia began in the 1860s. These migrants responded to the need for camel transport in the period when the colonial authorities were endeavouring to open up inland Australia. Afghan migrant workers were also involved in building the rail link between Alice Springs and Port Augusta.

The Afghan men came without women and without their religious leaders (Briscoe, 2005). They found "solutions" to both problems in the Aboriginal milieu. In the absence of religious leadership, the new arrivals started to build common places of worship, namely mosques, along the camel routes. In a predominantly white colonial context, these mosques could only be erected on the fringes of society, and these were marginal spaces already occupied by Australian Aboriginal peoples. Hence, the Afghans found themselves in close contact with Australian Aboriginal fringe-dwellers of the colony (Briscoe, 2005; Stevens, 2003), which stretched across vast parts of northern and central Australia. Briscoe (2005) describes how the building of the Overland

Telegraph Line facilitated both short and long-term relationships between the cameleers and Australian Aboriginal women. These relationships resulted sometimes in marriage and frequently in children.

The dawn of federalism

With the creation of federalism in Australia in 1901, new sets of laws came into effect and established the nation, as we know it today. Following the then modern spirit of the times, Section 116 of the Constitution formalised the separation of the church and the state. However, this development was, and is still, seen as a flexible separation, which only binds the Commonwealth and not the states. As Beck (2009) analyses, it is usually regarded as a weak guarantee of religious freedom, as Australia, the only exception among OECD countries, does not have a Bill of Rights.

Beck (2018) traces the history of the creation of the Australian Constitution, especially in relation to Article 116, which states:

> The Commonwealth shall not make any law for establishing any religion, or for imposing any religious observance, or for prohibiting the free exercise of any religion, and no religious test shall be required as a qualification for any office or public trust under the Commonwealth.

The crafting of this article that regulates our current understanding of freedom of religion came in part from the concerns of a Christian sect that wanted to work on Sunday. These are the Seventh-Day Adventists who regard Saturday (the Sabbath) as the day of rest. This was a time period when people could be arrested for working on the day of the Lord, in this case, Sunday. Beck (2018) interestingly begins his account with the case of a bricklayer by trade, also a Seventh-Day Adventist, who was arrested by a constable in Sydney in 1894, for mixing mortar and laying bricks. The *Sunday Observance Act 1677* passed in England was still in force in New South Wales at that time; however, it only tended to be enforced occasionally.

At the time of Federation, the Seventh-Day Adventists led the debates – in opposition to their fellow colonial churches – arguing that the federal government should have no powers to legislate on religion, as they were concerned about further persecution. Further, many of those involved in the Adventist cause were North Americans, who brought with them the American experience as a successful example of religions being protected from government interference. Thus, to cut a long story short, following a long series of public debates and consultations among various individuals and religious groups (see Beck, 2018), the constitution was created recognising God in its preamble. This was done to indicate that the Commonwealth of Australia is a Christian nation. However, to prevent the Commonwealth from being able to legislate with respect to religion, understood at the time as Christian, a provision was created, that is Article 116. The enactment of Sunday closing laws was thus no longer possible after Federation.

As a result of this, Australia became a secularised country, but in a specific and perhaps paradoxical way. Religion was occluded from politics and public institution not necessarily because of secular voices asking for religion, if not disappear, to at least be discreet, but by religious voices themselves. No Christian group could impose its credo on another one. Australia was in a sense a multi-Christian country. In their analysis, Chavura and Tregenza (2015) claim that the way religion has been treated after this time has been fundamental to the development of Australia as a modern society. Australia engaged with religion, but not at the political level (something that is slowly changing today, as explored in Chapters 11 and 12).

In its first national census in 1901, this multi-Christian make-up was starkly reflected. Australia had close to 2 million non-indigenous people,[2] and 96.1% of them were Christian. The dominant group was Anglicanism (39.68%), followed by the Catholics (22.75%) and the Methodists (13.36%). While there were 15,239 Jews (that is, 0.4%), there were no reported Buddhists, Hindus, or Muslims (Carey, 1996).

However, even though religion had its place in Australia, its citizens were known to have a lack of interest. According to Carey, a major factor contributing to this aloofness is that the Australian identity is strongly linked to a heroic form of masculinity which viewed religion as a feminine concern. Although there were attempts to create a masculine model of Christianity, a "muscular Christianity" as it was known at that time in England, it was seen as too closely linked to the imperial ideology from the UK. It too was perceived as unmanly and un-Australian, and after WWII, only a few groups remained, such as the Bush Brotherhood and the military Padres (Carey, 1996: 117; see also Chapter 9).

The impact of the dawn of federalism on religion is not only about Article 116, but also about the White Australia policy. Although there was no formal "White Australia" policy, there were various policy instruments devised to exclude non-white migrants (Jacobs, 2011). One of them was a dictation test that allowed an officer to administer a test of 500 words and use this as a basis for an entry rejection. While this had been used on around 200 occasions between 1901 and 1958, it was mainly a deterrent to prevent shipping companies from selling tickets to people who would likely not be accepted on the shore of Australia. This policy privileged UK and white European migrants with a view to maintaining racial purity and to control the economic impact of migrants on jobs and pay, especially at a time when there was open hostility towards non-white people, such as the Chinese workers in the gold fields (see also Chapter 4). This had of course an effect on religion, as the faiths that were exported in Australia were those of the white people, who tended to be mainly Christians, and helped to maintain the broadly Christian character of Australia (Bouma, 1996). While non-Christian communities existed at that time in Australia, they mainly started to grow when the White Australia policy was removed in the mid-1970s. Needless to state, this policy was one of exclusion of not only potential migrants but also Australian Aboriginal peoples who were expected by a large majority of white Australians to either die out or to have their "colour [...] bred out" (Jacobs, 2011: 13). Further to this, between federalism and 1946, Australian states passed legislation to "protect" Australian Aboriginal peoples. Violent dispossession moved to that of "protection." This was meant to control their movements and employment and allow officials to remove Aboriginal children from their families. The children of Australian Indigenous peoples who were removed from their families by governmental agencies and church missions between 1869 and 1969 are part of what is known as the Stolen Generations. This practice allowed a proselytising Christianity to take further steps to convert them and led to the further denigration of their culture and spirituality (Maddison, 2014).

On this point, Loos (2007) does not reject the fact that missionaries caused harm to the Australian Indigenous populations, but argued that they did not do more harm than some other groups of colonists who came in contact with them. For Loos, missionaries were indeed locked into the colonialist culture and the white supremacist ideology of their time. He admits that, in the 19th century, missionaries were not only interested in changing the belief systems of Indigenous peoples, but also wanted to eliminate their culture as well. However, Loos also offers another view on this colonial practice. The missionaries and their white helpers sometimes provided protection, however minimal, for Australian Aboriginal communities from the ragtag populations of miners and rapacious settlers whose main intentions were to exploit and remove Australian Aboriginal peoples from the land.

O'Sullivan (2005), in his analysis of the relations between the Catholic Church and the Australian Aboriginal peoples, claims that, although the determination to "exploit and exterminate" was central to the political sphere, the Church officially opposed it. The general directive given by the Catholic Church to missionaries was that they must stay aloof from the affairs of the state and from politics (Turcotte, 2009). However, as O'Sullivan (2005) illustrates, in practice, some prelates did indeed follow the political climate.

Civil religion and Gallipoli

The Gallipoli campaign (from 17 February 1915 to 9 January 1916 in Turkey) is central to Australian culture as it represents the first military action of the then "new" Australian military forces after Federation. It is often regarded as the beginning of the Australian national consciousness, and the day of the landing, the 25th of April, is now a public holiday, ANZAC Day, commemorating this battle and national identity (Donoghue and Tranter, 2015). While ANZAC is meant to honour war heroes, some critics have commented that it can at times glorify war and can also be sexist and racist (see Black, 1990).

This civil religion is basically a type of religion derived from the nation state in the form of nationalism, which has no connections to the supernatural world. As part of this civil religion, the state uses rituals, symbols, and language to promote a homogenous national identity. This religion includes, for example in other countries, the strong symbolism of the Statue of Liberty and Big Ben which are "sacred" to their nation in a similar way as the cross is for Christians. Other displays of civil religion are the singing of the national anthem at public gatherings, parades commemorating "patriotic" historical events, or monuments to commemorate great leaders or heroes of one's country. At the end of WWI, a new symbol of civil religion emerged, that of the Tomb of the Unknown Soldier, to represent all who have been killed in war.

To show, however, how civil religion can sometimes be linked to religion, Grace Davie (2000) notes a sharp contrast between the French and the UK cases. In Paris, the symbol is beneath the *Arc de Triomphe* and does not have any religious inscription. It reflects strongly the secular nature of this symbol. In Britain, the same symbol is just outside of the main door of Westminster Abbey where the religious and secular worlds meet. In Australia, plans were put together in the 1920s, but it was only in 1993 that one was brought home from a cemetery in France to commemorate the 75th anniversary of the end of the war. The Australian Unknown Soldier is in the Hall of Memory at the Australian War

Memorial in Canberra. While the museum is a secular place, "Known unto God" is nevertheless inscribed at the head of the tomb.

Similarly, Massam and Smith (1998) show in the Australian context how civil religion can be mixed with religion, as during WWII, many priests were linking the ANZAC spirit with belief in God so Australians at war could fight as good soldiers. Further to this, Bouma (2006) highlights the importance of ANZAC Day today and even links it to Australian spirituality and the much-celebrated annual trip to Gallipoli as a site of pilgrimage, as it is so much part of the Australian "soul." Emblematic of this is the fact that during the Covid-19 pandemic, the Prime Minister Scott Morrison has even named ANZAC Day Australia's most sacred day (Weng and Halafoff, 2020).

Hudson (2016: 67) calls this convergence the sacralisation of the secular, as it is accepted by both religious and non-religious people, and highlights that in the Australian context the sacred and the secular can often be porous. Also, as we have discussed earlier, as a result of the resistance to a religious authority that has been baked into the social memory of Australia, we can see similarities in the way this secular event is unofficially celebrated by some Australians which includes heavy drinking and gambling. These activities, as Black (1990) notes, are assertions of egalitarianism and rituals of rebellion against the authority, on top of being forms of expression dealing with the ambivalence of what wars were, especially their human costs.

Conclusion

This chapter has covered with broad strokes the history of religion in Australia before WWII. It started with the Australian Aboriginal peoples who had their spirituality strongly linked to the land. This period before European settlements marks a moment in history where religion was quite diverse. With the first fleet and the arrival of Christianity, there were attempts to homogenise religion in Australia, an attempt that was derailed with mass migration during the Gold Rush. Federalism then became another opportunity for some Christians to rehomogenise the country and prevent non-Christian groups from being able to migrate. This changed with WWII which slowly saw religious diversity take root in Australia. However, as we will explore in other chapters, the building of Australia as a modern nation is so entrenched within Christianity that it is still felt today, even if the Christian share of the population is in sharp decline.

Notes

1 The Yolngu are Indigenous people of north-eastern Arnhem Land.
2 Australian Indigenous people were not included in the census before 1967.

References

Austin-Broos, D. 2010. Translating Christianity: some keywords, events and sites in Western Arrernte conversion. *The Australian Journal of Anthropology, 21*(1):14–32.

Beck, L. 2009. Clear and emphatic: the separation of church and state under the Australian constitution. *The University of Tasmania Law Review*, 27(2): 161–196.

Beck, L. 2018. *Religious freedom and the Australian Constitution: origins and future.* London: Routledge.

Black, A.W. 1990. The sociology of religion in Australia. *SA. Sociological Analysis, 51*(S): S27–S41.

Bongiorno, F. 2006. In this world and the next: political modernity and unorthodox religion in Australia, 1880–1930. *ACH: The Journal of the History of Culture in Australia* (24–25). Gale Academic OneFile. Accessed 5 June 2021.

Bouma, G. 1988. The sociology of religion in Australia. *Australian Religion Studies Review, 1*(2): 44–49.

Bouma, G. ed. 1996. *Many religions, all Australian: religious settlement, identity and cultural diversity.* Melbourne: The Christian Research Association.

Bouma, G. 2006. *Australian soul: religion and spirituality in the 21st century.* Melbourne: Cambridge University Press.

Bouma, G.D. and Halafoff, A. 2017. Australia's changing religious profile—rising Nones and Pentecostals, declining British protestants in superdiversity: views from the 2016 census. *Journal for the Academic Study of Religion, 30*(2): 129–143.

Briscoe, G. 2005. Book reviews. *Aboriginal History, 29*: 169–71.

Carey, H.M. 1996. *Believing in Australia: a cultural history of religions.* Sydney: Allen & Unwin.

Charlesworth, M. 1997. *Religious inventions: four essays.* Melbourne: Cambridge University Press.

Chavura, S.A. and Tregenza, I. 2015. A political history of the secular in Australia, 1788–1945. In Chavura, S.A. and Tregenza, I. eds. *Religion after secularization in Australia.* New York: Palgrave Macmillan, pp. 3–31.

Cohen, H. 2016. The Strehlow-Hermannsburg/Ntaria Perplex: translation in a Lutheran-Aboriginal community. In Cox, J. and Possamai, A. eds. *Religion and non-religion among Australian Aboriginal peoples.* London: Routledge, pp. 109–128.

Davie, G. 2000. *Religion in modern Europe: a memory mutates.* Oxford: Oxford University Press.

Deen, H. 2011. *Ali Abdul v The King. Muslim stories from the dark days of White Australia.* Crawley: University of Western Australia Press.

Donoghue, J. and Tranter, B. 2015. The Anzacs: military influences on Australian identity. *Journal of Sociology, 51*(3): 449–463.

Drury, N. and Tillett, G. 1980. *Other temples, other gods: the occult in Australia.* Sydney: Methuen Australia.

Griffiths, B., Russell, L. and Roberts, R. 2017. Friday essay: when did Australia's human history begin? *The Conversation.* Retrieved from https://theconversation.com/friday-essay-when-did-australias-human-history-begin-87251

Hudson, W. 2016. *Australian religious thought.* Melbourne: Monash University Press.

Jacobs, K. 2011. *Experience and representation. Contemporary perspective on migration in Australia.* Farnham: Ashgate.

Latz, P. 2014. *Blind Moses. Aranda man of high degree and Christian evangelist.* Alice Springs: IAD Press.

Loos, N. 1992. The Australian Board of Missions, the Anglican Church and the Aborigines, 1850–1900. *Journal of Religious History, 17*(2): 194–209.

Loos, N. 2007. *White Christ black cross: the emergence of a black church.* Canberra: Aboriginal Studies Press.

Maddison, S. 2014. Missionary genocide: moral illegitimacy and the churches in Australia. In Havea, J. ed. *Indigenous Australia and the unfinished business of theology. Cross-cultural engagement.* New York: Palgrave, pp. 31–46.

Mansfield, B. 1989. Thinking about Australian religious history. *Journal of Religious History, 15*(3): 330–344.

Massam, K. and Smith, J.H. 1998. Images of God: civil religion and Australia at war 1939–1945. *Australian Religion Studies Review, 11*(2): 57–71.

McLachlan, C. 1988. The recognition of aboriginal customary law: pluralism beyond the colonial paradigm: a review article. *International and Comparative Law Quarterly,* 37 (2): 368–386.

McIntosh, I.S. 1996. Islam and Australia's aborigines? A perspective from North-East Arnhem land. *Journal of Religious History, 20*(1): 53–77.

Mol, H. 1985. *The faith of Australians.* Sydney: Allen & Unwin.

Naden, N. and Havea, J. 2014. Colonization has many names. In Havea, J. ed. *Indigenous Australia and the unfinished business of theology.* New York: Palgrave Macmillan, pp. 1–8.

O'Sullivan, D. 2005. *Faith, politics and reconciliation: Catholicism and the politics of indigeneity.* New Zealand: Huia Publishers.

Pattenden, R. 2014. Seeing otherwise: touching sacred things. In Havea, J. ed. *Indigenous Australia and the unfinished business of theology.* New York: Palgrave Macmillan, pp. 17–30.

Saunders, M. 1995. An Australian pacifist: the reverend Dr. Charles Strong, 1844–1942. *Biography, 18*(3): 241–253.

Stevens, C. 2003. [1989]. *Tin Mosques and Ghan Towns: a history of Afghan camel drivers in Australia.* Alice Springs, NT: Paul Fitzsimons.

Thompson, R. 2002. *Religion in Australia. A history*. Melbourne: Oxford University Press.

Turcotte, P.A. 2009. Conversion and mission: missionary insertion and the social conditions of Christianization. In Giordan, G. ed. *Conversion in the age of pluralism*. Leiden: Brill, pp. 307–328.

Weng, E. and Halafoff, A. 2020. Media representations of religion, spirituality and non-religion in Australia. *Religions*, *11*(7): 332. DOI:10.3390/rel11070332

4 Post-WWII migration to Australia

From being Christian to religiously plural

Introduction

As discussed in the previous chapter, one of the first actions of the newly formed Australian parliament, following Federation, was the introduction of the *Immigration Restriction Act* in 1901, which ushered in the White Australia policy. The logic behind the act – although not overtly targeting particular races – was to curtail the introduction of any more Afghan cameleers, who peaked at around 800 in 1890 (Scriver, 2004), and the emigration of Indian and Africans who formed the majority of the subjects in the British Commonwealth. This was achieved through a dictation test and the issuing of messages that stated "coloured people" cannot settle here. The net result of these policies was that Australia, by 1947, was one of the whitest nations outside of north-western Europe, with 97% of the population being British stock; non-Europeans constituted only 0.25% of the population, and the indigenous communities had declined from under 3% to around 1% of the total population (Jupp, 2002; Kirk, 2008). Subsequently, 88% of the population in 1947 identified as Christian, while only 0.5% identified as non-Christian (ABS, 1947).

However, after WWII, this began to change. In 1946, the United Nations formed the International Refugee Organization (IRO) to assist with approximately 1 million Europeans who were displaced from their home countries. The following year, the Australian government signed an agreement with the IRO to take 4,000 refugees. Over the next five years, this intake would expand to accommodate 170,000 displaced persons from many different European nations, the largest non-British contingent at that time (National Archives, 2020). This extensive intake was precipitated by the then Labour government's policy of "populate or perish," wherein it became clear that Australia's population needs, to help with the rebuilding following the war, could not be met by immigration from the British Isles. Hence, subsequent

DOI: 10.4324/9781003255338-4

governments in their demand for labour also made arrangements with Southern European countries such as Italy and Greece, and Turkey from the Middle East, which would see significant waves of non-British migration during the 1950s and 1960s (Kirk, 2008; National Archives, 2020; Price, 1975).

It is important to note that these initial waves of migration were still governed by the logic of the White Australia policy, and those allowed in constituted only a marginal easing or restrictions on race. Those who came in were either seen as white (Southern Europeans) or could pass as white (Turkey) in that they were seen as "somehow part of Europe" (Price, 1975: 56). Thus, it would not be until 1973, under the Labour government of Gough Whitlam, that there would be the removal of the emphasis on both whiteness and the need to preserve the "Christian ideals" and "inherited culture" of the nation, and thereby allow for more substantial migration from Asia and the wider Middle East. Indeed, the 1970s would herald the end of the White Australia policy and a turn towards a policy of multiculturalism that guided immigration policy in the 1980s and 1990s.

These successive waves of migration, and the eventual opening up to non-white and non-Christian peoples, led to Australia becoming one of the most ethnically and religiously diverse countries in the world, with people having immigrated from over 200 countries. Thus, with this in mind, this chapter details some of these migratory waves and explores the impacts that they have had on the religious make-up of the nation. In particular, this chapter focuses on how Christianity has become increasingly plural and on the implications of this internal diversity. Alongside this, there is also a focus on how Australia has become religiously plural more broadly with a host of small, but significant, religious minorities that have become part of the fabric of the nation. Finally, the chapter details how the opening up of the country also introduced both some non-traditional and new religious movements (NRMs) to Australia's religious and spiritual landscape.

1946–1973: a gradual opening

As touched on above, in the immediate aftermath of the war, Australia took in a considerable number of refugees, and this period was a watershed for the Jewish community. Up until 1933, the Jewish population had been largely static at around 23,000, which was about 0.5% of the population (Rutland, 2006). This was due to the increasing bipartisan racialisation of Jews as a possible "fifth column" that threatened Australia's British heritage, as non-British-born Jews were seen as "sweaters of labour, pawnshop specialists and social parasites" (Gouttman, 1993: 77) and largely unassimilable. In particular, this view was held of the Polish and Russian Jews who were regarded as "Eurasian" or "Asiatic" as opposed to white. Subsequently, between 1938 and 1945, Australia reluctantly took in around 9,000 Jews with a preference for North European Jews from Germany and Austria. Following the war, two more significant waves of Jewish displaced persons were allowed to immigrate to Australia, which saw the population increase considerably. Between 1946 and 1954, a total of 17,000 Jewish survivors migrated to Australia, followed by a further 10,000 by 1961 (Rutland, 2006).

However, despite the Jewish population almost trebling between 1938 and 1961 to around 61,000, it still remained only 0.5% of the population. This was because Jews were largely being excluded from the 170,000 displaced persons who were allowed in to bolster the labour market following the war (Rutland, 2006). These exclusions were based on racial grounds and targeted those who were from Soviet-occupied countries and those of Middle Eastern origins. The former were subjected to an "Iron Curtain embargo" that was established in December of 1949, while the latter were subjected to a policy established in 1951 by the Department of Immigration that required prospective Jewish migrants to show that they had at least 75% European heritage:

> [I]t has been found that a proportion of them [Jews] show distinct traces of non-European origin and their admission is generally restricted to the wives and minor children of residents of Australia. Applications for the admission of this class of persons, whether of British or alien nationality, should be referred, accompanied by evidence that they are at least of 75 per cent European origin, as in the case of Eurasians who are not Jews.
>
> (as cited in Stratton, 1996: 62)

In other words, Australia had a distinct hierarchy for the Jews, wherein Anglo-Jews, followed by German and fellow Northern European Jews, were acceptable and could be regarded as white, while Polish, Russian, and non-European Jews were the least desirable and cast as Asiatic (Stratton, 1996).

In contrast to the Jews, a major beneficiary of the opening up to non-British migration were the Italians. By 1950, the flow of displaced persons had been largely exhausted. As a result, the Australian government turned to Italy for their labour needs and brokered a bilateral deal in 1951. The Australian government subsidised 25% of the cost of the voyage, the Italian government also paid 25%, and the remaining 50% was provided as a loan. This underwriting of the programme by both governments was critical to its success. For while the first year only yielded 59 recruits, by the end of the decade, approximately 194,000 Italians partook of the "Assisted Passage Scheme," making them the largest cultural grouping after the British. The vast majority of these were from rural backgrounds, and worked as labourers in semi-skilled or skilled sectors and generally in labour-intensive industries, such as agricultural work, construction, and road building (Furlan and Faggion, 2016).

This turn to the Italians was considered acceptable as they were regarded as not too different from the British. Indicative of this thinking is the reflection of Arthur Calwell's[1] biographer Colm Kiernan, who noted:

> [A] driving force behind Calwell's immigration policy was a desire to create a heterogeneous society in which Irishness and Roman Catholicism would be as socially acceptable as Englishness and Protestantism. He wished for a more polyglot society which, however, would be basically white and European.
>
> (Gouttman, 1993: 80)

Here, it was emphasised that their Roman Catholicism would not be a bridge too far for a nation that was already predominantly Christian. For, while Christians comprised 88% of the population, the Church of England was the dominant denomination, constituting close to half of all Christians in Australia at that time with 44% of believers, followed distantly by Catholics (14.3%), Methodists (13.1%), and Presbyterians (11.1%) as the other denominations in double figures (see Table 4.1). Further, it is important to note that while Calwell's tenure as Minister for Immigration ended in 1949, his successor in the Liberal Menzies government, Harold Holt, was also of the view that significant immigrant labour was required to spur infrastructural economic development (Gouttman, 1993).

Indeed, Holt, one year after having signed a deal with Italy, inked a similar deal with Greece that would see some 250,000 Greek migrants make their way to Australia between 1952 and the early 1970s. Spurred by both the trauma of WWII and the civil war that followed, many astutely decided that their prospects in Greece were limited and they thus sought greener pastures; like the Italians, those who made the journey were young, unskilled, and from the countryside, and would go on to work in the production lines for large car and glass factories, the smelters, and the manufacturing industries. In particular, the initial waves were predominantly young bachelors, which caused an imbalance in the small but growing diaspora, which was problematic as there was stigma attached to Anglo-Saxon women marrying Greek men. However, this imbalance was rectified when the then President of the Greek Orthodox Community, Thesseus Marmaras, represented the government in Greece in 1954, at the request of Holt, to encourage Athens to allow the immigration of Greek women (Tamis, 2005).

This move would ultimately lead to unrestricted female migration by 1961, which saw thousands of Greek women migrate that resulted in an increase in marriages and fundamentally changed the composition of the community (Tamis, 2005). Indeed, the removal of the restriction on female migration from Greece corresponds with a considerable spike and peak in Greek migration during the 1960s (see Figure 4.1).

Further, this surge in numbers would see the Greek Orthodox Church become the largest of the Eastern Orthodox Churches in Australia, with 152 regional and urban parishes and ecclesiastical communities across Australia (Tamis, 2009). In contrast, the Italians would

Table 4.1 Christian denominations in 1947

Denominations	*Population*	*%*
Church of England	2,957,032	44.3
Catholic	956,540	14.3
Methodist	871,425	13.1
Presbyterian	743,540	11.1
Catholic, Roman	613,186	9.2
Baptist	113,527	1.7
Protestant, Undefined	73,270	1.1
Church of Christ	71,771	1.1
Lutheran	66,891	1.0
Other Christian groups[a]	205,754	3.1
Total	6,672,936	100.0

Source: ABS, census (1947).

[a] This category contains all Christian groups that fell under 1% of the Christian population and includes Australian Church, Brethren, Catholic (Apostolic), Catholic (Greek), Christadelphian, Christian Scientist, Congregational, Latter-Day Saints, New Church, Other (Undefined Christians), Quaker, Salvation Army, Seventh-Day Adventist, Swedenborgian, and Unitarian.

be taken into what had been a predominantly Irish Catholic Church (Bouma, 1995), which for some formed a bridge from the old world to the new and allowed them to navigate the prejudice they encountered in Australia (Furlan and Faggion, 2016). However, that said, this incorporation of the Italians was not always smooth, with some of the Irish clergy seeing them as fundamentally different and unwelcome. For example, historian Patrick O'Farrell noted:

> Within many parishes migrants were subject to strong pressures to assimilate, to adopt Australian religious ways and to drop their own. This pressure conflicted in particular with the Italians' desire to retain their own form of worship – notably their saints' days, statues and habits of devotion. Some parishes bluntly refused to accommodate such differences of Catholic behaviour; in very few were they welcome. As a consequence, many Italian Catholics – disposed by their background to anti-clericalism – deserted the parish churches, and the regular practice of their religion. Where they remained, their participation in, and contribution to, Australian Catholic life was relatively small.
>
> (as cited in Cappello, 2002: 70)

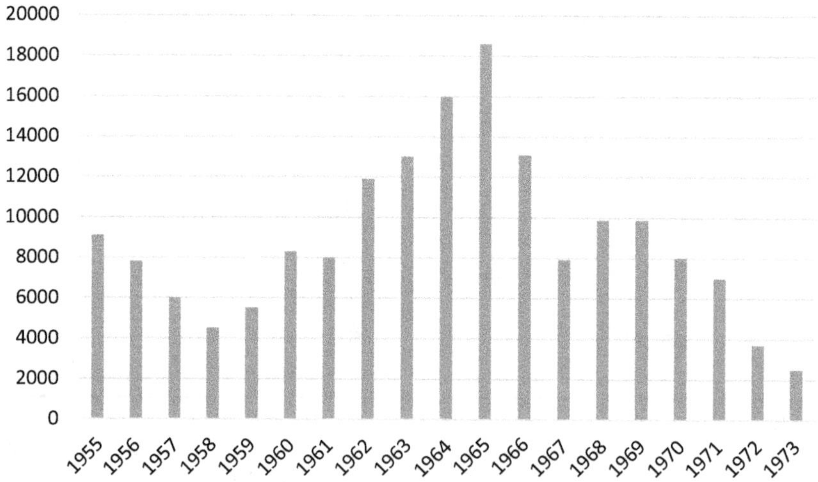

Figure 4.1 Greek migrants to Australia, 1955–1973.
Source: Adapted from Lianos (1975).

On this point, Cappello (2002) notes that O'Farrell's less than charitable view of the contribution of Italian Catholics in Australia could be on account of the fact that there was a struggle between the Irish and Italian clergy for supremacy, and that the influx of Italians caused a pivot away from the Irish towards a broader Australian Church. Indeed, historically there appears to have been a long-standing tension between the Irish and Italian clergy, with the appointment of two Italian Bishops in the 19th century leading to allegations of Rome seeking to hatch a plot to undermine Irish control. For, at the time of Federation in 1901, the Catholic Church was strongly Irish born, constituting two-thirds of the 2,050 priests, and the church would have to wait till 1942 for its first Australian-born archbishop (Cahill, 2009). Thus, with the veracity of O'Farrell's jibe notwithstanding, what is clear is that there were most certainly schisms and that an increasingly diverse Christian landscape was being formed.

Further pluralisation of Christianity

As a result of these waves of migration from both Italy and Greece, the Christian landscape changed quite markedly with the establishment of large and distinct Greek Orthodox and Roman Catholic communities. The former, in particular, grew from very humble beginnings, with only 17,012 residing in Australia as of 1947 to 338,632 in 1971, a growth of 1891% that saw the Greek Orthodox move from just 0.25% of the overall Christian population to just over 3%. Equally impressive was the growth of the Roman Catholic community. Although coming off a much higher base of 613,186 adherents, the population more than doubled to 1,529,232, representing a 149% growth rate over two decades and a 4.72% increase in the share of the overall Christian population. Further, this growth in conjunction with the growth in the local Catholic community, which also saw a 100% growth rate, meant that the Catholics and Roman Catholics combined almost equalled the numbers of the Church of England (see Table 4.2).

Previously the Church of England was significantly larger than any other denomination. Comprising 44.3% of the Christian population in 1947, Anglicans were three times more numerous than the next denomination in local Catholicism (14.33%) and almost double both Catholic communities combined (23.52%). However, by 1971, the gap between the Anglican and wider Catholic community had narrowed considerably to near parity, with a differential of only 4.65%. The Anglican community only had a 33.69% growth rate, which saw its share

Table 4.2 Change in the Christian population by denomination, 1947–1971

Christian denominations	*1947*	*% of Christians*	*1971*	*% of Christians*	*% Change*
Baptist	113,527	1.70	175,969	1.60	−0.10
Brethren	13,002	0.19	22,963	0.21	0.02
Catholic (Roman)	613,186	9.19	1,529,232	13.91	4.72
Catholic	956,540	14.33	1,913,402	17.41	3.08
Churches of Christ	71,771	1.08	97,423	0.89	−0.19
Church of England	2,957,032	44.31	3,953,204	35.97	−8.34
Congregational	63,243	0.95	68,159	0.62	−0.33
Orthodox	17,012[a]	0.25	338,632	3.08	2.83
Jehovah's Witness			35,752	0.33	
Lutheran	66,891	1.00	196,847	1.79	0.79
Methodist	871,425	13.06	1,099,019	10.00	−3.06
Presbyterian	743,540	11.14	1,028,581	9.36	−1.78
Salvation Army	37,572	0.56	65,831	0.60	0.04
Seventh-Day Adventists	17,550	0.26	41,617	0.38	0.12
Protestant (Undefined)	73,270	1.10	243,202	2.21	1.11
Other Christian	57,375[b]	0.86	180,546	1.64	0.78
Total Christian	6,672,936	88.04	10,990,379	86.16	−1.88

Source: Australian Bureau of Statistics.

[a] In the 1947 census, the Orthodox category was listed as Catholic (Greek); in Table 4.1, this category was included in Other Christian as it was under 1% of the population.

[b] The category of Other Christian for the year 1947 comprises the following: Australian Church, Catholic (Apostolic), Christadelphian, Christian Scientist, Latter-Day Saints, New Church, Quaker, Swedenborgian, Unitarian, and Other Christian (Undefined).

of the overall Christian population contract by 8.34%, as other dominations grew more rapidly. Thus, while Anglicans were still numerically superior, it was a much more even playing field, with four other denominations – Catholics, Roman Catholics, Methodists, and Presbyterians – all having more than 1 million adherents. Moreover, the Christian landscape had become increasingly plural with the rapid rise of the Greek Orthodox community and strong growth amongst the Protestant and Lutheran communities, which both grew by 232% and 194%, respectively, during the same time frame.

In other words, what was previously an Anglican hegemony then became a joint affair with the Catholic community, and, as Gary Bouma (1995: 293) notes, this did not lead to competition but rather to "tolerance, mutual understanding and accommodation." This tendency towards cooperation and acceptance of the smaller bit part players is a result of the fact that Australia is only nominally a Christian country, having never taken on Anglicanism as the Church of the State. Rather, as discussed earlier, in the formative years of the colonies, governors preferred not to choose one church over another, and would provide funding across the board to avoid conflict. Thus, Anglicans, despite being the largest denomination, were subject to disestablishment along with all the other denominations, and this egalitarianism carried through to Australian Federation (see Carey, 1996; Chapter 3).

Pluralisation of religion: a Turkish beginning

In conjunction with this pluralisation of Christianity, Australia also began to open up to other religions in the late 1960s. By this time, both Italian and Greek migration began to taper off with improved economic circumstances in Italy, while migrants from Greece preferred to migrate to other countries (see Baldassar and Pyke, 2014; Lianos, 1975). Subsequently, the government in 1967 signed an "assisted migration agreement" with Turkey. This arrangement was born out of pressure in Turkey on account of the unemployment problem and the fact that the doors to Europe were being closed, combined with Australia's desire to continue to expand the workforce. Further, this move to include migrants from beyond Western Europe was the first step towards the dismantling of the White Australia policy, as it enabled the first major Muslim community to settle in Australia (İçduygu, 2008; Tao, 2017).

Beginning in 1968, the programme saw the number of Turkish-born migrants increase from 1,544 in 1961 to 11,589 in 1971 (Deen, 2012). This represented a significant increase in the Muslim population, which, in 1971, only numbered 22,311, or 0.17% of the overall population (see Table 4.4). This injection of Muslim migrants effectively put Islam on the map, as it was not even listed as a religion in the 1966 census. Rather, Muslims were incorporated into the larger subcategory of "Other" under "non-Christian." Thus, this burst of Turkish migration would be the beginning of rapid growth for the Muslim diaspora in Australia. However, further development in this regard would not be led by the Turkish community. For, from 1975 onwards, the numbers reduced considerably, with only a few hundred coming each year, mainly for family reunification and marriage flows (İçduygu, 2008). Rather, further growth would be on account of the full dismantling of the White Australia policy and a shift to a multicultural agenda under the stewardship of Prime Minister Gough Whitlam and his Labor government (1972–1975), which was then followed by the Fraser (1975–1983), Hawke (1983–1991), and Keating (1991–1996) governments. Indeed, as Poynting and Mason (2008) note, this period was shaped by a bipartisan support for the policy of multiculturalism – a development that would end with the election of the Howard government (1996–2007), which sought to bring "white politics" back to the centre (see Jakubowicz, 2002; see also Chapter 11). Therefore, for our purpose, the following section focuses on developments up until 1996, as this period laid the foundation for Australia's cultural and religious pluralism.

The shift to a multicultural Australia: 1973 to 1996

In 1973, the Whitlam government officially ended the last vestiges of the White Australia policy through the introduction of a raft of immigration reforms. These included the provision of access to assisted passage for non-Europeans and access to citizenship after three years, and the *Race Discrimination Act* was introduced in 1975, making it illegal for people to discriminate on the basis of race, colour, or ethnic origins (Tavan, 2004). However, as Jones (1997, 2003) notes, the supporters of White Australia policy were not entirely defeated by this point. Rather, they were simply outmanoeuvred and the situation would become point of contention again in the 1980s and early 1990s, on account of Geoffrey Blainey, John Howard, and later Pauline Hanson raising the issue of Asian immigration. Further, the opening up of Australia to a more diverse array of migrants was kick-started by two crises.

The first of these crises was the arrival of boat people from Vietnam in 1976 after the fall of Saigon. The numbers were small, with the first boat to arrive carrying five men who landed in Darwin in April, and only 111 would reach Australia that year. This number would increase the following year with a further 868; however, with an election looming on 10 December, the Fraser government was keen to stem the influx of Vietnamese asylum seekers. This was due to extensive media coverage that suggested that the nation was losing control of its borders, a situation that was nothing short of a moral panic as the numbers to this point were less than 1,000 arrivals. As a result, Fraser undertook two measures to curb the flows. Alongside instituting boat holding strategies with Indonesia, he sought to deter asylum seekers by undertaking a substantial intake of Indo-Chinese people from overseas camps (K. Betts, 2001).

Subsequently, between 1978 and 1982, with intakes of Vietnamese displaced by the Viet Cong averaging around 8,000 a year,[2] over 50,000 had been resettled in Australia. This growth in Vietnamese migration would continue into the early to mid-90s under the Hawke/Keating governments (discussed below), but would slow significantly after 1996 with the election of the Howard government, which instituted tough family reunion rules (Jakubowicz, 2004).[3] Nevertheless, by then, the Vietnamese-born population had become one of largest diasporas in Australia at that time,[4] having grown from a humble 2,472 in 1976 to 150,941 in 1996 (see Table 4.3).

In conjunction with the Vietnamese crisis, there was also a third wave of Lebanese migration to Australia on account of an outbreak of civil war in 1976. The war claimed 50,000 lives and displaced 600,000 people, many of whom had fled to Cyprus, where Australia set up processing facilities (Franklin, 2006). In response, Australia accepted 4,000 of them in 1976, and by 1981, around 18,500 visas were issued to Lebanese migrants, which resulted in net migration of around 16,200 (J. Betts and Krayem, 2019).

This intake was significant as it was fundamentally different from those who had come before. The first wave that arrived in small groups from the late 19th century up until WWII, which amounted to approximately 2,000, was predominantly Christian. Similarly, the second stream that arrived between 1947 and 1975 – most of which had arrived after the Arab–Israeli War of 1967 and saw the diaspora grow to 33,000 – was also predominantly Christian. However, the third wave had a relatively even mix of Christian and Muslim refugees. As a result, the Lebanese Muslim population grew from just under 7,000 to around 15,600 by 1981 (K. Betts and Healy, 2006), a boost which represented a significant jump in the overall Muslim population (see Table 4.4).

Table 4.3 Growth in the Vietnamese population, 1976–1996

Census year	*Born in Vietnam*	*% Change*
1976	2,427	
1981	41,096	1593
1986	83,028	102
1991	121,813	47
1996	150,941	24

Source: Adapted from Jakubowicz (2004).

This expansion of immigration to include people from Asia and the Middle East continued under both Hawke and Keating, particularly the former. During Hawke's tenure, immigration peaked at a high of 145,320 in 1988/89 before dropping to 121,560 in 1990/91 (Murphy, 1993), and was driven by family reunion intake, which had doubled and was taken up largely by those from the Vietnamese and Lebanese diasporas, as well as those from the Philippines and Hong Kong (Birrell, 1994). These intakes saw that each community continued to rapidly increase in size. Further, this expansion of immigration to include many from Asia under Hawke was driven by a strong sense of equality and social justice and a firm belief in the value of multicultural society:

> "Multicultural" is more than a descriptive term to designate a society made up of different ethnic groups. It is also an approach to policy formulation and resource allocation which seeks to provide for equality of access and opportunity. It designates a society which supports a common group of institutions, legal rights and obligations, while leaving individuals free to maintain their religion, language and cultural customs. A multicultural society is a vital and tolerant and progressive community in which all groups, be they aboriginal [sic], Anglo-Celtic, European, Asian, Latin American, or Middle Eastern, or from any other of the ethnic groupings we find in our society today, make an important contribution to the richness, the depth and traditions of our nation.
>
> (Hawke, 1984, as cited in Moran, 2017: 68–69)

Similarly, under Keating, who was guided by the same ethos, Asian migration continued to grow apace, despite a significant reduction in the overall immigration intake to less than 70,000 in 1991 and a moderate increase to only 92,000 by 1994. For example, between 1990/1991

Table 4.4 Muslim population growth, 1971–1996

Year	*Total Muslim Population*	*Total Population*	*%*
1971	22,311	12,755,638	0.17
1976	45,202	14,033,083	0.32
1981	76,792	14,923,260	0.51
1986	109,523	16,018,350	0.68
1991	147,507	17,284,036	0.85
1996	200,885	17,892,423	1.12

Source: Australian Bureau of Statistics & Haveric (2019).

and 1994/1995, Vietnam added a further 39,000, Hong Kong 40,000, Philippines 24,000, and India 21,000 (Jupp, 2002).

Thus, a natural outgrowth of this increased acceptance of cultural diversity under the rubric of multiculturalism actioned by Gough Whitlam, and then implemented by Fraser, Hawke, and Keating, has also led to Australia becoming increasingly religiously diverse. Indeed, as Bouma (1994) notes, the Christian plurality of the 1950s and 60s is now accompanied by the religious plurality that was brought about by the 1970s and 1980s which introduced significant numbers of Muslims, Buddhists, and Hindus.

As can be seen in Table 4.5, over the course of just 25 years, Australia shifted from simply having a category titled "Other religions" that comprised 0.11% in 1971,[5] to have clearly identifiable Buddhist and Hindu communities in 1996, representing 1.12% and 0.38% of the population, respectively. Similarly, the Muslim population also saw rapid growth, more than quadrupling in size between 1971 and 1986, and then almost doubling again between 1986 and 1996, a development that represented an overall growth rate of no less than 800% (see Table 4.4).

However, while these developments represent significant growth and increased religious pluralism, it is important to note that these numbers were still small in relation to the wider population and that Australia was still very much a nominally Christian country with 70.32% of the population identifying as such in 1996, albeit a significant decline from 86.16% of Australians defining themselves as Christian 25 year earlier. Much of this shift can be attributed to significant growth of those in the "no religion" category. Interestingly, since 1971, the instruction of "if no religion, write none" was introduced to the census which saw an immediate sevenfold increase from 0.8% in 1966, and a progressive increase to more than 16% in 1996 (ABS, 2006; see also Chapter 7).

New migrant religious movement and new religious movements (NRMs)

Migrants from a non-world religion coming to Australia also brought with them what are called New Migrant Religious Movements. These are not part of the main religions and enlarge the scope of diversity. Indeed, some Vietnamese imported Caodaism, a religion that mixes elements of Catholicism and spiritualism, and some Iranian communities brought with them the Baha'i faith, a religion from a Persian

Table 4.5 Population by religious denomination in 1971 and 1996

Religious denomination	*1971*	*% of population*	*Religious denomination*	*1996*	*% of population*
Christian:			*Christian:*		
Anglican	3,953,204	30.99	Anglican	3,903,324	21.82
Baptist	175,969	1.38	Baptist	295,178	1.65
Brethren	22,963	0.18	Brethren	22,063	0.12
Catholic	3,442,634[b]	26.99	Catholic	4,798,950	26.82
Churches of Christ	97,423	0.76	Churches of Christ	75,023	0.42
Jehovah's Witness	35,752	0.28	Jehovah's Witnesses	83,414	0.47
			Latter-Day Saints	45,112	0.25
Lutheran	196,847	1.54	Lutheran	249,989	1.40
			Oriental Christian	31,342	0.18
Orthodox	338,632	2.65	Orthodox	497,015	2.78
			Pentecostal	174,720	0.98
Presbyterian	1,028,581	8.06	Presbyterian and Reformed	675,534[c]	3.78
Salvation Army	65,831	0.52	Salvation Army	74,145	0.41
Seventh-day Adventists	41,617	0.33	Seventh-day Adventist	52,655	0.29
Uniting Church[a]	1,167,178	9.15	Uniting Church	1,334,917	7.46
Protestant (Undefined)	243,202	1.91	Other Protestant	50,216	0.28
Other Christian	180,546	1.42	Other Christian	219,167	1.22
Total	*10,990,379*	*86.16*	*Total*	*12,582,764*	*70.32*

Non-Christian:			*Non-Christian:*		
Buddhism			Buddhism	199,812	1.12
Hinduism			Hinduism	67,279	0.38
Islam	22,311	0.17	Islam	200,885	1.12
Judaism	62,208	0.49	Judaism	79,805	0.45
Other religions	14,404	0.11	Other religions	68,647	0.38
Total	*98,923*	*0.78*	*Total*	*616,428*	*3.45*
No religion	855,676	6.71	No religion	2,948,888	16.48
Indefinite	29,413	0.23	Inadequately described	54,164	0.30
Not stated	781247	6.12	Not stated	1,550,585	8.67
			Overseas visitor	139,594	0.78
Total population	**12,755,638**	**100.00**	**Total Population**	**17,892,423**	**100.00**

Source: Australian Bureau of Statistics.

[a] This category contains both the denominations Congregational and Methodists. In 1977, the Uniting Church was formed through a merger of the Methodists, Congregationalists, and the Presbyterians to give effect to the *Basis of the Union* (1971) (see Emilsen, 2009).

[b] Catholic and Roman Catholic are combined here as there was no distinction in the 1996 census.

[c] The significant decline amongst the Presbyterians was on account of the formation of the Uniting Church in 1977. Only around 31% of the pre-1977 membership continued as Presbyterians (see Prentis, 2009).

origin that recognises all religions in the world (see Possamai and Possamai-Inesedy, 2007).[6]

There were also religions that were brought to Australia and were not necessarily connected to any specific ethnicity. For example, as there has been a revival of nature religions (also called witchcraft) in the UK and the US, the same happened in Australia (see Hume 1997 and Chapter 8). This move has even divided the Australian neo-pagan community into those who follow the calendar from the northern hemisphere and those who follow the southern one.

Other movements also came and even changed the way religion has been defined in Australian courts of law (see below). In Anglo-Saxon cultures, these groups can sometimes be called "cults", which has a strong pejorative connotation in everyday life (see Dillon and Richardson, 1994; Pfeifer, 1992), whereas the terms "New Religious Movements" (NRMs) and "Minority Religions" are more objective appellations used by scholars to describe the same phenomenon. The term "Cults" refers to religious groups with an authoritarian leadership which suppress rational thought, organise deceptive recruitment techniques and coercive mind control, and isolate members from conventional society and former relationships. It is a word used to scare, to worry, and to sell in the milieu of sensationalist journalism. For Barker (1986: 332), the term became highly derogatory after the mass suicide/murder of followers of Jim Jones in Guyana. While numerous NRMs had formally been treated individually, following this killing, they have all tended to be negatively termed "cults," even if there exists a considerable diversity among them. If most anti-cult movement' pronouncements tend to be about "destructive cults," they also have the tendency to lump many NRMs together as though they were a single entity, "the sins of one being visited on all" (Barker, 1995b: 297).

The term NRMs tends to describe new forms of religions which have developed during the 1960s in the Western world. Even if some of these groups, such as Theosophy and Spiritualism, have appeared in the 19th century (see Chapter 2) and are thus called old NRMs (Chryssides, 1999), they still remain within the confines of this appellation as they have "fully" emerged in the public sphere around this period. Within these groups, two large subtypes tend to typify the phenomenon. The world-rejecting NRMs appear to create a sense of community, their membership tends to be more demanding, and the tension with the external world can be high. On the other hand, world-affirming NRMs do not ask of its members a rejection of mainstream society and believe that human beings have a (godly) potential within themselves that can be developed.

Table 4.6 lists some of the NRMs as reported in the Australian census (see also Table 8.1). Not all of these movements are reported, and many members of these movements might not even declare their affiliation when filling out the form. Interestingly, from the five listed in this table, all have experienced a decline in the last census. We will come back to this observation in Chapter 8 where we explore the possibility that new spiritualities are having a stronger interest from religious seekers.

Some of these NRMs have created tension in Australia. For example, several legal battles have surrounded the case of the Church of Scientology (Kohn, 1996; Possamai and Possamai-Inesedy, 2009), the Children of God or the Family (Kohn, 1996; Sheen, 1996), and Ananda Marga (Richardson, 1996), and/or have been in tension with the broader Australian society such as the Hare Krishna movement (Locke, 1983; Salter, 2008).

A specific case here is worth elaborating on as it changed the way Australia understands religion in legal issues (Possamai and Possamai-Inesedy, 2009). In Victoria in 1983, the Church of Scientology faced a legal battle on the issue of being defined as a religion for tax purposes in the Church of the New Faith v Commissioner for Payroll Tax (Vic.). The court was asked to decide if the church was a religious

Table 4.6 New religious movements in Australia, 1996–2016

New religious movements	*1996*	*2001 (%Growth)*	*2006 (% Growth)*	*2011 (% Growth)*	*2016 (% Growth)*
Eckankar	829	747 (−9.89)	679 (−9.10)	674 (−0.74)	562 (−16.62)
Satanism	2,091	1,798 (−14.01)	2,247 (+24.97)	2,454 (+9.21)	2,443 (−0.45)
Scientology	1,488	2,032 (+36.56)	2,506 (+23.33)	2,163 (−13.69)	1,681 (−22.28)
Spiritualism	8,141	9,279 (+13.98)	9,844 (+6.09)	11,551 (+17.34)	10,101 (−12.55)
Theosophy	1,423	1,627 (+14.34)	1,638 (+0.68)	1,485 (−9.34)	893 (−39.87)
Total	**13,972**	**15,483 (+10.81)**	**16,914 (+9.24)**	**18,327 (+8.34)**	**15,680 (−14.44)**
Population (%)	17,892,423 (0.08)	18,769,249 (0.08)	19,855,288 (0.09)	21,507,717 (0.09)	23,401,892 (0.07)

Source: Australian Bureau of Statistics.

institution for the purpose of tax exemption. The church was first listed as a foreign company as the Church of the New Faith Incorporated in 1969 in Victoria. When the Church of the New Faith was asked to pay taxes from 1975 to 1977, it objected on the basis that it was a religion, and thus its wages were not liable to payroll tax. After many rejections to this objection, the church applied for an appeal at the High Court of Australia. The court investigated whether this organisation was, during the relevant period, a religious institution. The court focused on whether "the beliefs, practices and observances which were established by the affidavits and oral evidence as the set of beliefs, practices and observances accepted by Scientologists are properly to be described as a religion". Taking into account that religion had received little judicial exegesis in Australia since 1943 (Company of Jehovah's Witnesses Inc. v. The Commonwealth), that religions in Australia were no longer exclusively Christian and theistic since it has recognised itself as a multicultural country since the early 1970s, and that protection is required for the adherents of religions rather than for the religions themselves, the court held that the beliefs, practices, and observances of this church did constitute a religion in the state of Victoria. Through this case, the legal definition of religion in Australia was re-defined by Acting Chief Justice Mason and Justice Brennan to include two elements:

1 belief in a supernatural Being, Thing, or Principle and
2 the acceptance of canons of conduct to give effect to that belief (though canons of conduct which offend against the ordinary laws are outside the area of any immunity, privilege, or right conferred on the ground of religion).

Justices Wilson and Deane, instead of a single definition of religion, referred to some guiding principles. These are:

- a particular collection of ideas and/or practices involving belief in the supernatural,
- ideas that relate to the nature and place of humanity in the universe and the relation of humanity to things supernatural,
- ideas accepted by adherents requiring or encouraging the observation of particular standards or codes of conduct or participation in specific practices having supernatural significance,
- adherents constituting an identifiable group or identifiable groups, regardless of how loosely knit and varying in beliefs and practices these adherents may be, and

- adherents themselves seeing the collection of ideas and/or practices as constituting a religion.

By applying a definition of religion that is more inclusive of non-Christian faiths, the Church of Scientology was able to be recognised as a religion and in the end won the case.

Conclusion

Thus, three distinct trends can be seen from the gradual opening following WWII and the subsequent dismantling of the White Australia policy. The first is that Australia was becoming more religiously plural through rapid growth in adherents of Islam, Hinduism, and Buddhism on account of increased migration from the Middle East and Asia, along with a mix of some non-world religious traditions and NRMs. The second is that Christianity, despite its increased plurality, was very much in decline. Lastly, Australia was simultaneously becoming less religious with a sharp rise in "religious nones" (see Chapter 7). In other words, Australia, following WWII, was simultaneously becoming more religiously diverse, less Christian, and increasingly irreligious, and, as will be shown in the following chapter, these trends have continued and become much more pronounced.

Notes

1 Arthur Calwell was the first Minister for Immigration after the Department's establishment on 12 July 1945. The Department of Immigration aimed to increase the net population by 2% annually (Tamis, 2005).
2 Barnes (2001) notes that during this period some intakes ranged between 10,000 and 12,000.
3 By the 2001 census, the growth of the Vietnamese diaspora through migration had been reduced to just 2.6%, bringing the total to 154,831 (see Jakubowicz, 2004).
4 By the early 1990s, the Vietnamese were the seventh largest immigrant group behind the British, Germans, Italians, Greeks, members of the former Yugoslav republics, and the Chinese (Jones, 1997).
5 In the 1976 census, there was still only the category of Other non-Christian, and this was 0.22%.
6 These movements are, however, small in number. Caodaism in 2001 had only 824 adherents and, as of the 2016 census, has declined to 605. The Baha'i community, in contrast, has grown incrementally over the years, rising from 7,484 members in 1991 to 13,989 in 2016.

References

ABS. 1947. Part XVI - Religion *1947 Census of Australia*. Retrieved from https://www.ausstats.abs.gov.au/ausstats/free.nsf/0/BDB6D970204DD4C0CA2578410019B05B/$File/1947%20Census%20-%20Volume%20I%20-%20Part%20XVI%20Religion.pdf

ABS. 2006. Religious Affiliation. *1301.0- Year Book Australia, 2006*. Retrieved from https://www.abs.gov.au/ausstats/abs@.nsf/bb8db737e2af84b8ca2571780015701e/bfdda1ca506d6cfaca2570de0014496e!OpenDocument

Baldassar, L. and Pyke, J. 2014. Intra-diaspora knowledge transfer and 'new' Italian migration. *International Migration, 52*(4): 128–143.

Barker, E. 1986. Religious movements: cult and anticult since Jonestown. *Annual review of Sociology, 12*(1): 329–346.

Barker, E. 1995. The scientific study of religion? You must be joking!. *Journal for the Scientific Study of Religion, 34*(3): 287–310.

Barnes, D. 2001. Resettled refugees' attachment to their original and subsequent homelands: long-term Vietnamese refugees in Australia. *Journal of Refugee Studies, 14*(4): 394–411.

Betts, J. and Krayem, M. 2019. Strategic othering: framing Lebanese migration and Fraser's "mistake". *Australian Journal of Politics & History, 65*(1): 100–114.

Betts, K. 2001. Boat people and public opinion in Australia. *People and Place, 9*(4): 34–48.

Betts, K. and Healy, E. 2006. Lebanese Muslims in Australia and social disadvantage. *People and Place, 14*(1): 24–42.

Birrell, R. 1994. Immigration control in Australia. *The Annals of the American Academy of Political and Social Science, 534*(1): 106–117.

Bouma, G.D. 1995. The emergence of religious plurality in Australia: A multicultural society. *Sociology of Religion, 56*(3): 285–302.

Cahill, D. 2009. The Scriptural, Historical and Ecclesiological Foundation of the church's structure. In Jupp, J. ed. *The encyclopedia of religion in Australia*. Melbourne, VIC: Cambridge University Press, pp. 227–235.

Cappello, A. 2002. Rome or Ireland?: the religious control of the Italian community. *Journal of the Australian Catholic Historical Society, 23*(2002): 58–72.

Carey, H. M. 1996. *Believing in Australia: a cultural history of religions*. St. Leonards, NSW: Allen & Unwin.

Chryssides, G. 1999. *Exploring new religions*. Cassell: London.

Deen, H. 2012. Excavating the Past: Australian Muslims. *The La Trobe Journal, 89:* 63–80.

Dillon, J. and Richardson, J. 1994. The "Cult" concept: A politics of representation analysis. *Syzygy: Journal of Alternative Religion and Culture, 3*(3–4): 185–197.

Emilsen, W. W. 2009. Uniting church. In Jupp, J. ed. *The encyclopedia of religion in Australia*. Melbourne, VIC: Cambridge University Press, pp. 582–591.

Franklin, M. 2006. Fraser was warned on Lebanese migrants. *The Australian*. Retrieved from https://www.theaustralian.com.au/in-depth/cabinet-papers/fraser-was-warned-on-lebanese-migrants/news-story/0e447d68c5d9b8a47218dc3f03cff0fc

Furlan, R. and Faggion, L. 2016. Post-WWII Italian Immigration to Australia: The Catholic Church as a Means of Social Integration and Italian Associations as a Way of Preserving Italian Culture. *American Journal of Sociological Research*, *6*(1): 27–41.

Gouttman, R. 1993. A Jew, and coloured too! Immigration of 'Jews of middle east origin' to Australia, 1949–58. *Immigrants & Minorities*, *12*(1): 75–91.

Haveric, D. 2019. *Muslims making Australia home: Immigration and community building*. Issue: 28. Melbourne Univ. Publishing.

Hume, L. 1997. *Witchcraft and paganism in Australia*. Melbourne: Melbourne University.

İçduygu, A. 2008. Circular migration and Turkey: An overview of the past and present-some demo-economic implications. In *CARIM-AS 2008/10*: Robert Schuman Centre for Advanced Studies, San Domenico di Fiesole: European University Institute.

Kohn, R. 1996. Cults and the new age in Australia. In Bouma, G. ed. *Many Religions, All Australians: Religious Settlement, Identity and Cultural Diversity*. Melbourne: Christian Research Association, pp. 149–162.

Jakubowicz, A. 2002. White noise: Australia's struggle with multiculturalism. In Levine-Rasky, C. ed. *Working through whiteness: International perspectives*. Albany: State University of New York Press, pp. 107–125.

Jakubowicz, A. 2004. Vietnamese in Australia: a generation of settlement and adaptation. *Making Multicultural Australia*. Retrieved from http://www.multiculturalaustralia.edu.au/library/media/document/id/731.Vietnamese-in-Australia-a-generation-of-settlement-and-adaptation

Jones, G.W. 1997. "Australian identity", racism and recent responses to Asian immigration to Australia. In *Working Papers in Demography No. 71*. Research School of Social Sciences, Australian National University.

Jones, G.W. 2003. White Australia, national identity and population change. In Jayasuriya, L., Walker, D. and Gothard, J. eds. *Legacies of White Australia: Race, culture and nation*. Crawley, WA: University of Western Australia Press, pp. 110–128.

Jupp, J. 2002. *From white Australia to Woomera: the story of Australian immigration*. Cambridge University Press.

Kirk, N. 2008. Traditionalists and progressives: labor, race, and immigration in post-World War II Australia and Britain. *Scandinavian Journal of Gastroenterology*, *39*(1): pp.53–71.

Lianos, T.P. 1975. Flows of Greek out-migration and return migration. *International Migration*, *13*(3): 119–133.

Locke, R.G. 1983. Who am I in the city of mammon? the self, doubt and certainty. In a *Spiritualist cult* in Black, A. and Glasner, P. eds. *Practice and belief. Studies in the sociology of Australian religion*. Sydney: Allen & Unwin, pp. 108–33.

Moran, A. 2017. Multiculturalism as social justice: the Hawke and Keating Governments. In Moran, A. ed. *The public life of Australian multiculturalism*. New York: Springer, pp. 67–108

Murphy, P.A. 1993. Immigration and the management of Australian cities: the case of Sydney. *Urban Studies, 30*(9): 1501–1519.

National Archives. 2020. Refugees displaced by World War II. Retrieved from https://www.destinationaustralia.gov.au/stories/motivations/refugees-displaced-world-war-ii

Pfeifer, J.E. 1992. The psychological framing of cults: schematic representations and cult evaluations. *Journal of Applied Social Psychology, 22*(7): 531–544.

Possamai, A. and Possamai-Inesedy, A. 2007. The Baha'i faith and Caodaism: migration, change and de-secularization (s) in Australia. *Journal of Sociology, 43*(3): 301–317.

Possamai, A. and Possamai-Inesedy, A. 2009. Scientology down under. In Lewis, J. ed. *Scientology*. New York: Oxford University Press, pp. 345–361.

Poynting, S. and Mason, V. 2008. The new integrationism, the state and Islamophobia: retreat from multiculturalism in Australia. *International Journal of Law, Crime and Justice, 36*(4): 230–246.

Prentis, M. 2009. Presbyterians. In Jupp, J. ed. *The encyclopedia of religion in Australia*. Melbourne, VIC: Cambridge University Press, pp. 523–545.

Price, C. 1975. Australian immigration: 1947–73. *International Migration Review, 9*(3): 304–318.

Richardson, J.T. 1996. Journalistic bias toward new religious movements in Australia. *Journal of Contemporary Religion, 11*(3): 289–302.

Rutland, S.D. 2006. *The Jews in Australia*. Cambridge University Press.

Salter, B. 2008. "Haris" in Saris: the status of women in the Hare Krishna Movement in Australia. *Australian Religion Studies Review, 21*(2): 217–236.

Scriver, P. 2004. Mosques, ghantowns and cameleers in the settlement history of colonial Australia. *Fabrications, 13*(2): 19–41.

Sheen, J. 1996. Living within the tensions of plurality: religious discrimination and human rights law and policy. In Bouma, G. ed. *Many religions, all Australian: religious settlement, identity and cultural diversity*. Kew: The Christian Research Association, pp. 163–180.

Stratton, J. 1996. The Colour of Jews: Jews, Race and the White Australia Policy. *Journal of Australian Studies, 20*(50–51): 51–65.

Tamis, A. 2005. *The Greeks in Australia*. Melbourne: Cambridge University Press.

Tamis, A. 2009. Greek orthodoxy in Australia. In Jupp, J. ed. *The Encyclopedia of Religion in Australia*. Melbourne, VIC: Cambridge University Press, pp. 477–492.

Tao, K. 2017. Fifty years of Turkish migration. *Australian National Maritime Museum*. Retrieved from https://www.sea.museum/2017/10/05/fifty-years-turkish-migration

Tavan, G. 2004. The dismantling of the White Australia policy: Elite conspiracy or will of the Australian people? *Australian Journal of Political Science*, *39*(1): 109–125.

5 Australia as a Christian, a post-Christian, and a non-religious country

Introduction

Australia has included a question on the religion of its citizens since the first national census in 1911. This chapter details the increase and decrease of various religions and argues that in light of the data (especially the results of the 2016 census), Australia can be regarded paradoxically and synchronously as a Christian, a post-Christian, and a non-religious place.

Using techniques from human geography, this chapter first showcases the growth (de-secularisation) and decline (secularisation) of religion across states. It uses the data to illustrate that Australia is becoming both secular and more religious, depending on where you live. Indeed, religious changes do not happen homogenously in the whole of Australia. With regard to Christianity, the more religious people tend to live in Queensland and New South Wales (NSW). The less Christians states, but still over 50%, are South Australia, Victoria, and Tasmania.

To further understand these paradoxes, this chapter then concentrates on one case study per perspective. On the matter of Australia being Christian, the only Christian group that is still growing is Pentecostalism. All others are in decline. This section gives an overview of this growth and lays the foundation for further discussion on this group in Chapters 9 and 10. This chapter then moves to the notion of Islamophobia to illustrate that if Australia is increasingly recognised as a post-Christian and multifaith country, it does not mean that everyone is "tolerated." While non-Christian religions are growing, some experience challenges, especially Islam. This chapter then explores the growing non-religious phenomenon among youths to try to understand potential future trends in Australia, before coming back in Chapter 7 to a more detailed discussion of what non-religion means. It

DOI: 10.4324/9781003255338-5

then concludes by pointing to the likelihood that both non-Christian religions, and non-religion will continue to grow while Christians, with the exception of the Pentecostals, will continue to decrease in number.

What can the census tell us?

Australia, a former English penal colony where the Anglican religion was first used as a tool for social control – despite claims of a separation of church and state (see Chapter 3) – saw its religious homogeneity changing after the WWII as post-war migration and conversion to NRMs transformed its cultural, religious, and ethnic profile. In 1947, Anglicans represented 39% of the population. As listed in Table 5.1, in 2016, they have dropped to 13.3% and are no longer the largest religious group in Australia. Catholics, on the other hand, thanks to migration (see Chapter 4), have become the largest group, with 22.6% of the population.

What is also worth noting is that Australia is becoming less and less a Christian country, with those professing to be Christian falling from 88% of the population in 1947 to 52.1% in 2016. This decrease can be read by some as Australia being a post-Christian country. However, others would still call it a Christian country as the religion is still above 50%. The drop of 9% from 61.1% in 2011 to 52.1% in 2016 can be explained by the fact that less people identify themselves as Christian and also by the fact that the wording of the question on religion changed in 2016 (see Chapter 7). Whereas previous census questions listed the "no religion" category as an option at the bottom of the list to choose from, in 2016, the Australian Bureau of Statistics put it at the top. It can be assumed that some people who were raised as Christian but no longer practise and believe might have opted for the easier and quicker answer that is the top box. In previous surveys, they would have ticked a religious category at the top for ease as well. While this might explain the significant drop from 2011 to 2016, it does not undermine the 2016 results. Rather, these people would have been categorised as religious in previous censuses, when they were not. Therefore, we can then assume that Australia has been even less Christian than presented in the previous censuses.

In just a mere quarter of a century, from 1991 to 2016, the non-Christian religions have more than tripled. These include Buddhism, Hinduism, and Islam, which have grown without attracting public and secular group notice from the mid-1970s to the early 1990s. The

Table 5.1 Australian census, 1911–2016

% in	*1911*	*1947*	*1966*	*1991*	*2006*	*2011*	*2016*
Anglican	38.4	39.0	33.5	23.9	18.7	17.1	13.3
Catholic	22.4	20.7	26.2	27.4	25.8	25.3	22.6
MCPRU[a]	26.5	22.1	19.4	12.9	8.7	7.7	6.0
Pentecostal +[b]	–	–	–	0.9	2.7	3.3	3.7
Christianity total	96.9	88.0	88.2	74.1	63.9	61.1	52.1
Nones	0.2	0.3	0.8	12.9	18.7	22.3	30.1
Other religions	0.8	0.5	0.7	2.6	5.6	7.2	8.2
No response	2.1	11.2	10.3	10.4	11.8	9.4	9.6

Source: Australian Bureau of Statistics – various census reports compiled by G. Bouma in Bouma and Halafoff (2017).

[a] Methodist, Congregational, Presbyterian, Reformed, and Uniting.

[b] Pentecostal, plus "Christian," "Apostolic Church," "Church of God," "Australian Christian Churches," "New Church Alliance," "Faith Churches" so described and not further defined.

Australian government, while managing migrant intake, expected that when religious migrants came to Australia, they would simply lose their religious beliefs, especially when moving from an agrarian region of a country to more urban Australia. However, when migrants arrived and were in need of connecting with people with the same language and culture, a point of regular meeting became the church, mosque, temple, and so on. By becoming more religious than they were in their country of origin, they were able maintain a sense of cultural connection to their homeland (Bouma, 2006). This is significant, for in 2016, more than a quarter of Australians were born overseas and more than half were either born overseas or had at least one parent born outside of the country (Bouma and Halafoff, 2017: 133). In conjunction with the decrease of Christianity in the census, this is read as Australian being a post-Christian country due to its increase of non-Christian religions.

The 2016 census data thus indicate that Australia is becoming less Christian and that non-Christian groups are growing. Further to this, it is important to note that Australia, in combination with becoming more non-Christian, is also, paradoxically, becoming less religious, as already indicated above. Indeed, the "no religion" category has grown from 6.7% of the population in 1971, to 30.1% in 2016. The non-religious now are the largest category from the census and has exceeded the Catholics for the first time (see Chapter 7). This can also be read as Australian being a non-religious country.

At the present moment in Australia, there is a growth of religious diversification and religious revitalisation, especially among Pentecostals, Buddhists, Muslims, and neo-pagan groups. This diversity has been present for a very long time if we take into account the history of this country before colonialism. As already explored in Chapter 3, and as Bouma (2013: 143) states, this country "has been multilingual, multicultural and multifaith for over 45,000 years," as there was diversity among the Australian Aboriginal peoples on the continent. When the convicts were transported in the 18th century, they also brought with them religious diversity. What made Australia less diverse is in fact the White Australia policy of the first three quarters of the 20th century. Nevertheless, Pew's 2010 Religious Diversity Index ranked Australia quite highly, placing it in position 35 out of 232 countries, a rank that landed Australia in the top 15%.

With this increased vitality comes increased differentiation, and thus increased competition between religious groups. Further, spirituality, as a more personal approach to the religious phenomenon, has grown over the last few years (see Chapter 8), and this is not well represented in the census data. Many people who claim to be non-religious on the census may in fact be spiritual (see Chapter 7).

Despite this decrease in Christianity in terms of people who identify as such in the census, it does not mean that it is disappearing. On the contrary, as Marion Maddox (2009) has demonstrated, even in secular liberal societies such as Australia, where a strong division between church and state is supposedly definitive, religion has still a part to play in politics: religion, especially Christianity, is shown to be a significant factor in voting decisions, and religion is intruding more and more into the public sphere (see Chapters 11 and 12).

Looking at the various states in Australia, we can discover some interesting patterns. To visualise the trends across states, we have compressed the religious profile of Australia into three broad categories according to census data: the Christian, non-Christian religions, and non-religious groups. Figure 5.1 details the percentage of Christianity in various states. The darker the colour, the higher the percentage. It indicates that NSW and Queensland are not only the most Christian states (above 60%) but that they are also above the national average.

Figure 5.2 provides information about the non-Christian groups. Again, the darker the colour, the higher the percentage. NSW, while being heavily Christian (above 60%), is also one of the most non-Christian states (above 10%). NSW could thus be argued to be both Christian and post-Christian. Queensland, on the other hand, while being one of the most Christian states (above 60%), is the least non-Christian one.

In Figure 5.3, we can see that the most non-religious state is Tasmania (above 40%), followed by South Australia. The lower the level of non-religious residents, the lighter colour on the map. NSW leads in this regard with less than 30% falling into the non-religious category.

From this exercise, it can be inferred that NSW is the most religious state, be it Christian or non-Christian, and that Queensland is the most Christian state in terms of its religious homogeneity. Victoria is the most non-Christian religious state while at the same time being less religious with only a count around that of the national average and a higher contingent of non-religious than the national average of 30.1%. Tasmania is less religious with a higher contingent than national count in the non-religious category, whilst having around the national average (52%) for Christians and the lowest non-Christian community in the country. Western Australia and the Northern Territory are a mix of these three characteristics. Geographically speaking, ACT is a less Christian and more non-religious enclave than the encompassing state of NSW.

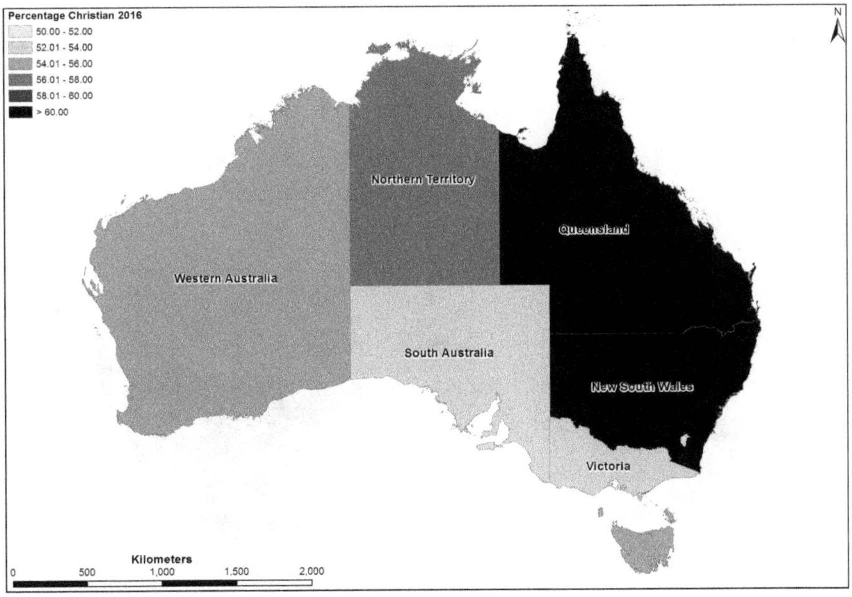

Figure 5.1 Percentage of Christians across states.
Source: Australian Bureau of Statistics.

Research on these differences between the states is not abundant. Porter (2011) studies Anglicanism and observes a contrast between the Sydney Anglicans and the rest of Australia. She claims that Sydney's synod has moved away from mainstream Anglicanism and has become a more conservative Protestant congregation. But what would cause these differences? Porter (2011) analyses the input of Bishop Peter Jensen and other recent factors such as the education provided by Moore Theological College, an institution that has been training men and women since 1856 for Christian ministry and mission. She traces this to the different social memory of Sydney compared with the rest of Australia. When the transport of convicts stopped in 1868, out of the 160,000 convicts, only 25,000 were females. This created a very male-centred society. The convicts also came from urban settings in Britain and a working (and criminal) class background, wherein there was considerable contempt for the established religion of their home country, as the Church of England was a church for the gentry and the middle classes. The contacts of preachers with the working class were mainly to uphold law and order, and this continued in Australia (see Chapter 3). This created a sense in the host country that established religion was used as a tool of social control. Tension with Catholics was

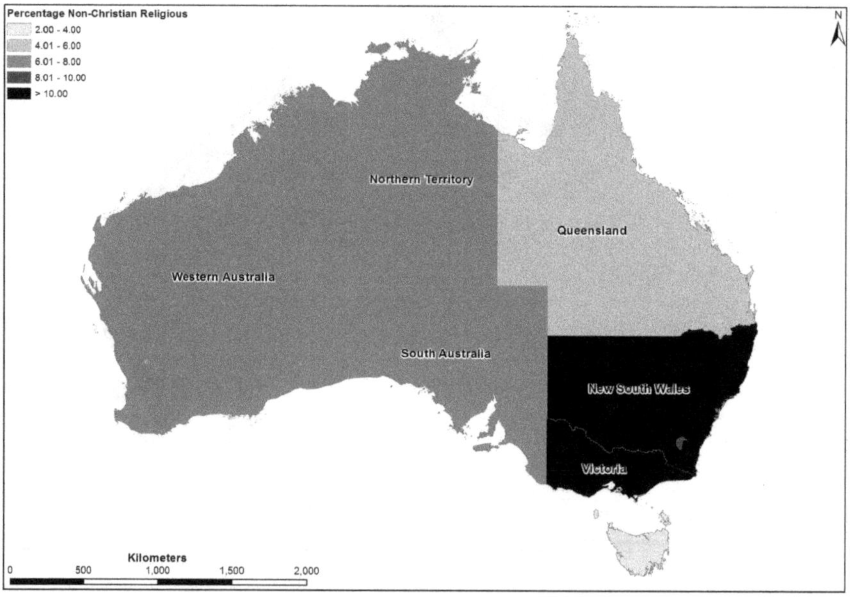

Figure 5.2 Percentage of non-Christians across states.
Source: Australian Bureau of Statistics.

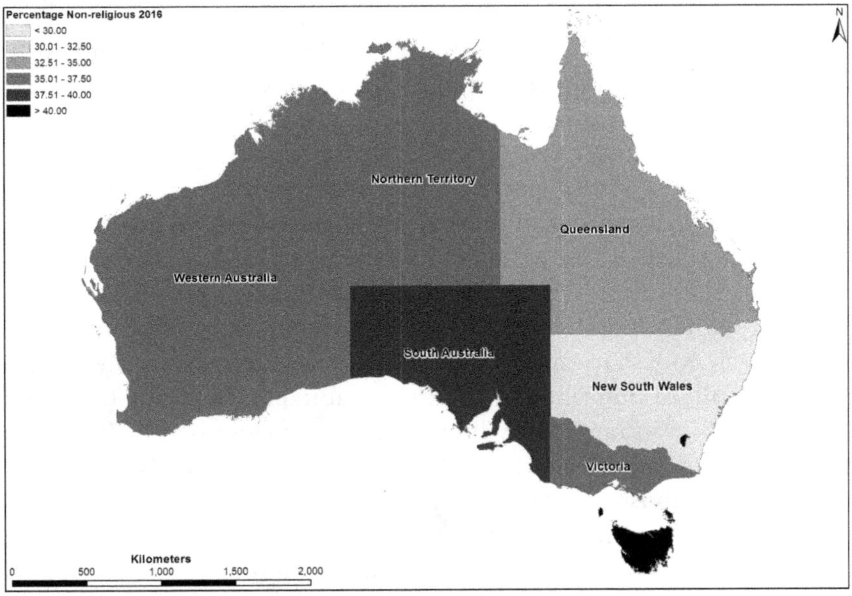

Figure 5.3 Percentage of non-religious across states.
Source: Australian Bureau of Statistics.

strong, as their request for Catholic priests to minister them was only accepted in 1820. These tensions created a legacy of "us and them" between the first white Australians and the Anglican Church. Although the religious landscape of Australia has changed, especially after WWII, the vestiges of this legacy have remained, especially in Sydney. Porter (2011) sees this as a source for the more conservative leaning in Sydney as compared to, for example, Melbourne where the free settlers (e.g. industrious churchgoing Presbyterians) worked better together with the church to build a prosperous community.

Half a century ago, Mol attempted to answer the provocative question: "Is Sydney a pragmatic and godless city, trying to live down its convict origins, while Melbourne is the home of the more reserved, god-fearing church-goer"? (1971: 125). This inquiry was based on some anecdotes from his reading of commentaries, but he did not find significant differences in his survey research. He did point out, however, that Melbourne was the bastion of atheism in the late 19th century where the influence of Darwin, Spencer, and Huxley was most felt.

Much later, in his account of the two largest cities in Australia, Bouma (2013) makes reference to two different social memories, in which contestation for state privilege (especially from Anglicans) has been stronger in NSW history than in Victoria where the Presbyterians (also called the Church of Scotland) were wealthier and more influential. Bouma highlights the legacy of the first Archbishop of Melbourne, Moorhouse, who had begun to soften relationships with other Protestant denominations, while NSW faced stronger sectarian rivalry, especially between Protestants and Catholics. He also points out two different modes of interreligious relations in Australia's two largest cities, due to differences in leadership and in theology. The history of inter-church cooperation has been longer and stronger in Melbourne. This leads him to describe the Victorian capital as the irenic (i.e. aimed at peace) city contrary to Sydney as the pugnacious one (i.e. being eager to argue), and that the theologies in the capital of NSW tend to be more exclusivist, as reflected by the Sydney Anglican leadership rarely participating in interfaith activities (Bouma, 2013: 149). Sydney also has a stronger history of tension, with Anglicans and Protestants being antagonistic towards Catholics. Bouma also reflects on Muslim organisations in Sydney being more prone to internal conflict than their counterpart in the south.

In a study on Sydney, Stevenson et al. (2010) mapped religious identification and discovered that this metropolis is more religious than the rest of the country. This is mainly caused by its patterns of non-Christian immigration, even though Christianity has decreased and the "No Religion" category has grown. Subsequently, they argued that Sydney is more and more a post-Christian city even if NSW is among the most Christian states in Australia.

With this overview in place, we now move to explore one case study for each of the three contemporary characteristics of Australia to shed more light on current changes.

A new Christianity?

As indicated by the census, the large majority of Christian groups are in decline. The Pentecostals, however, are an exception. Looking at the current census data, the Pentecostals represent 1.1% of the population (see Chapter 9 and Table 9.2). Bouma and Halafoff (2017) observe this growth but argue that this group is part of a broad Christian category that has remained invisible in various statistical analyses. This more inclusive categorisation comprises the "Apostolic Church," the

"Church of God," "Australian Christian Churches" (which used to be the "Assemblies of God"), and many other charismatic churches which are part of a broad Pentecostal movement. They have combined these categories to reflect the now more impressive growth of this larger and larger Christian group. In their estimation, they moved from being less than 1% in 1991, to have grown to 3.7% in 2016. This is the one of the rare Christian groups that is growing in Australia, and with high profile adherents like the current Prime Minister, Scott Morrison, the Pentecostal community is likely to continue to grow.

Singleton (2020) traces its influence in Australia to a much earlier time period. He argues that the movement started in Australia following the Azusa Street Revival in Los Angeles (1906–1915), and that there were revivals as well in Victoria, NSW, and Queensland from the 1920s. The Assemblies of God was then founded in 1937. It started to expand in this country in the late 1960s and early 1970s. It is today one of the most popular options among young Christian adults. According to Singleton (2020), its strength lies in adapting to social and cultural changes, as we will see in Chapter 10, with their use of social media. Hutchinson, Rocha, and Openshaw (2020) also argue that Australia, if on the periphery on a Eurocentric map, is deeply entangled in the global flows of this religion. Three of the largest charismatic megachurch networks today in the world are Hillsong, C3, and INC, which all have roots in Australia.

Australia is not unique in this regard and is part of a growing world phenomenon. Focusing on Pentecostalism in Latin America, for example, Jesús Garcia-Riuz and Patrick Michel (2012) demonstrate how this religion is creating a new type of globalised individual who answers to the call of the new global world and its logic of market expansion. Neo-Pentecostal groups have been successful in Latin America through advancing the social mobility of both their leaders and parishioners. Pentecostalism supports a prosperity gospel which gives a theological justification to neoliberalism and which ignores structural inequality (Jennings, 2017). It spreads from North America to the Global South (Freston, 2004) and across the Global South, from Brazil to South Africa (Freston, 2005). It is seen as an exporter of American capitalism that aims to break down traditional and indigenous ways of living (Sharpe 2013). Some prosperity teachers even revise the traditional view that Jesus led an ascetic life and even that he was in fact wealthy. To justify their views, they quote verses from the New Testament, such as 3 John 1: 2, "Beloved, I wish above all things that thou mayst prosper and be in health, even as thy soul prospereth," and John 10:10, "I am come that they might have life, and that they might have it more abundantly" (as cited in Sharpe, 2013: 165). They also preach sermons and organise group classes on how to deal with finances and gain entrepreneurial skills. In the United States, Einstein (2008) claims that Evangelical Protestantism has become the largest religious group in the country, representing 36% of all religious practitioners. While other denominations are in decline, Einstein attributes this group's success to the development of seeker churches, also known as mega-churches. This is a trend that has seen these groups "megasize" their brands and teach (and preach) about prosperity. Einstein quotes John Osteen, one of the Baptist ministers who played a central role in spreading this new gospel:

> It's God's will for you to live in prosperity instead of poverty. It's God will for you to pay your bills and not be in debt. It's God will for you to live in health and not in sickness all the days of your life.
> (as cited in Einstein, 2008: 123)

This message is a far cry from a gospel of condemnation and damnation, and we will come back to this new Christianity more specifically when analysing their effective use of social media in Chapter 10, and their impact on Australian politics in Chapter 11.

Backlash against non-Christian religions: Islamophobia

Australia is a success story in terms of migration and deep equality (see Chapters 1 and 12). This has also impacted on the growth of Christian religions (e.g. migrants from Vietnam, the Philippines, and Lebanon) but mainly on non-Christian religions (e.g. migrants from Vietnam for Buddhism and from Lebanon for Islam) as seen in Chapter 4. One group which stands out among this wide mix at the moment is Islam.

Riaz Hassan's (2018) recent report provides some very telling findings. Islam represents 2.6% of the whole Australian population, that is 604,244 who identified as such. Among them, 37.2% were Australian-born. The other top countries of origin are Pakistan (9.3%), Afghanistan (7.2%), Lebanon (5.8%), and Bangladesh (5.7%). Altogether, they have come from 183 countries, making this religious group one of the most ethnically diverse in Australia. Of interest to the discussion above, 44.4% of the whole Australia

Muslim population live in NSW and 32.6% in Victoria, the two most non-Christian states.

The terrorist attacks in the United States on 11 September 2001 unleashed racially based attacks on Australians who have a Muslim background. Many Muslims, especially after this event, have experienced forms of everyday racism such as discrimination at work, media stereotyping, verbal abuse and harassment, threats of violence, veil-tearing, and physical assault (Tabar et al., 2010). Some specific cases in Australia, among many, have been the media coverage from 2001 to 2002 of "Muslim Gang Rapes" in Sydney (Dagistanli and Grewal, 2012), the 2007–2009 Islamic School Controversy in South West Sydney (Al-Natour and Morgan, 2012), and the 2007 "Lindsay Leaflet Scandal" where a politician sought to use the fear against Muslims as a political strategy by linking them with the opposing party, though ultimately failed and fell afoul of the authorities (Dunn and Kamp, 2012). Almost 20 years after 9/11, a recent analysis on Australia media documents found that Islam still tends to be strongly and negatively associated with terrorism and violence (Weng and Halafoff, 2020).

To understand the level of hostility towards this religion, Hassan uses the concept of Islamophobia which is a term that "denotes negative and hostile attitudes towards Islam and Muslims" (2018: 42). He discovered that almost 70% of Australians have a low level of antagonism against Muslims, 20% are undecided, and that 10% show signs of being highly Islamophobic. As stated in the executive summary of his report (2018: 12):

> The survey found that people are more likely to be Islamophobic if they are older, have not completed Year 12, are not employed in a professional or managerial role, or if they belong to a non-traditional Christian denomination. People who have regular contact with Muslims are less likely to be Islamophobic, and so are people who have tolerant attitudes towards migrants or who are not very worried about terrorism.

In recent research on religion and Generation Z in Australia, Singleton et al. (2021) found that their Muslim respondents still reported experiencing ongoing Islamophobia. The same was found for their Jewish participants with regard to anti-Semitism.

Islamophobia is in a sense connected to a fear of terrorism conducted since the beginning of this century by groups like al-Qaeda and ISIS, but it is more than this. Of course, this does not prevent various governments around the world from attempting to control these extremist and radical elements. To securitise Muslim radicalism, many Western governments have put in place various measures aimed at "domesticating" Islam in the West, including deradicalisation programmes (Akbarzadeh, 2013; Humphrey, 2013). New anti-terror laws have been pushed through, and governments have increased surveillance (Richardson, 2013). Between 2002 and 2007, Australia introduced 44 separate pieces of counterterrorism legislation, which was more than that in the US, the UK, and Spain, although, to date, unlike the US, the UK or Spain, Australia has never experienced a major terrorist attack on home soil (Misra, 2018). Further, since the advent of Islamic State (ISIS) and the issue of foreign fighters, this programme of laws has continued to expand, with the number of law changes reaching 60 by 2014 (Battersby, 2018).

As already touched on in Chapter 1, if the word "Shari'a" is mentioned, the issue becomes even more antagonistic. Discussions in the West about allowing Shari'a courts alongside common law have often become heated (Possamai et al., 2015). Shari'a is in fact more a way of life than a system of laws, and is practised as part of a Muslim's daily adherence. In Western countries, many populist politicians and journalists have used this as a claim that Muslim people are changing "their" country. These debates are often sensationalist and overlook that Muslims are obliged to follow the laws of their host country (for the first generation) and country of birth (for subsequent generations). In practice, Shari'a law is often used adjacent to local laws (for instance, finding a Shari'a-compliant financial system that does not invest in alcohol and pornography, or having a Shari'a court acknowledging that a female Muslim is religiously divorced, even if already divorced legally, so she can remarry someone from her community). As an example, in the UK, Bano (2012) surveyed 22 Shari'a councils and found that they mainly tend to be part of the whole gamut of services offered by the mosque in which they are based. Their focus is on reconciliation and mediation services, and the councils do not operate as distinct or unofficial legal bodies. As such, their activities are not about introducing Islamic law into English law. They complement England's legal system and do not replace civil law.

The respondents of a study in Sydney by Possamai et al. (2016) were reflective about their interaction with Shari'a and the impact this interaction has on Australian society and the ensuing perception non-Muslims in Australia have of Muslims. In stark contrast to the public's association of Shari'a with beheadings, stonings, and amputations, the only engagement the respondents have with these is their frustration at the media for perpetuating this idea of Shari'a. What was particularly significant was that some respondents believed it was not worth pursuing a parallel system of Australian law and Shari'a. Many of the interviewees felt that any attempt towards establishing Shari'a courts in Australia would be counterproductive in the current political climate. They were not opposed to Shari'a but were, however, concerned about it inciting further Islamophobia in Australia. Any benefit the courts would bring to Muslims would be outweighed by the political and social backlash the issue would produce. Some respondents were also against a parallel system on the basis that it would further isolate Muslims from Australian society. In Melbourne, Johns et al. (2015) investigated the experience of citizenship and belonging of Muslims. They discovered that their informants are following liberal democratic models of civic virtue and are committed to improving the social conditions of the locality which they inhabit. To work towards this "common good," the informants detailed their lived practices of Shari'a as a positive way of living in Australia.

In another recent report on research conducted in Sydney, Dunn et al. (2015) argue that the majority of Australian Muslims live their lives as ordinary citizens. By this, they mean that they are not marginal, disaffected, and radicalised. In this city in which we find an everyday multiculturalism, the everyday concerns of Muslim Australians are ordinary, that is, they do not differ from other Australians.

The youth and the future of the non-religious in Australia

In their research on religion and Generation Z in Australia, Singleton et al. (2019) discovered in their national telephone survey of 1,200 people aged 13–18 that 52% of the participants do not identify with a religion. If these youth were themselves filling out the census data, instead of their parents, the overall proportion of the no religion in Australia could be higher than 30%. However, this does not mean that they do not believe in something, as only a quarter of the participants have no belief at all in a transcendent being or God. While they tend to not affiliate themselves with a religious group, it does not mean that they are secular. The most popular beliefs in this group of respondents are karma (50%) and reincarnation (29%), and they are not necessarily Buddhists or Hindus. Gen Z is also less Anglo-Australian than previous generations and is less likely to follow mainline Christian churches.

If overall they do not tend to be religious in a conventional sense, they still believe in a higher being (Singleton et al., 2021).

Overall, they are also supportive of religious diversity, as 91% have agreed with the statement: "Having people of many different faiths makes Australia a better place to live" and 74% of them have a positive attitude towards Islam, Buddhism, and Hinduism. Only a small minority of 5% had negative views. For the large majority, people should be free to be religious and not fear prejudice for their beliefs and practices. But contrary to the highly politicised religious freedom debate, especially since the legalisation of same-sex marriage in 2017 (see Chapters 11 and 12), the possibility of increasing the right of religious groups to be exempted from certain discrimination laws is for them not acceptable (Singleton et al., 2021). They do not agree that staff or students should be discriminated because of their gender and/or sexual identity and tend to be against these religious exemptions.

This generation has for all of their life known Australia as a diverse country (Halafoff et al., 2020). This is contrary to the baby boomers who were born just after WWII and who started to live religious diversity (as in not limited to Christianity) in their early adulthood. For Generation X, raised during 1960–1980, they were young when this started, but not fully integrated into this new view of their society. Anglicans, Presbyterians, Reformed, Uniting, Baptists, and Lutherans in Australia are in decline in terms of their numbers simply because they attract the older generation. Catholics, Pentecostals, Muslims, Hindus, Sikhs, and Buddhists tend to include more youth, and this is partly due to recent migration patterns.

However, the youth are not a homogenous group. For example, with regard to the Muslim youth and the discussion above about Islamophobia, Tittensor et al. (2020) have highlighted that following 9/11 the Australian government instituted an unprecedented raft of counterterrorism measures, which introduced both preventative mass surveillance and pre-crime offences. While not directly targeting Muslims in name, in practice, it has had negative unintended consequences for Muslim diaspora communities. Drawing on 23 interviews with Muslim youth, they found that Muslim Australians are retreating into their ethno-religious identities as a result of a feeling of misrecognition. This climate of fear and anxiety is also leading to self-censorship in Muslim youth and to a sense of disconnect between them and the current leadership. These developments are significant as the age profile of the Australian Muslim community is comparatively young, with 82% under the age of 45

(495,444), while around 37% are Australian-born (223,554) (Hassan, 2018). This means there are likely many young Muslims who are impacted by this generational and cultural divide and who are turning to social media and other cyber-fora that function as virtual religious communities (Aly, 2012) allowing for the articulation of transnational and supranational Muslim networks. The future of this youth subgroup might be different than youth more broadly.

This caveat notwithstanding, if we extrapolate from the current composition of Australia and project into the future when this Generation Z will be established, we could hypothesise a society even more open to diversity with an increase of people not identifying with a religion, but not necessarily ruling out alternative beliefs and notions of spirituality. Also, Anglicans and Protestants (excluding Pentecostals) are likely to further decrease as their members age and do not attract Australian youths. Depending on the growth of Pentecostals, Australia is likely to become less and less Christian.

Conclusion

Australia is no longer the Christian country it was before WWII. Migration patterns and changes of attitudes towards religion have changed to the point that this country is paradoxically still Christian, but also post-Christian and non-religious. It is Christian because they still have the majority in terms of peoples' identification in the census, but it is not the same dominant religion as it was at the birth of federalism. We now have more non-Christian religions and people claiming to have no religion. While these three characteristics could be argued to be paradoxical, it is, however, three identities that are coexisting together. This can sometimes create some tension as explored above with Islamophobia.

Also, the way religion has entered politics in Australia has changed Australia's approach to religion. This will be further explored in Chapter 11 where we will focus on the Christianisation process of the parliament despite the decline in Christian identification in Australia, and in Chapter 12 the various de-secularisation processes in Australia.

We are now moving to contemporary religion and Australian Aboriginal peoples. In this chapter, we will explore not only their religious diversity but also a paradox in the theoretical construction of the social scientific study of religion that could have changed the development of this cohort of disciplines as detailed in Chapter 2.

References

Akbarzadeh, S. 2013. Investing in mentoring and educational initiatives: the limits of de-radicalisation programmes in Australia. *Journal of Muslim Minority Affairs, 33*(4): 451–463.

Al-Natour, R.J. and Morgan, G. 2012. Local Islamophobia: the Islamic School Controversy in Camden, New South Wales. In Morgan, G. and Poyting, S. eds. *Global Islamophobia: Muslims and Moral Panic in the West.* Farnham: Ashgate, pp. 101–118.

Aly, A. 2012. Fear online: seeking sanctuary in online forums. In Hayes, A. and Mason, R. eds. *Cultures in refuge: seeking sanctuary in modern Australia.* Farnham, Ashgate, pp. 163–178.

Bano, S. 2012. *An exploratory study of Shariah councils in England with respect to family law.* Reading: University of Reading.

Battersby, J. 2018. Terrorism where terror is not: Australian and New Zealand terrorism compared. *Studies in Conflict & Terrorism, 41*(1): 59–76.

Bouma, G. 2006. *Australian soul: religion and spirituality in the 21st century.* Cambridge University Press.

Bouma, G. 2013. Australian Anglicans and religious plurality: exclusive theologies vs. theological affirmations of diversity-a tale of two cities. *Journal for the Academic Study of Religion, 26*(2): 139–156.

Bouma, G.D. and Halafoff, A. 2017. Australia's changing religious profile—rising Nones and Pentecostals, declining British Protestants in superdiversity: views from the 2016 census. *Journal for the Academic Study of Religion, 30*(2): 129–143.

Dagistanli, S. and Grewal, K. 2012. Perverse Muslim masculinities in contemporary orientalist discourse: the vagaries of Muslim immigration in the West. In Morgan, G. and Poyting, S. eds. *Global Islamophobia: Muslims and Moral Panic in the West.* Farnham: Ashgate, pp. 119–142.

Dunn, K.M., Atie, R., Mapedzahama, V., Ozalp, M. and Aydogan, A.F. 2015. *The resilience and ordinariness of Australian Muslims: attitudes and experiences of Muslims report.* Sydney: Western Sydney University https://www.westernsydney.edu.au/__data/assets/pdf_file/0003/990129/Sydney_Muslims_report.pdf

Dunn, K.M. and Kamp, A. 2012. A failed political attempt to use global Islamophobia in Western Sydney: the 'Lindsay leaflet scandal'. In Morgan, G. and Poyting, S. eds. *Global Islamophobia: Muslims and Moral Panic in the West.* Farnham: Ashgate, pp. 143–160.

Einstein, M. 2008. *Brands of faith: marketing religion in a commercial age.* New York: Routledge.

Freston, P. 2004. Evangelical Protestantism and democratization in contemporary Latin America and Asia. *Democratization, 11*(4): 21–41.

Freston, P. 2005. The Universal Church of the Kingdom of God: a Brazilian church finds success in Southern Africa. *Journal of Religion in Africa, 35*(1): 33–65.

García-Ruiz, J. and Michel, P. 2012. *Et Dieu sous-traita le Salut au marché: De l'action politique des mouvements évangéliques en Amérique latine*. Paris: Armand Colin.

Halafoff, A., Singleton, A., Bouma, G. and Rasmussen, M.L. 2020. Religious literacy of Australia's Gen Z teens: diversity and social inclusion. *Journal of Beliefs & Values*, *41*(2): 195–213.

Hassan, R. 2018. *Australian Muslims: the challenge of Islamophobia and social distance*. Adelaide: International Centre for Muslim and non-Muslim Understanding, University of South Australia.

Humphrey, M. 2013. Migration, security and insecurity. *Journal of Intercultural Studies*, 34(2): 178–95.

Jennings, M.A.C. 2017. Great risk for the kingdom: Pentecostal-Charismatic growth churches, pastorpreneurs, and neoliberalism. In Pascal, A-M ed. *Multiculturalism and the convergence of faith and practical wisdom in modern society*. Pennsylvania: IGI Global, pp. 236–248.

Johns, A., Mansouri, F. and Lobo, M. 2015. Religiosity, citizenship and belonging: The everyday experiences of young Australian Muslims. *Journal of Muslim Minority Affairs*, *35*(2): 171–190.

Maddox, M., 2009. An argument for more, not less, religion in Australian politics. *Australian Religion Studies Review*, *22*(3): 345.

Misra, A. 2018. Australia's counter-terrorism policies since September 11, 2001: Harmonising national security, independent oversight and individual liberties. *Strategic Analysis*, *42*(2): 103–118.

Mol, H. 1971. *Religion in Australia: a sociological investigation*. Melbourne: Thomas Nelson.

Porter, M. 2011. *Sydney Anglicans and the threat to world Anglicanism: the Sydney experiment*. London: Routlegde.

Possamai, A., Richardson, J.T. and Turner, B.S. eds. 2015. *The sociology of shari'a: case studies from around the world*. Leiden: Springer.

Possamai, A., Turner, B.S., Cheng, J.E., Voyce, M. and Dagistanli, S. 2016. Shari'a and everyday life in Sydney. *Australian Geographer*, *47*(3): 341–354.

Richardson, J.T. 2013. Managing minority religious and ethnic groups in Australia: implications for social cohesion. *Social Compass*, *60*(4): 579–590.

Rocha, C., Hutchinson, P. and Openshaw, K. 2020. Introduction: Australian Charismatic movements as a space of flows. In Rocha, C., Hutchinson, P. and Openshaw, K. eds. *Australian Pentecostal and Charismatic Movements. Argument from the margins*. Leiden: Brill, pp. 1–21.

Sharpe, M. 2013. Name it and claim it: prosperity gospel and the global Pentecostal reformation. In Clarke, M ed. *Handbook of research on development and religion*. Cheltenham: Edward Elgar Publishing, pp. 164–179.

Singleton, A. 2020. Strong Church or Niche Market? The demography of the Pentecostal Church in Australia. In Rocha, C., Hutchinson, P. and Openshaw, K. eds. *Australian Pentecostal and Charismatic Movements. Argument from the margins*. Leiden: Brill, pp. 88–105.

Singleton, A., Halafoff, A., Rasmussen, M.L and Bouma, G. 2021. *Freedoms, faiths and futures. Teenage Australians on religion, sexuality and diversity*. Sydney: Bloomsbury Academic.

Singleton, A., Rasmussen, M.L., Halafoff, A. and Bouma, G. 2019. The AGZ study: Project report. Australia: Australian National University, Deakin University and Monash University.

Stevenson, D., Dunn, K., Possamai, A. and Piracha, A. 2010. Sydney: An examination of a "post-secular" world city. *Australian Geographer, 41*(3): 323–350.

Tabar, P., Noble, G. and Poynting, S. 2010. *On being Lebanese in Australia: identity, racism and the ethnic field*. Beirut: Lebanese American University Press.

Tittensor, D., Hoffstaedter, G. and Possamai, A. 2020. Hyper-securitisation and belonging: understanding the Plight of Young Muslims in Melbourne, Australia. *Journal of Muslim Minority Affairs, 40*(3): 480–496.

Weng, E. and Halafoff, A. 2020. Media representations of religion, spirituality and non-religion in Australia. *Religions, 11*: 332. DOI:10.3390/rel11070332.

6 Australian Aboriginal peoples and contemporary religion

Introduction

In Australia, one of the most advanced countries in the world, Australian Aboriginal peoples' overall life expectancy is shorter, due to poorer health, and they typically have lower levels of educational attainment, and are more incarcerated than non-Indigenous people. Although the inequalities have been shrinking over the years, a gap still remains (SCRGSP, 2016). This is an outcome of Australia's colonial legacy and its social memory of white superiority. Indeed, Australia was declared *terra nullius* by the British Empire in the 18th century which means that they did not consider this country to be inhabited. The hunter gatherers were not deemed to be organised in a "civilised" way and did not cultivate any fields, contrary to the Maoris in New Zealand for example (Onnudottir et al., 2013). They were seen as part of the flora and fauna of the country until they received the right to vote in the 1960s. Before that time, it was assumed that those who were called the "full blood" would disappear from this evolving society and the "mixed blood" needed to be taken away from their parents. They were part of the Stolen Generations and were sent to Christian missions to get a Christian and Western education. It was only in 2008 that Kevin Rudd, the then prime minister of Australia, gave an official apology which helped revitalise pride for Australian Aboriginal peoples in being indigenous. This has been reflected in the census data in which Australian Aboriginal peoples are more prone to acknowledge their background and report it. Indeed, between the 2006 and 2016 censuses, the numbers increased by close to 43%, from 455,024 people to 649,168 (see Table 6.1). This is explained not only by a desire to be recognised and accepted as part of the fabric of Australia, but also due to a lower mortality rate and higher fertility rate.

DOI: 10.4324/9781003255338-6

On the issue of faith, Australian Aboriginal peoples have not remained static and not all are practising their traditional religion. Some of them are Christian and might go to church on a Sunday but still follow their "old" spirituality; sometimes the two faiths are combined or practised alongside each other. Other Christian groups, do not want to be involved in these "old" spiritualities as they are seen as pagan and too close to witchcraft (Cox and Possamai, 2016). Some of them have converted to Islam and Buddhism and others are "not religious." Checking the 2016 census data, the proportion of non-religious Indigenous peoples is even higher than non-religious non-Indigenous peoples (see below). This means that one is more likely to report on the census that he or she is not religious if he or she is an Indigenous person. As all peoples in a society, they are affected by change, and changes in religious patterns affect everyone.

To explore this development, this chapter first retells the classic story of one of the founding books in the sociology of religion, that of Durkheim's (2001) *The Elementary Forms of the Religious Life*, first published in 1912. Then we propose a revisionist approach to this book and claim that if its focus had not been so colonialist and Western, the whole approach to the social scientific study of religion in the world would have been totally different. Our argument is that the secularisation thesis might not even have had to eventuate and would not have had to wait until the 21st century to be discredited. The later sections of this chapter explore census data and detail the contemporary religious composition of Australian Aboriginal peoples, which is, as for the rest of the country, Christian, post-Christian, and non-religious (see Chapter 5).

Australia as a forgotten major source of social theory

Emile Durkheim (1858–1917) is the founder of the functionalist school of thought. In a nutshell, functionalism sees society as a system divided into a series of parts and subparts that fit together. As each organ in a human body has its place and function, each institution (e.g. family, religion, government) and other social groups have a specific function to perform for the benefit of a society as a whole. Durkheim believed that a society is more than the sum of its parts because if all parts of a society perform their function and are well connected to other parts like the organs of our bodies, what comes out is a new whole. Indeed, to reuse the biological metaphor, if one can imagine all the body parts put together inside out and piled together in a box, one will certainly realise that it is the synchronised orchestration of all of these various parts that makes up the body. Further, the element that holds all of these parts and subparts together is a type of social glue or social cement which Durkheim equated to social norms and values; as will be shown shortly, religion is a critical part of this glue.

Durkheim's key work on religion comes from his seminal book, *The Elementary Forms of the Religious Life* (Durkheim, 2001). He started his argument with the premise that all societies divide the world into two distinct categories: "sacred" and "profane." With regards to the former he (Durkheim, 2001: 36–37) stated:

> By sacred things one must not understand simply those personal things which are called gods or spirits; a rock, a tree, a spring, a pebble, a piece of wood, a house, in a word anything can be sacred. A rite can have this sacred character as well; in fact, no rite exists that does not have it to some degree. There are words, speeches, and formulas that can be spoken only by consecrated persons; there are gestures and movements that cannot be executed by everyone.

Religion, for Durkheim, was seen to act as a social glue that held everyone within a specific society together around these sacred things. But how did this social glue start? Why did people begin to believe in the first instance? To answer these questions, Durkheim analysed the accounts of anthropologists who studied this religion, believing that to study a complex phenomenon such as religion one must begin by analysing its simplest form. Like many thinkers of his time, he viewed this religion as the most simple and "primitive" religion (which has, of course, been proven otherwise, see Hume, 2002). Studying the texts available at this time period, Durkheim realised that each Australian Aboriginal clan followed the rule of exogamy (i.e. members cannot marry within the same clan) and each of them had a totem. This totem was an animal or a plant and represented the sign by which an Aboriginal group identified itself to, and against, other groups with different totems. The totem was also seen as a sacred symbol.

Like many thinkers of his time, Durkheim was strongly influenced by social Darwinism, the idea that as humans evolve from a "primitive" shape, societies do too, from hunter-gatherer ones to agrarian ones, to city-based ones, and to scientifically developed ones. For him, "primitive" religions evolved from magic to become institutionalised religions, from oral rituals to well-developed theologies. If a religion was organised through a structure and had written text to provide guidance to its believers, it was seen as a step-up towards advancement from a religion based on oral traditions and located within a clan, rather than spread across countries, and carried, for example, by missionaries. But more had to be done towards evolving further, and science, education, and urbanism were seen as the key factors towards this end goal of a perfect rational society where science had all the answers. But what of religion in this scientific utopia in a time period that viewed modernity in a more monolithic fashion (see Chapter 2)? It could not have a place, as belief in a god cannot be seen as matching the need of rational and educated people. Like Australian Aboriginal peoples were expected to disappear (see below) through the "civilisation process" in Australia, religion had to disappear as well.

The main source of inspiration for Dukheim's book is the religion of the Arrernte of Central Australia as reported by Walter Baldwin Spencer (1860–1929) and Francis James Gillen (1855–1912). Gillen worked for years in a telegraph station as the station master in what was not yet Alice Springs and was situated next to a water hole (which would later give the name to the town a few kilometres away, Alice being Gillen's wife name). This station still exists and can be visited. It played a key role in linking communication between the city of Darwin in the north (receiving messages from Europe) and Adelaide in the south (transmitting messages to the rest of the country). When this line opened in 1872, it reduced the isolation of Australia from the rest of the world. Any social scientists visiting this place should bear in mind that this place was also at the cradle of one of the most important European social theories that influenced a whole field of knowledge. Spencer was a biologist who joined the W.A. Horn Scientific Expedition which left Adelaide in May 1894 to explore Australia. He then met Gillen and convinced him to conduct research with him on the local Indigenous people whom he had known for years.

Over the years, many groups of Australian Aboriginal peoples had gathered in this centripetal point and Gillen got to know them well and was able to speak their language. Spencer later met this man and both decided to study scientifically the rituals of these Indigenous peoples. They analysed their rituals and took pictures. These greatly influenced Durkheim which helped shape his theory on rituals, which would later become fundamental to the social sciences. The pictures taken in Australia were depicting the Aboriginal peoples as very traditional. Around the same period, not too far from Alice Springs, in the Hermannsburg Mission, Carl Strehlow (1871–1922) was a Lutheran pastor who was also a linguist.

However, because of his religious convictions, he did not want to observe these "pagan" rituals.[1]

Nevertheless, Carl Strehlow spent years with these communities and got to know their language. He interviewed them and learned about their belief system of which he wrote about. He also took pictures of Australian Aboriginal peoples but in a more contemporary setting, wearing the Western clothes of that time. This work which demonstrated how Australian Aboriginal peoples could be part of the Western world, albeit Christianised but still practising their traditional spiritualities in a hybrid fashion. This, as Kreinath (2012) has so well demonstrated, was not used at all in Durkheim's work. Indeed, Durkheim's interest was located in the spirit of the times which could not imagine old ways of being adapting themselves to a changing world. Durkheim believed that with the development of modernity, religion would slowly disappear, and as such, a "primitive" religion could not have its place. Indeed, he, like many authors of that time, crystallised Australian Aboriginal peoples in their "exotic" past and did not take on board the more "mundane" present.

If Durkheim had been able to use the work of Strehlow more adequately, he could have started questioning the secularisation thesis and began realising that religion can change without going through a social Darwinist path, and without having to disappear.

This missing out on such a theoretical opportunity is akin to Durand's (1996) claim that a crucial moment in the history of social theory could have enchanted the Middle Ages instead of putting it on a path towards the instrumental rationality that led to a disenchanted industrial period. Circa AD 1300, after the Dark Ages, penetration of Arab texts into the Latin world was very advanced. These works were remnants of Ancient Greece and became the basis of a return to mythopoeic thought in the Renaissance. They were also the basis for new synthetic developments in Christianity. As the Greek texts were missing at that time, and because Christianity until that time could not deal with the works of pagans, Christian theologians had to decide which works among these numerous translations in Arabic of ancient pagan philosophers, such as Aristotle, were suitable for expression and elaborations of their credo. They finally adopted the Latin Averroism, being the thought of the Muslim Andalusian Ibn Rushd known as Averroes (AD 1126–1198), born in Cordoba in Spain, who was one of the translators of Aristotle's work from Greek to Arabic, but interpreted in a more rational way, one that would lay the path towards a version of disenchanted scientific knowledge. This was chosen instead of the influence of the

Persian Avicenna (AD 980–1037) who, by a combination of Aristotelianism and Neo-Platonist ideas, praised the idea of a mundus imaginalis and its consequence, the active imagination/intuition. Thus, as Durand (1996) has hypothesised, if the latter translation had been used, the industrial world would have been more enchanted.

Aristotelianism, through the interpretation of Averroes, then became hegemonic in the Western world. Its adaptation to the Bible story was so complete that to claim that Aristotle's work, as translated by Averroes, was wrong, was to claim that the Bible was wrong. What the Bible could not explain, only Aristotle could. For example, the Galenic system that was inspired by a blend of Hippocrates' and Aristotle's theories could not be criticised, even if a sick person was dying from bloodletting, that is, a Galenic prescription. Proposing a heliocentric view of the universe was not a danger to Catholic exegesis in itself, but was a crime because Aristotle's system was geocentric. History abounds of many "ifs," and this case with Durkheim, as seen above, is certainly one of them.

But these theoretical blinkers on how religion could change among Australian Aboriginal peoples were not limited to this French sociologist. In contrast to the desert region, for example, where Spencer conducted the research that influenced Durkheim, Swain (1991: 152–153) claimed in the 1990s that there was a dearth of data with regard to religion and Aboriginal peoples in the most urban regions of Australia.

> It is estimated that the [Aboriginal] population in the South-East of Australia had been culled by a staggering 96 per cent a full generation before the first serious ethnographic accounts of the region were produced. Yet until the 1960s, virtually every report was written about the alleged nature of 'traditional' Aboriginal societies. Scholars simply ignored the reality that the people they consulted lived on missions, stations and government reserves and maintained a radical transformed culture.
>
> (Swain, 1991: 151)

Swain makes reference to the poverty of research in relation to the study of religious change and Australian Aboriginal peoples as researchers tended to be attracted mainly to the "unicorn of Aboriginal studies: Australian Aboriginal peoples untouched by the non-Aboriginal world" (Swain, 1991: 156) and missed the fact that Aboriginal religions have not remained static. In her research in Arrernte, Austin-Broos (2009: 21) makes reference to the gaze of Australian anthropologists and their ethnography of authentic tradition to follow the procedures of land rights so their research would be accepted in courts of law.

As a continuous innovator in the field of sociology of religion in Australia in 1982, Mol is probably the first sociologist (rather than anthropologist) dealing with contemporary and religious issues. In his 100-page book, he dedicates close to 30 pages to his three ideal types of what he called the European effect on Aboriginal religion. He makes reference to the missionary effect, which for him has not greatly contributed to a new Aboriginal identity, as he saw "the transition from their traditional belief to Christian beliefs [as] too great" (Mol 1982, 77). This reflection, as we will see in the next section, should indeed be revised. In his second type, the sectarian effect, Mol makes references to evangelical groups such as Pentecostalism and notices some hybrid processes between ancestral beings from the Dreaming and biblical theology. In his last ideal type, the secular effect, he observes the impact of, for example, trade unions on Aboriginal cultures and the modernisation of some of their traditional rituals.

To shed further light on this phenomenon, Onnudottir et al. (2013) and Cox and Possamai (2016) analysed census data and conducted some fieldwork. The next section is a summary of these findings. The data have also been updated to include the most recent census results from 2016.

Contemporary religion and Indigenous peoples in census data

Census data is the best available source of knowledge when trying to understand religious trends among Indigenous peoples in Australia, but unfortunately it is not perfect, as it does not capture hybrid approaches (e.g. being both Christian and involved in Aboriginal traditional religion at the same time), as the question only asks for one answer. Cox and Possamai (2016) also discovered in their fieldwork that when Australian Aboriginal peoples practise their traditional spirituality and answer the survey questions about religion, they would often put Christianity as their religion and would not include their traditional ways as they do not see the latter as part of this Western construct of religion. These spiritualities are for them more their ways of being, or their business, rather than a religion. This would explain the small amount of people claiming to be part of this tradition as detailed in Table 6.1. From 1996 to 2006, there was a decrease in Indigenous people claiming to be part of an Aboriginal traditional religion (from 7,274 to 5,209). In the 2011 census, we find a reversal of this trend, with a growth rate of 35% from

Table 6.1 Contemporary main religions and Australian Aboriginal peoples

	1996		*2001*		*2006*		*2011*		*2016*	
	N	%	N	%	N	%	N	%	N	%
Aboriginal traditional religion	7,274	2.06	5,015	1.22	5,209	1.14	7,017	1.28	7,770	1.19
Christianity	252,222	71.45	282,697	68.95	290,619	63.87	341,735	62.33	347,568	53.54
Buddhism	485	0.14	1,245	0.30	1,423	0.31	2,268	0.41	2,948	0.45
Islam	621	0.18	622	0.15	1,010	0.22	1,142	0.21	1,502	0.23
No religion	60,648	17.17	65,070	15.87	93,591	20.57	131,737	24.02	230,929	35.57
Total	352,997	100.00	410,002	100.00	455,024	100.00	548,372	100.00	649,168	100.00

the 2006 census. The total in the 2016 census is 7,770 people, which is still less than the 1996 census, and represents a small percentage of the Indigenous population, that is 1.19%.

Further to this discussion about the meaning of the word "religion" in an Australian Aboriginal language, the linguist David Moore (2016) discusses the word "Altjira" which has been the basis of a dispute between anthropologists and missionaries in central Australia. This word is the closest to "religion" in the Aranda language but does not mean "religion" in the Western sense. It is thus very difficult to translate. Spencer and Gillen (see above) translated this word as "Dream" and made reference to the Dreamings as a religious system of all Australian Aboriginal peoples. This term has been widely used to describe the religious system of Australian Aboriginal peoples and has led to the trivialisation of Aboriginal religion and legal systems (Moore, 2016: 103). As Morton (2000: 758) explains "… Aboriginal peoples have been romanticised and celebrated in terms of their deep spirituality, but they have also been denigrated for being primitive and childlike. Either way, the Dreaming is largely, if not exclusively, a shadow that others have cast upon them." On the other hand, missionaries like Strehlow used this word as a key term for "God," but this search for a Christian God did reflect a Christian theological bias of seeking the presence of God in all cultures. The problem with the word "religion" is not only found in Australian Aboriginal languages. Words such as Dharma in Sanskrit ["that which carries the universe"], Dat in Hebrew ["judgement"], Thrèskeia in Greek ["following of cultural prescriptions"], and Dīn in Arabic ["debt, obligation to follow God"] are translated as religion, but these are only approximations and do not adequately reflect the meaning of these words in their original context (Debray, 2005).

Having acknowledged the difficulty of using the word religion in the context of Australian Aboriginal peoples, let's nevertheless come back to the 2016 Australian census in which 649,168 people identified as Australian Indigenous. Christianity has gone down from 71.45% in 1996 to 53.5% in 2016. This is on par with the national trend, from 63.9% in 2006 to 52.13% in 2016. The religious nones are the second highest (non)religious group in the census, and the number has gone up from 17.17% in 2006 to 35.57% in 2016. While they were slightly below the overall population in 2006 (18.6%), they are now more than 5% above the national percentage in 2016 (30.1%). There has clearly been a rapid increase, as Figure 6.1 clearly shows, among Australian Aboriginal peoples.

Islam amongst Indigenous Australians had significant growth (62%) in 2006, with an increase from 622 people in 2001 to 1,010. Since then, the growth has continued in 2011, with 1,142 peoples and in 2016 with 1,502. Compared to the overall Muslim population in Australia (2.6%), as seen in Table 6.2, the percentage of Muslims among Australian Aboriginal peoples (0.23%) is not as strong. As discussed in Onnudottir et al. (2013), there have been some articles in newspapers about Australian Aboriginal peoples converting at a high rate, but the census data reveal another picture in terms of percentage. Buddhism had a strong peak in 2001 (157% growth) and has since continued to grow steadily (2,268 Indigenous peoples in 2011 and 2,948 in 2016). This major religion had the highest growth rate (57%) in 2011. While research on Australian Aboriginal peoples tends to focus more on Christianity (see Charlesworth et al., 2005) and Islam (see Onnudottir et al., 2013; Stephenson, 2010), there is nothing to date about Buddhism. There are also small numbers of Indigenous peoples claiming to be from other faiths such as the Baha'i faith and Hinduism, but they have not been included in the table.

The results of these censuses undermine the colonial construct of what an "authentic" Aboriginal person is, as the contemporary everyday life of Australian Aboriginal peoples is no longer restricted to their traditional spirituality and Christianity. Various strata of Australia,

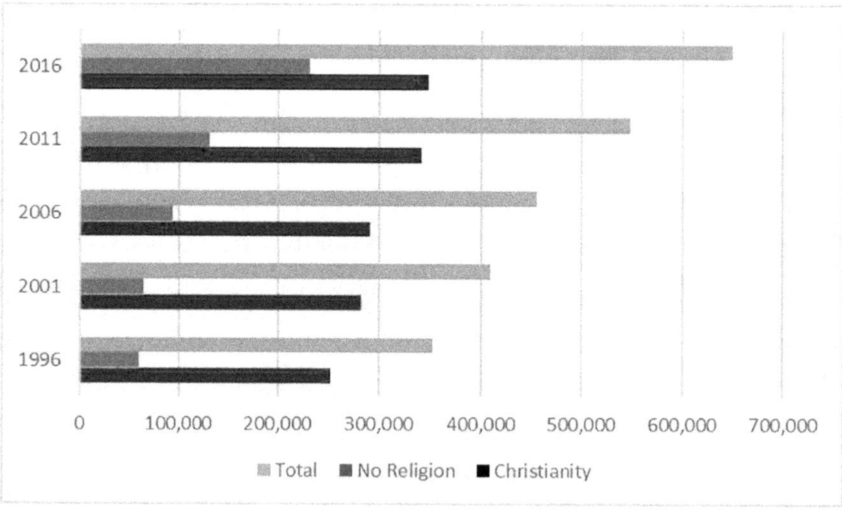

Figure 6.1 No religion and Christianity.
Source: Adapted from Onnudottir, H., Possamai, A. and Turner, B. (2013: 26).

Table 6.2 Comparison with overall population

	2006		2011		2016	
	Overall Australian population	Aboriginal and Torres Straight Islanders	Overall Australian population	Aboriginal and Torres Straight Islanders	Overall Australian population	Aboriginal and Torres Straight Islanders
Christianity	63.9%	63.87%	61.14%	62.33%	52.13%	53.54%
Islam	1.7%	0.22%	2.21%	0.21%	2.6%	0.23%
No religion	18.6%	20.57%	22.3%	24.02%	29.62%	35.57%
total no.	19,855,000	455,024	21,598,000	548,372	23,402,000	649,168

especially those with a New Age inclination, see Indigenous people as deeply spiritual. While it would certainly be the case for many Indigenous people, the reality of the census points to a different story that removes this romantic gaze. Overall, according to census data, Indigenous peoples are more prone to be religious nones than non-Indigenous ones.

How do we make sense of this finding? Berndt (1979: 28) commented in the 1970s that because early missionaries did not recognise Australian Aboriginal religions as religions, they "hastened the downhill plunge toward increasing secularization." Similarly, Edwards (2002: 27) contends that in the urban environment of the 21st century many Australian Aboriginal peoples have experienced a loss of spirit:

> I have had increasing contact with Aboriginal people who are more removed from their traditions. A common response from many of my Aboriginal students has been 'I have lost my culture'.

Cox and Possamai (2016) interviewed Australian Aboriginal peoples who claim to have no religious affiliation in the census and discovered a double break in the chain of memory of these people. Drawing on the work of Danièle Hervieu-Léger (2000), and as already discussed in Chapter 2, modernity is seen as oppositional to traditional societies. The latter are epitomised as "societies of memory," in which cultural heritage could be reproduced from one generation to the next. Institutional religions were thriving in this context and were able to retain their established positions. On the other hand, for Hervieu-Léger, societies in modernity are societies of change and have greatly impacted institutional religions. These are now faced with difficulties in passing on their traditional teachings, that is, in continuing their chains of memory. Religion, it could be argued, has lost its memory. With regard to the Western context, Christianity has been declining, and this is reflected in census data about the Indigenous and the non-Indigenous peoples in Australia. As discussed in the introduction, Australia is imbued with a social memory that is Christian since the First Fleet. With the decrease of Christianity, non-Indigenous people in Australia are going through a break in this chain of memory from a Christian one to a non-religious one. Some Indigenous participants interviewed in this research, however, make reference to two breaks, one from Christianity and the other from their Aboriginal spirituality. Indeed, in some cases, Indigenous Australians have moved away not only from traditional religion but also from Christianity. We see among these informants a double chain of memory that has broken down, or two secularising processes. Overall, and contrary to general trends in the Western world, we are seeing Indigenous peoples in Australia who are losing (or mutating) both of their faiths. In Australia, as adherence to Christianity is falling (at around the same rate for Indigenous and non-Indigenous people), self-identification as religious "nones" is rising (faster among Indigenous populations), and claims to Aboriginal traditional spirituality are decreasing in the census.

Coming back to Christianity, we can find types of understandings that are not captured by the census. For example, James Cox (2014) describes the Rainbow Spirit Theology which merges Aboriginal spirituality with Christianity. They follow the New Testament and are greatly inspired by Jesus Christ. However, their traditional stories are seen as equivalent to those recounted in the Hebrew scriptures and can be interpreted as their equivalent of the Old Testament. In this theology, the Australian Aboriginal peoples are oppressed like the Israelites who were dispossessed of their land. The creator was expressed in their Aboriginal ways, and ceremonies in which the rainbow-serpent (understood in this context as the Rainbow Spirit) played a significant role. This Spirit gives life to the land and to all living creatures. As another example, Cohen (2016) describes the "Jesus's footprint," an impression in a rock adjacent to the Finke River in central Australia. It is evidence for the Arrernte people that Jesus visited them a long time ago before the Europeans arrived. These Australian Aboriginal peoples have interpreted the Lutherans to have come to them to remind them that they had forgotten this visit. Today, this footprint is a popular landmark that attracts tourist buses. In the Northern Territory, Magowan (2016) finds that for the Yolngu exchanges have taken place between ancestral and Christian performing arts. She observed dances that were connected to kin authority but imbued with Christian spiritual concerns. In another study, Cox and Possamai (2016) spoke to an elder in central Australia who described his Christianity and his traditional spirituality, drawing two parallel lines in the sand. He lives both side by side but without linking them. While being part of two belief systems implies a hybrid approach, the types of hybridity can be quite different.

Australian Aboriginal religion across states

If we analyse the statistics between states, we can discover some interesting trends. In Table 6.3, NSW (44.3%) and Victoria (32.6%) have three-quarters of the whole Muslim population in Australia, and are the two most post-Christian states as seen in Chapter 5. Though, while the Australia Muslim Aboriginal population is on par in NSW (43.1%), this is not the case in Victoria (17.2%). However, we can find that the Australian Muslim population is higher in terms of its percentage in Queensland (15.3% compared to 7.4% of the whole Muslim population) and in Western Australia (14.6% compared to 8.4% for the whole Muslim population); that is, we find a higher concentration. This indicates that the rates of conversion (or reversion to Islam) are happening less in Victoria and that this trend is not homogenous across Australia. In Onnudottir et al. (2013), three reasons for the increase of the rate of conversion to Islam by Australian Aboriginal peoples were provided. The first was due to a revival of the Black Power Movement in Australia from which a section finds a solution in Islam to contest the current oppression of Aboriginal populations. This is strongly inspired by the work of Malcom X in the 1960s and his Nation of Islam. The second reason is not necessarily a conversion, but a reversion to the religion of their ancestor. Indeed, there is a hidden history of Islam in Australia in which the Afghan cameleers mixed with Australian Aboriginal females (see Chapter 3). When the White Australia policy came into place at the beginning of the 20th century, and no more non-white Muslim people could migrate, their children continued their work. Today, some Australian Aboriginal peoples want to revert to the Muslim religion of their ancestor. The third reason is that, like other types of converts, Australian Aboriginal peoples find an attraction to this religion which provides a system of beliefs suited to their values and lifestyles.

With regard to "no religion," we can see in Table 6.3 that Victoria, which is among the most non-religious states in Australia (see Chapter 5), another interesting trend. While 27.06% of the overall no-religion population lives there, it is only 10.20% of the Australian

Table 6.3 No religion per state

2016	*NSW*		*Victoria*		*Queensland*		*South Australia*	
No religion	N	%	N	%	n	%	n	%
Indigenous peoples	72,668	31.4	23,565	10.20	61,808	26.76	16,969	7.34
Overall no-religion population	1,879,561	27.10	1,876,739	27.06	1,374,431	19.82	594,312	8.57

2016	*Western Australia*		*Tasmania*		*N.T.*		*A.C.T.*		*Total*	
No religion	n	%	n	%	N	%	n	%	n	%
Indigenous peoples	29,051	12.58	11,396	4.93	12,554	5.43	2,868	1.24	230,929	100
Overall no-religion population	804,270	11.59	192,520	2.77	67,169	0.96	143,741	2.07	6,933,715	100

Table 6.4 Islam per state

2016	*NSW*		*Victoria*		*Queensland*		*South Australia*	
Islam	n	%	N	%	n	%	n	%
Indigenous peoples	648	43.1	258	17.2	230	15.3	76	5
Overall Muslim population	267,658	44.3	197,032	32.6	44,880	7.4	28,547	4.7

2016	*Western Australia*		*Tasmania*		*N.T.*		*A.C.T.*		*Total*	
Islam	n	%	n	%	n	%	n	%	n	%
Indigenous peoples	220	14.6	21	1.4	33	2.1	10	0.6	1502	100
Overall Muslim population	50,647	8.4	2,497	0.4	2,338	0.4	9,882	1.6	604,242	2.6

Aboriginal population. In NSW, among the least non-Christian states (see Chapter 5), the trend is slightly different, with 27.10% of the overall population and 31.4% of the Australian Aboriginal one. Another interesting trend is in the Northern Territory, with 5.43% of the Australian Aboriginal Population without a religion; that is five times more than the overall population of that territory (0.96%). The other states and territory, in contrast, are on par with regard to the distribution of these two groups.

While there are indeed national trends in relation to how religion changes in Australia, there are also some differences from state to state, already seen in Chapter 5.

The new age and Australian Aboriginal peoples

New Agers in Australia, that is people who are interested in alternative spiritualities (see Chapter 8), have approached religions and philosophies in an eclectic way. They can be interested in Sufism and tarot card readings, and then move to Buddhism and Catholicism, with a touch of beliefs in reincarnation and astrology. Among this reservoir of beliefs to explore is Australian Aboriginal spirituality. An interest for this local spirituality became part of a trend at the end of the last century and has been contested.

According to anthropologist Diane Bell (in Richards, 1995: 61):

> [...] we're talking about highly problematic renditions of beliefs and life ways and people, spiritual selves being put into books, being put onto tapes, being put onto videos, sold across the counter to hungry, desperate people who have very little understanding of what's really going on and in many ways don't want to know. [...] It is insidious and dangerous.

Further, some commentators such as Cuthbert and Grossman (1996) and Marcus (1988, 1996) underscore the power relation in "cultural appropriation". This is the processes by which meanings are transformed within specific hierarchical structures of power, and in this case within the structures of race (Marcus, 1988), and sees in the "New Age" a quest for cultural inclusiveness that erases all differences and that often reduces indigenous practices to shallow therapeutic devices. Likewise, Sutton (2010) explores the exchanges between New Age religions and Aboriginal "spirituality" and deplores the many ways in which white "spirituality" has carelessly and flagrantly borrowed from "Aboriginal Dreaming" to suggest that Aboriginal religions were in fact "New Age." For these authors, this quest "invades" the space of Australian Aboriginal peoples, is neocolonialist, and is a romantic "expropriation" of Aboriginal culture that avoids and even undermines issues such as land rights and self-determination. The resultant claim that these New Agers can therefore be like "indigenes" appears to be an "unintended" form of racism (see, for example, Gallagher, 2000 and Taylor, 1997) and an attempt to appropriate an identity which is now a source of power.

Possamai (2005) discussed indigenous culture with several New Age informants who were aware of these issues. Susie was very interested in Aboriginal spirituality and she wanted to learn more from it:

> Feeling like this whole country [Australia] has kind of been abused a lot and that both on a practical and on a spiritual level you have to bring some of its traditional culture back.

Another participant, Elisabeth, thinks it is questionable to appropriate and commodify indigenous culture. Both desire to learn about indigenous spirituality, but only from Indigenous peoples.

On the other hand, Lynne Hume (2000: 131) discovered that "it is not only Westerners who are making connections between the New Age and Aboriginal worldviews. Some Australian Aboriginal individuals are offering New Age-style workshops of self-discovery."

This debate had some social consequences such as those reported by Sutton (2010), who observed that issues with regard to linking "authentic" Aboriginal spiritualities to their land have been further complicated when "New Age" spiritualities have been perceived to permeate traditional spiritualities, as happened during the hearing of the Simpson Desert (Wangkangurru) Land Claim in Alice Springs in 1997.

Conclusions

This chapter has explored religious change among Australian Aboriginal peoples. It argued that this was already happening in the late 19th century as reported in the work of the missionary Strehlow. If this had been picked up more appropriately by Emile Durkheim for his seminal work in the sociology of religion, the theory of secularisation would have been quite different. Today, as recent census results demonstrate, Indigenous peoples in Australia follow similar trends as the rest of Australia, such as the decrease in Christian numbers, the increase of the no religion and the non-Christian religions, although at different rates. The following chapter explores in more detail the growth of non-religion in Australia.

Note

1 Yet, while he closed his eyes to these pagan practices from his Christian parishioners, his son, T.G.H. Strehlow (1908–1978), grew up learning these practices and later became a famous anthropologist (see Cox, 2018).

References

Austin-Broos, D. J. 2009. *Arrernte present, Arrernte past: invasion, violence, and imagination in indigenous central Australia*. Chicago: University of Chicago Press.

Berndt, R.M. 1979. *A profile of good and bad in Australian aboriginal religion*. Adelaide: Charles Strong Memorial Trust.

Charlesworth, M., Dussart, F. and Morphy, H. eds. 2005. *Aboriginal religions in Australia. An anthology of recent writings*. Aldershot: Ashgate.

Cohen, H. 2016. The Strehlow-Hermannsburg/Ntaria Perplex: translation in a Lutheran-Aboriginal Community. In Cox, J. and Possamai, A. eds. *Religion and non-religion among Australian Aboriginal peoples*. Abingdon, Oxon: Routledge, pp. 109–127.

Cox, J. 2014. *The invention of God in indigenous societies*. Durham: Acumen.

Cox, J. L., and Possamai, A. 2016. Religion, Cultural Hybridity and Chains of Memory. In Cox, J. L. and Possamai, A. eds. *Religion and non-religion among Australian Aboriginal peoples*. Abingdon, Oxon: Routledge, pp. 179–203.

Cox, J. 2018. *Restoring the chain of memory. T.G.H. Strehlow and the repatriation of Australian indigenous knowledge*. Sheffield: Equinox Publishing.

Cox, J. L., & Possamai, A. 2016. Religion, Cultural Hybridity and Chains of Memory. In J. L. Cox & A. Possamai (Eds.), *Religion and Non-Religion among Australian Aboriginal Peoples*. Abingdon, Oxon: Routledge, pp. 179-203.

Cuthbert, D. and Grossman, M. 1996. Trading places: locating the indigenous in the New Age. *Thamyris*, *3*(1) : 18–36.

Debray, R. 2005. *Les communions humaines. Pour en finir avec la religion*. Paris: Fayard.

Durand, G. 1996. *Science de l'homme et tradition*. "Le nouvel esprit anthropologique". Paris: Albin Michel.

Durkheim, E. 2001 [1912]. *Elementary forms of religious life*. Oxford: Oxford University Press.

Edwards, W.H. 2002. *Recovering spirit: exploring aboriginal spirituality.* Charles Strong Memorial Trust. Adelaide: Charles Strong Memorial Trust.

Gallagher, A. 2000. Weaving a tangled web? Pagan ethics and issues of history, 'race' and ethnicity in pagan identity, Diskus 6. http://www.uni-marburg.de/religionswissenschaft/journal/diskus/gallagher.html.

Hervieu-Léger, D. 2000. *Religion as a chain of memory.* Cambridge: Polity Press.

Hume, L. 2000. The Dreaming in Contemporary Aboriginal Australia. In G. Harvey (Ed.), *Indigenous religions: A Companion.* London: Cassell, pp. 125-138.

Hume, L. 2002. *Ancestral power: the dreaming, consciousness and aboriginal Australians.* Melbourne: Melbourne University Press.

Kreinath, J. 2012. Discursive formation, ethnographic encounter, photographic evidence: The centenary of Durkheim's basic forms of religious life and the anthropological study of Australian Aboriginal religion in his time. *Visual Anthropology, 25*(5): 367–420.

Magowan, F. 2016. Valuing spiritual intimacy: convergences and counterpoints of Christianity in an economy of Yolngu performance. In Mogowan, F. and Schwarz, C. eds. *Christianity, conflict, and renewal in Australia and the Pacific.* Leiden: Brill, pp. 102–125.

Marcus, J. 1988. The journey out to the centre. The cultural appropriation of Ayers Rock. *Kunapipi, 10*(1): 29.

Marcus, J. 1996. New age consciousness and aboriginal culture: primitive dreaming in common places. *Thamyris, 3*(1): 37–54.

Mol, H. and Mol, J.J. 1982. *The firm and the formless: Religion and identity in aboriginal Australia* (Vol. 2). Waterloo, ON: Wilfrid Laurier University Press.

Moore, D. 2016. '*Altjira*, dream and god' in Cox, J. and Possamai, A. eds. *Religion and non-religion among Australian Aboriginal peoples.* Oxon: Routledge, pp. 85–108.

Morton, J. 2000. Dreaming. In M. Kleinhart and Neale, S. eds. *The Oxford companion to Aboriginal art and culture.* Oxford: Oxford University Press, pp. 577–578.

Onnudottir, H., Possamai, A. and Turner, B. 2013. *Religious change and indigenous peoples: The making of religious identities.* Aldershot: Ashgate.

Possamai, A. 2005. *In search of new age spirituality.* Aldershot: Ashgate.

Richards, D. 1995. Whitefella dreaming. *HQ Magazine* May–June: 61–67.

SCRGSP (Steering Committee for the Review of Government Service Provision). 2016. *Overcoming Indigenous Disadvantage: Key Indicators 2016.* Canberra: Productivity Commission.

Stephenson, P. 2010. *Islam dreaming: Indigenous Muslims in Australia.* Sydney: UNSW Press.

Sutton, P. 2010. Aboriginal spirituality in a new age. *The Australian Journal of Anthropology, 21*(1): 71–89.

Swain, T. 1991. Aboriginal religions in time and space. In Black, A. ed. *Religion in Australia. Sociological perspectives,* Sydney: Allen & Unwin, pp. 151–165.

Taylor, B. 1997. Earthen spirituality or cultural genocide?: Radical environmentalism's appropriation of Native American spirituality. *Religion, 27*(2): 183–215.

7 Non-belief

"Religious nones", atheists, and the spiritual but not religious

Introduction

As touched on in Chapter 4, when the census introduced the category of "no religion" in 1971 there was a significant spike in the number of people who selected this designation. Indeed, there was a sevenfold increase from 0.8% in 1966 to 6.71% in 1971, and it has continued to rise steadily ever since. By 1996, the figure had reached 16.48%, and as of the 2016 census, this figure had almost doubled. Those who now have no confession stand at 30.1%, almost one-third of the population. But, perhaps most importantly, this now places the "religious nones" as the largest (non)religious category, outstripping both Catholicism and Anglicanism which have declined to 22.6% and 13.3%, respectively (ABS, 2018). We have also observed in Chapter 6 that Australian Aboriginal peoples are more prone to claim to be from a non-religious affiliation (35.6%) than the overall population (30.1%). Further, it is projected that by 2050, the unaffiliated, whether indigenous or not, will reach 40.4% and will be the second largest category behind all Christians combined, which is projected to stand at 47% (Pew-Templeton, 2016), a trajectory that suggests that Australia will in due course become a majority secular nation.

However, as with any group in relation to religion, it is important to recognise that they are not monoliths. Just as the Christian community is incredibly diverse, the "religious nones" are no exception. The no religion category is a container that can hold many different meanings, some of which can even be incompatible and contradictory. Within the non-religious community, there is thus a variety of different groups, with some being "spiritual but not religious," others agnostic, and some being atheists. In relation to the latter, contrary to the hype generated by public figures such as Richard Dawkins and Christopher Hitchens with their respective books *The God Delusion* (2006)[1] and *God is Not*

DOI: 10.4324/9781003255338-7

Great (2007) that set out a militant atheist position, it has been found that they only constitute a small number of those identifying as "religious nones" and that the vast majority of atheists are not especially anti-religious (Ezzy et al., 2020). Therefore, in this chapter, we look to provide an overview of the diversity of those who claim no religion, then unpack what each of these different categories mean in turn, and where possible provide the contours of the communities involved.

Secular diversity

While the number of those who have identified as "religious nones" has grown over time, it is unclear what has really gone up. Indeed, putting "No Religion" in the census can mean various things for people who fill out the form, and can be interpreted variously by social scientists. Ideally, as will be shown, further qualification of people's beliefs (such as "I am not religious but I believe in a spiritual reality") or their religious identities (for example, "I am not religious but I consider myself to belong to _______ because I was raised in this faith") would be welcome in such a national instrument.

The complications in this fluid category do not stop here. The census data provide two glimpses into secularism: No Religion and Religious Affiliation Not Stated. The first category, No Religion, includes those who stated that they had no religion, as well as those who said they were agnostics, atheists, humanists, and rationalists (see below). Some social commentators might argue that secularism should be operationalised only for those who have made a specific declaration of non-belief, such as those who specifically say they are atheists or agnostics. However, the results from the Pew Forum's 2007 United States Religious Landscape Survey would contradict such a strategy. In this survey, 5% of Americans claimed that they did not believe in a God or in a spirit, yet only one quarter of these non-believers would specifically call themselves atheist. The second category, Religious Affiliation Not Stated, could also be read as a possible indication of secularism. However, Bouma (2006: 55) warns that

> [i]nterpreting a non-response poses serious problems and should be avoided. Some people feel that their religion and spirituality are to be kept private. Moreover, some religious groups discourage their members from responding to the census. Given the use of census data by the Nazis to facilitate the Holocaust, some feel uneasy about giving this information.

We do not know if people who did not state their religion are religious, non-religious, or unsure. Some people might feel reluctant to provide personal information. Others might simply feel that they are not religious, but they are not part of the No Religion category either. They might simply opt out of answering this question if the various categories from the census do not reflect their way of thinking.

The No Religion category is thus a container that can hold many different meanings, some of which can even be incompatible and contradictory. In this catch-all category, we can have people who engage with religion and people who do not at all (Bullivant, 2012). Lim, MacGregor, and Putnam (2010) discuss the heterogeneity of this category based on survey research in the United States. They claim that it is unclear who the religious "nones" are with respect to their stance vis-à-vis religion. To help with their research, they created two subcategories. The liminal nones are people who identify themselves as "none" at one time but might claim a religious preference at another time, and the stable nones are those who are constant when they identify themselves as having no religion.

Further, the dynamics within this broad group have changed quite markedly. In 1981, the first Australian Values Survey was conducted which found that only 14% of respondents agreed that God was not important in their lives, 38% regarded themselves as non-religious, and only 5% were avowed atheists. In contrast, 57% categorised themselves as religious persons. Moving forward to 2018, this script has been flipped. Those disregarding the importance of God climbed to 35%, the number of religiously inclined dropped 20 points to 37%, while the number of atheists grew fourfold to 20%. As result of this growth in atheism, those who defined themselves as non-religious remained relatively steady, moving from 38% in 1981 to 43% in 2018 (Sheppard et al., 2018). Though it should be noted that the "not religious" and "atheist" categories combined constituted a 20-point increase for "religious nones" overall, with a 63-37 split in 2018, as opposed to a 57-43 that favoured the religious in 1981.

Interestingly, despite two-thirds of respondents declaring themselves as non-religious or atheist, over half declared a belief in God (57%) and that there is life after death (55%). This suggests, given that only 37% claimed to be religious, that there is a significant minority of respondents within the non-religious category who could be qualified as agnostics, which are often regarded as being on the pathway to atheism. For example, Silver et al. note in their taxonomy of non-belief that there are seeker-agnostics whom some regard as being in an "ontological transitional state from religion or spirituality to atheism" (2014: 994). Similarly, Martin (2007) observes that agnosticism is compatible with atheism in that it entails negative atheism, as agnostics do not believe in God, which makes them, by definition, negative atheists (see below).

Adding an additional layer of complexity are recent studies that have found another category in the "spiritual but not religious." In a report by McCrindle (2017), commissioned by a Christian consortium that included Christian Schools Australia and Ministry Training Strategy, it was found that 14% of respondents (n = 1,024), when asked about which religion they identify with, selected "I have spiritual beliefs but I don't identify with any religion." Intriguingly, this figure was relatively stable across all age categories, with the category of "Builders" (those born between 1925 and 1945) recording a rate of 16%, while Generation Z (those born between 1995 and 2009) were only slightly lower with 13% being spiritual but not religious (see Table 7.1).

At first glance this dynamic makes sense, as the younger generations are becoming increasingly irreligious, which generally means eschewing anything tied to religion, including the spiritual. As Pew (2018) has noted, there is globally an age gap in relation to religion where those under the age of 40 are likely to regard faith as less important, and religion and spirituality are usually connected or overlapping (see Roof, 2003; Wuthnow, 2007). This explains why there might be more individuals from the traditionally religious "Builders" category that have transitioned to being just spiritual.

However, another study undertaken just on Generation Z (n = 1,200) found a much higher proportion of teens aged between 13 and 18 regarded themselves as spiritual but not religious, with 18% selecting this designation (Singleton et al., 2018). A possible reason for this discrepancy between the two studies, aside from sampling, is that scholars have identified two types of spirituality in that there are dwellers and seekers. The former, typically older generations, look to their congregation for religion and spirituality, whereas the seekers – typically younger generations who have not been born into a faith community – are people who are not anchored to a particular congregation and are prepared to shop around and tinker, and to find new ideas and patch them together to find inspiration. As a result of this lack of anchoring for the younger generations, spirituality becomes increasingly uncoupled from any particular religious tradition and a category in and of itself (Roof, 2003; Wuthnow, 2007).

Further, Wuthnow, albeit dealing with the American context and with adults largely from Generations Y and X (21–45-year-olds), speculates

Table 7.1 Religion and spirituality by age group

Religious identification	*Gen Z*	*Gen Y*	*Gen X*	*Baby Boomers*	*Builders*	*Average*
Christianity	46%	32%	42%	53%	63%	47%
Spiritual beliefs but don't identify with any main religion	13%	14%	14%	14%	16%	14%
None, I do not identify with any religion or spiritual belief	34%	36%	38%	28%	18%	31%

Source: McCrindle (2017).
Note: Gen Z (7–22 years; 1995–2009); Gen Y (23–37 years; 1980–1994); Gen X (38–52 years; 1965–1979; Baby Boomers (53–71 years; 1946–1964; Builders (72+; 1925–1945).

that around one-sixth of those who are religiously uninvolved fall into the category of spiritual seekers who are not religious. If accepted, this would suggest that the figure is roughly around 17% for the 'spiritual but not religious' community (2007: 134). The two studies noted above fit within the 3% margin of error utilised for studies with samples of around 1,000, which places them in the range of Wuthnow's supposition of one-sixth being spiritual but not religious. Lending further support for this estimate is another study on the Generation Y in Australia, which also found that 14% of them, then aged between 13 and 25, were secular and "actively" spiritual (Mason et al., 2007a: 70).[2] In other words, all of the studies across the generations appear to support the finding by McCrindle that the category is indeed relatively stable across the various generations.

Therefore, in parsing the various different sets of statistics, we have a rough guide to the breakdown of the "no belief" community that is beginning to form. Around 20% are avowed atheists, and roughly 14% are spiritual but not religious. This leaves the remainder as non-religious nor spiritual, which constitutes 29%. However, within this group, there is the subset of the agnostic as noted earlier, which is not often accounted for. In this regard, the study by Mason et al. on Generation Y is instructive. Within the non-religious category they identified three subgroups: *non-religious*, *ex-religious*, and *undecided*. The non-religious, namely those who have never believed in God or the spiritual, constituted 10%; the ex-religious, namely those who have given up on both, represented 4%; the undecided (agnostics) polled 14% (2007a: 207–208) – a breakdown that rather neatly fills out the remaining 29% of the wider non-religious camp, particularly if we take into consideration the usual margin for error that easily accounts for the one-point discrepancy.

Thus, from this brief survey, it can be seen that non-belief is far from straightforward, with a variety of categories and subcategories, and with this framework in place we can now turn our attention to unpacking what each of these designations mean.

Non-religious

According to Singleton (2015), those who regard themselves as non-religious are highly secular and have a much higher rate of disbelief in God (70%) or the afterlife (59%) or are equivocal. Alongside this, three quarters of "nones" never attend religious services, while 86% never or rarely pray. In accordance with this, over half of "nones" (53%) regard themselves as extremely non-religious, while a further 39% describe themselves as somewhat non-religious or simply as non-religious. Finally, only 4% regard themselves as somewhat religious, which aligns with the ex-religious subgroup (see Table 7.2).

Atheists

As Nixon (2014: 24) notes, there is a dearth of empirical studies on atheism in Australia, and if we were to go by the census, the figure of those who designate as such appears to be significantly underreported. In contrast to the Australian Values Survey, which recorded a fourfold increase from 5% in 1981 to 20% in 2018, the 2016 census counted only 67,592 under the banner of "secular beliefs," which incorporates agnosticism, atheism, humanism, and rationalism. This figure represents less than 1% of all religious "nones" (see Table 7.3) and substantially less than those reported in the 2011 census, where the figures have been disaggregated in a special report. Previously, 58,889 (1.2%) listed as atheist, 34,632 (0.7%) were agnostic, 7,663 (0.2%) selected humanist, and 2,435 (0.1%) rationalist (ABS, 2013).[3]

A reason for this possible underreporting in the census could be that there is stigma attached to designating oneself as an atheist. Gervais and Najle (2018) note that possible judgement about one's morality in relation to non-belief can lead people to present themselves differently

Table 7.2 Adult population of non-religious in Australia by belief and practice

Item	*No affiliation (n = 740)*
Belief in God	
No	70%
Can't Choose	20%
Yes	8%
Belief in Afterlife	
No	59%
Maybe	8%
Yes	30%
Attendance at religious services	
Never	75%
Rare occasions	21%
A few times per year	<1%
Monthly	0%
Regular	0%
Frequency of Prayer	
Never/Rarely	86%
Several times a year	6%
Monthly	3%
Nearly weekly	1%
Daily	2%
Describes Self as...	
Extremely/Very non-religious	53%
Somewhat non-religious	15%
Neither religious nor non-religious	24%
Somewhat religious	4%
Extremely/very religious	0%

Source: Adapted from Singleton (2015, p. 241).

in anonymous questionnaires. Bullivant (2008) echoes this observation and adds that there can also be confusion about what the terms atheist and agnostic mean, as he found in the research he conducted in Oxford, not everyone uses classic definitions for these terms. In the context of the 2016 census, these issues are potentially at play as there is only one option for "religious nones," which is the label "No Religion," and in order to designate oneself as an atheist, additional information needs to be placed in the open-ended box titled "Other (please specify)" (see Figure 7.1). Therefore, it is probable that a significant portion of those who do see themselves as atheists, or were unsure as to the term that

Table 7.3 Religious "nones" in the 2016 census

Secular beliefs and other spiritual beliefs and no religious affiliation	*No*	*%*
No religion, so described(b)	6,933,708	98.48
Secular beliefs(c)	67,592	0.96
Other spiritual beliefs(d)	39,416	0.56
Total	7,040,717	100

Source: ABS (2016).

best applies to them, simply did not provide the additional information (e.g. atheist, humanist) and have been absorbed into the wider "No Religion" category.

It thus can be difficult to fully understand what is below the surface when putting "No Religion" in the census as it can mean various things for people who fill out the form and for this reason it would be good to have more detailed categories as noted above.

Further, previous polls have also placed the number of atheists as much higher than the census. As early as 2002, a poll suggested that atheists and agnostics constituted 24% of Australians (as cited in Zuckerman, 2007: 48), while a 2008 poll found 9.7% of Australians to be "strong atheists" (Smith, 2012: 11). Given this it seems reasonable to suggest that the number of atheists in Australia is relatively large and possibly sits somewhere between 9.7% and the 20% mark indicated by the World Values Survey in 2018. Thereby, a conservative range would be between 2.27 million and 4.68 million.

Nevertheless, speculation aside, what can be stated with a greater degree of certainty is what atheists in Australia believe. Nixon, in seeking to fill the empirical lacuna regarding the atheist community, undertook 39 in-depth interviews with self-declared atheists and found that 95% described themselves as negative atheists and agnostic atheists. The former means that they simply see no evidence to believe in God, while the latter refers to a lack of belief in God but are open for evidence to dissuade them from their lack of belief. In contrast, only two participants took a positive approach to atheism, which is simply the view that "there is no God." Alongside this, only 11 of the participants (28%) associate additional meanings to being an atheist, such as rationalism, humanism, and a sense of awe with life (Nixon, 2014: 149). This finding, while certainly not generalisable, does line up with Bullivant's observation that atheists tend to be "disbelieving without belonging"

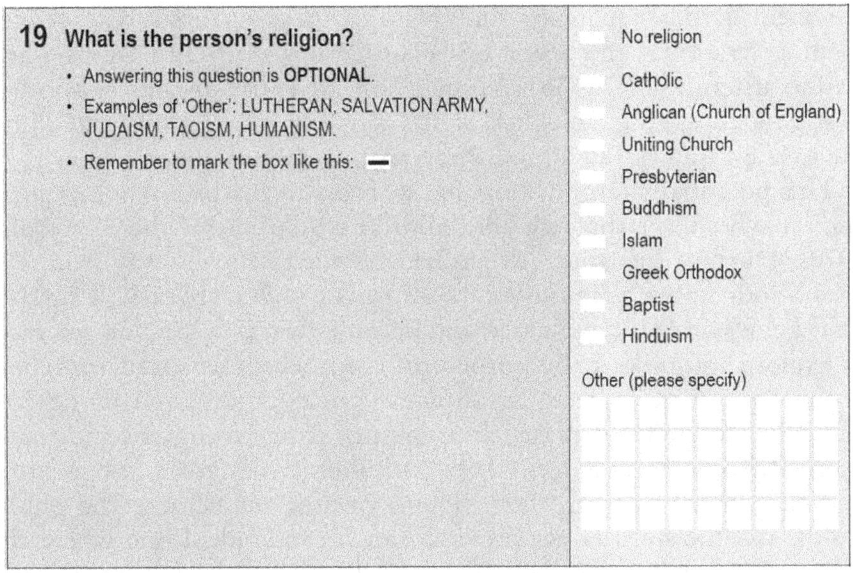
19 **What is the person's religion?**

- Answering this question is **OPTIONAL**.
- Examples of 'Other': LUTHERAN, SALVATION ARMY, JUDAISM, TAOISM, HUMANISM.
- Remember to mark the box like this: ▬

No religion
Catholic
Anglican (Church of England)
Uniting Church
Presbyterian
Buddhism
Islam
Greek Orthodox
Baptist
Hinduism
Other (please specify)

Figure 7.1 Religious affiliation question in the 2016 census.
Source: ABS (2015).

(2008: 365) to a particular tribe and suggests that those involved in organised atheism are a minority.

Though, perhaps most intriguingly, Nixon (2014) notes that even in increasingly secular Australia there is still a stigma about "coming out" as atheist and that 15 participants (38%) used the term agnostic as a defence mechanism against offending people. This lends further credence to the notion that the catch-all approach of the census is not telling the full story in relation to atheists and the heterogeneity of the religious nones more broadly.

Spiritual but not religious

Like atheists, the spiritual but not religious are most likely significantly underrepresented in the census. As outlined above, studies have ranged between 14% and 18%, and another study by the National Church Life Survey (NCLS) in 2016 (n = 1,258) fell in the middle with 16.9% (Bouma & Halafoff, 2017). This relatively consistent set of results across a number of studies suggests that there could be somewhere between 3.28 million (14%) and 4.21 million (18%) in this category. Interestingly, Bouma and Halafoff note that the "spiritual but not religious" can be despised by the religious who see them as inadequate or shallow, and the secularists who regard them as irrational and see it as a phase that will eventually pass and lead to atheism (2017: 138). As such, this raises the distinct possibility of stigma also being a blocker, with many again being subsumed into the overarching No Religion category.

This potentially large cohort has its roots in the baby boomer generation who went through the cultural revolution of the 1960s and 1970s. During this time, people had begun to move away from the bricks-and-mortar religious establishments which were seen as rigid in their beliefs and ritual practice and became reflexive looking for ways to explore and unlock the purpose of their lives. In particular, people at this time were looking for something experiential and immediate and coincided with increased awareness of Eastern religions and traditions (Parsons, 2018; Roof, 1999). As Fuller (2001) notes, the spiritual became a private realm, the religious institutions became the public realm, and the spiritual journey became an individual one where the aim was continual personal growth. Further, those who are spiritual but not religious tend to be eclectic in that they dabble and experiment rather than making a firm commitment to a particular practice, and it is not unusual for the spiritual seeker to disregard the religious philosophy that accompanies activities such as meditation. A good outline of the spiritual but not religious is succinctly put by Zinnbauer et al. as being:

> less likely to evaluate religiousness positively, less likely to engage in traditional forms of worship such as church attendance and prayer, less likely to engage in group experiences related to spiritual growth, more likely to be agnostic, more likely to characterize religiousness and spirituality as different and nonoverlapping concepts, more likely to hold nontraditional "new age" beliefs, and more likely to have had mystical experiences.
>
> (1997: 561)

Reflective of this eclecticism are the results from Mason, Singleton, and Weber's (2007b) study of alternative spirituality amongst Generation Y in Australia. They found that Eastern practices like yoga, tai-chi, and meditation were popular and often disconnected from their cultural contexts. Alongside this, they also found a high belief in reincarnation (29%), communicating with the dead (25%), and astrology (24%). In relation to reincarnation, similar to the practice of other Eastern traditions noted above, there was often little connection with either Hinduism or Buddhism, with 70% and 84%, respectively, of those who adhere to the belief system having never explored either tradition.

A further reflection of the experimentalism of the category is the fact that 48% reported dabbling in three alternative spiritual practices, 43% reported four of five, while only 9% engaged in six or more alternative beliefs and practices. Interestingly, this eclecticism was found to extend to traditional religious beliefs, with 78% believing in life after death and 63% accepting the presence of angels. However, Mason et al. (2007b) note that the belief in life after death was possibly a result of four out of five participants believing in reincarnation, and that the vast majority of those who believed in angels were not religious in the traditional sense. Two-thirds of the participants did not identify with a denomination or routinely engage in Christian practices.

To add to this complexity, Cox and Possamai (2016) conducted fieldwork among Australian Aboriginal peoples to understand the meaning that was attached to non-religion, especially when filling out the census form. This research was prompted by the discovery that, as explored in the previous chapter, Australian Aboriginal peoples are more likely to opt for this option than the overall Australian population. They spoke to a few committed Christians who distinguished themselves from being religious. For them, religion is human-making, that is their way for humans to make their way to God, whereas Christianity is God-made, that is God's way down to humans. Within this perspective, Christian faith and religion are not part of the same category. One informant explicitly stated that he put "no-religion" in the census as he regards himself as Christian and not religious.

Conclusion

Here it can be seen that Australia has become increasingly secular in recent decades. Indeed, in just 50 years since the introduction of the no religion category in the census, this has become the largest cohort in the nation. However, at the same time, the brief survey above has shown that to be secular is not singular. Rather, the category is extremely heterogeneous with variety of different categories and subcategories. While the non-religious group is still the dominant secular cohort, both the atheists and the spiritual but not religious have become significant minorities within the secular camp, with the former growing fourfold from 5% in 1981 to 20%. Further, given the possible underreporting in both the atheist and spiritual categories, combined with the fact that some regard the spiritual camp as one of the fastest-growing segments of contemporary society (see Parsons, 2018), much research still needs to be done.

Notes

1 Reportedly, by August 2008, Dawkins has sold over 2 million copies of *The God Delusion* (Bullivant, 2008: 363).
2 In the sample (n = 1219), Mason et al. initially had a much higher reading of 28% who designated as secular but spiritual. However, through 26 follow-up interviews, this figure was qualified down to 14% who were actively engaged with spirituality, whilst the remaining 14% were regarded as being unengaged. They explain that "unengaged" means they either inherited a nominal interest from their parents, or had a nominal or marginal engagement with groups or organisations that embody spirituality. In short, this 14% did not typically engage in spirituality (Mason et al., 2007a: 70).
3 Interestingly, ABS reports that there was a drive by the Atheist Foundation of Australia for people to choose no religion on the census in 2011, which saw the figure almost double from 31,300 atheists in 2006 (ABS, 2013).

References

ABS. 2013. Losing my religion?. *4102.0- Australian Social Trends, Nov 2013*. Retrieved from https://www.abs.gov.au/ausstats/abs@.nsf/Lookup/4102.0Main+Features30Nov+2013

ABS. 2015. Religious affiliation. *2008.0- Census of population and housing: nature and content, Australia, 2016*. Retrieved from https://www.abs.gov.au/ausstats/abs@.nsf/Lookup/by%20Subject/2008.0~2016~Main%20Features~Religious%20affiliation~111

ABS. 2018. 2016 Census data reveals "no religion" is rising fast. Retrieved from https://www.abs.gov.au/AUSSTATS/abs@.nsf/mediareleasesbyReleaseDate/7E65A144540551D7CA258148000E2B85

Bouma, G. 2006. *Australian soul: religion and spirituality in the 21st century*. Melbourne: Cambridge University Press.

Bouma, G.D. and Halafoff, A. 2017. Australia's changing religious profile—rising Nones and Pentecostals, declining British Protestants in superdiversity: views from the 2016 Census. *Journal for the Academic Study of Religion, 30*(2): 129–143.

Bullivant, S. 2008. Research note: sociology and the study of atheism. *Journal of Contemporary Religion, 23*(3): 363–368.

Bullivant, S. 2012. Not so indifferent after all? Self-conscious atheism and the secularisation thesis. *Approaching Religion, 2*(1): 100–106.

Cox, J. and A. Possamai eds. 2016. *Religion and non-religion among Australian Aboriginal peoples*. Oxon: Routledge.

Dawkins, R. 2006. *The God delusion*. Boston: Houghton Mifflin Co.

Ezzy, D., Bouma, G., Barton, G., Halafoff, A., Banham, R., Jackson, R. and Beaman, L. 2020. Religious diversity in Australia: rethinking social cohesion. *Religions, 11*(2): 92.

Fuller, R.C. 2001. *Spiritual, but not religious: understanding unchurched America*. New York: Oxford University Press.

Gervais, W.M. and Najle, M.B. 2018. How many atheists are there?. *Social Psychological and Personality Science, 9*(1): 3–10.

Hitchens, C. 2007. *God is not great: how religion poisons everything* (1st ed.). New York: Twelve.

Lim, C., MacGregor, C.A. and Putnam, R.D. 2010. Secular and liminal: discovering heterogeneity among religious nones. *Journal for the Scientific Study of Religion, 49*(4): 596–618.

Martin, M. 2007. General introduction. In Martin, M. ed. *The Cambridge Companion to Atheism*. New York: Cambridge University Press, pp. 1–7.

Mason, M., Singleton, A. and Webber, R. 2007a. *The spirit of generation Y: young people's spirituality in a changing Australia*. Mulgrave: John Garrat Publishing.

Mason, M., Singleton, A. and Webber, R. 2007b. The spirituality of young Australians. *International Journal of Children's Spirituality, 12*(2): 149–163.

McCrindle, M. 2017. Faith and belief in Australia: A study on religion, spirituality and worldview trends. *Baulkham Hills, Australia: McCrindle Research Pty Ltd*. Retrieved from https://mccrindle.com.au/wp-content/uploads/2018/04/Faith-and-Belief-in-Australia-Report_McCrindle_2017.pdf

Nixon, A.G. 2014. *New atheism as a case of competitive postsecular worldviews* (PhD Thesis). Sydney: Western Sydney University.

Parsons, W.B. ed. 2018. Introduction: framing the volume. In Parsons, W. B. ed. *Being spiritual but not religious: past, present, future(s)*. Abingdon, Oxon: Routledge.

Pew Research Center. 2018. The age gap in religion around the world. Retrieved from https://www.pewforum.org/2018/06/13/the-age-gap-in-religion-around-the-world/

Pew-Templeton. 2016. Global religious futures. Retrieved from http://www.globalreligiousfutures.org/countries/australia/religious_demography#/?affiliations_religion_id=0&affiliations_year=2050

Roof, W. C. 1999. *Spiritual Marketplace: baby boomers and the remaking of American religion*. Princeton, NJ: Princeton University Press.

Roof, W. C. 2003. Religion and spirituality: Toward an integrated analysis. In Dillon, M. ed. *Handbook of the sociology of religion*. Cambridge: Cambridge University Press, pp. 137–148.

Sheppard, J., McAllister, I. and Makkai, T. 2018. *Australian values study -2018*. Canberra: Australian National University, Social Research Centre.

Silver, C.F., Coleman III, T.J., Hood Jr, R.W. and Holcombe, J.M. 2014. The six types of nonbelief: a qualitative and quantitative study of type and narrative. *Mental Health, Religion & Culture*, *17*(10): 990–1001.

Singleton, A. 2015. Are religious 'nones' secular? The case of the nones in Australia. *Journal of Beliefs & Values*, *36*(2): 239–243.

Singleton, A., Halafoff, A., Bouma, G. and Rasmussen, M.L. 2018. New research shows Australian teens have complex views on religion and spirituality. *The Conversation*. Retrieved from https://theconversation.com/new-research-shows-australian-teens-have-complex-views-on-religion-and-spirituality-103233

Wuthnow, R. 2007. *After the baby boomers: how twenty-and thirty-somethings are shaping the future of American religion*. Princeton University Press.

Zinnbauer, B.J., Pargament, K.I., Cole, B., Rye, M.S., Butter, E.M., Belavich, T.G., Hipp, K.M., Scott, A.B. and Kadar, J.L. 1997. Religion and spirituality: unfuzzying the fuzzy. *Journal for the Scientific Study of Religion*, *36*(4): 549–564.

Zuckerman, P. 2007. Atheism: Contemporary numbers and patterns. In Martin, M. ed. *The Cambridge companion to atheism*. New York: Cambridge University Press, pp. 47–65.

8 Alternative spiritualities, ecology, and individualism

Introduction

At the turn of the millennium, a number of social commentators were of the view that the world was witnessing a spiritual revolution. According to Paul Heelas (2002), this was grounded in the fact that various studies in Western countries were reporting low numbers of either atheists or agnostics in conjunction with poor attendance at traditional places of worship. For example, he notes that regular worship at bricks-and-mortar institutions had collapsed in both the UK (10%) and Sweden (2%), but that each country was still only reporting 24% and 15% in the atheist/agnostic category, respectively. As a result, he surmised that there were substantial numbers of people that were "betwixt and between" who were not attending institutionalised places of worship, nor were they entirely unbelieving. Thus, for Heelas, this meant there is a substantial body of people who could be "spiritual, but not religious." Similarly, in Australia, David Tacey (2004) was of the view that there was a "rising waters of the spirit" as people were fed up by the dryness of secular modernity and the aridness of institutional religion and wanted to return to the spiritual.

When both Heelas and Woodhead (2003) sought to test the assertion of a spiritual revolution in the town of Kendal in the UK, it was found that only 1.7% of the population of 28,000 was engaged in alternative spiritual practices (e.g. yoga, tai chi, aromatherapy). According to the authors, the Kendal figures do not seem to deviate from the UK national picture. While it is clear from the study that the congregational domain is declining while the holistic milieu is growing, it is far from being a spiritual revolution; it is more of a "mini-revolution." Taking into account their own findings and those of others, they claim that whether it be Kendal or the UK nationally, if

DOI: 10.4324/9781003255338-8

the holistic milieu continues to grow at the same rate since it started in the 1970s, and if the congregational milieu still declines at the same rate, the "full-blown" spiritual revolution in the UK will only take place during the third decade of the third millennium. By "full-blown" revolution, the authors understand a situation in which the congregational domain and holistic milieu have become much the same size. Further, the authors also discovered that the relatively small growth of the holistic milieu does not compensate for the larger decline of the congregational domain. Indeed, the fall in numbers of Christian churchgoers is much higher than the growth of the New Age and other New Religious Movements (NRMs). As Bruce (2002: 81) states, "even the most generous estimates of the New Age are unlikely to have the new spiritual seekers filling the space left by the decline of just one denomination." The New Age, as it appears, does not provide a spiritual refuge for all dissatisfied Christians: many of these church-leavers can also become non-religious.

As we touched on in the previous chapter, the census in Australia requires respondents to provide additional information in the open-ended "Other" section following the selection of "No Religion," to designate himself or herself as something else. Therefore, while we know that around 30% selected no religion in 2016, we do not know how many of these regard themselves as spiritual only. We can only speculate about the real numbers, as they too have to write out their spiritual orientation in the open-ended "Other" section (Ezzy, 2019).

However, the statistics that we do have from the census are instructive. They show that there was an upturn in alternative spiritualities (see below), but not to the extent that Heelas and Tacey have suggested. Rather, as we will show, it might again be better to regard developments as more of a "mini revolution" that has already peaked. Further, as we noted in the previous chapter, many of those who are engaged in a variety of spiritual practices tend to be disengaged from the foundations that gave rise to them. Put another way, they are not always deeply immersed in those practices. As such, we will also look to outline how spirituality has become something of a capitalist commodity that is to be consumed. Though before we move to unpacking the current state of play, it is necessary to explain what constitutes the "new spiritualities" that scholars like Heelas, Tacey, and Woodhead are referring to, as there is a lot of confusion and slippage across a range of different categories.

New spiritualities

Often when there is discussion of spirituality, the expressions "NRMs" and "New Age" are invoked. These are only partially correct in relation to the rise of "new spiritualities" in that they both helped to lay the foundation for its emergence (Possamai, 2019). For example, NRMs and occult movements such as the Theosophical Society and Spiritualism have long traditions in Australia arriving in the 19th century (see Chapter 3), and exhibit many of the same characteristics in that they draw from Eastern traditions, but are different. For instance, the Theosophical Society is eclectic in that it draws from both Christianity and Hindu/Buddhist concepts such as karma and reincarnation. There is a divine God who resides in everyone and everything, and can be unlocked through spiritual practice. Similarly, Spiritualism sought to blend a Trinitarian understanding of God with mediumship that involved the contacting of spirits, in conjunction with meditation and spiritual healing. Nevertheless, while both engaged in syncretism they did not stray too far, in that they both had chapters or churches and remained to some extent within the confines of traditional institutional religion. Indeed, Spiritualism still had Sunday services, hymn books, and ministers (Humphreys and Ward, 1995).

This gradual move away from traditional understandings of God to the more esoteric and spiritual developed further during the advent of the New Age movement, which took place in the 1960s and 1970s. As scholars note, while the movement drew from the same influences as its forebears in Theosophy and Spiritualism, it was also driven by a counterculture that rejected both Western materialism and ecclesiastical domination and sought out independent models. As a result, a major thrust of the New Age era was a search for personal spiritual growth and development, or the sacralisation of the self. Therefore, there were two parallel developments. While some did join movements founded by gurus such as Bhagwan and Maharishi Yogi, or the human potential movement (a blend of Western psychology developed by Maslow and transcendental meditation), many others took a more democratic approach. The latter, driven by a distaste of authority, would not limit themselves to any one spiritual pathway, doctrine or dogma, as they regarded them all as simply different, rather than superior or inferior and ultimately leading to the same end, infinite spiritual awakening (Amaral, 2015; Gleig, 2014; Jespers, 2014).

In his research on the New Age movement in Melbourne, Possamai (2005) used the theory of Aldous Huxley on his philosophia perennis and coined the concept of perennism to describe the fundamental three elements that link these spiritualities together. He suggested that the notions of monism (or oneness), the human potential ethic and the knowledge of the self, serve as significant interrelated elements that specify a fundamental paradigm of the extraordinary array of contemporary spiritual actors he interviewed in Australia in 1996–1997.

This eclecticism on the part of the New Age followers sees them choose from a dazzling range of practices that can be embraced simultaneously and fit under the rubric of "mind, body, spirit" that are all geared to a better understanding of the self. These included a variety of alternative practices such as reiki, shamanic experiences, meditation, performances with water, crystals, flowers, and tai chi. In some instances, the practices also involved the use of hallucinogens to aid with the experience (Amaral, 2015; Gleig, 2014). Further, this tendency towards an alternative lifestyle meant that some of these practices operated on the margins, outside of mainstream society, and sometimes would take place in rural locations (see St John, 1997). Reflective of this are gatherings that are organised by New Agers in Australia; since the mid-1970s, there has been a biannual gathering called ConFest established by Jim Cairns that speaks directly to the counterculture and the focus on the individual:

> The purpose of the festival is to show the urgent need to SHAPE ALTERNATIVES NOW. Ways must be found because of the violent, acquisitive, alienated, industrial society which now poses a threat to survival. People have for centuries searched for equality and the right and ability to determine their own development. Individuals must accept responsibility for themselves. Personal happiness and equality, as much as a good society, depend upon self realisation. The most vital factor today is a sense of true identity. This is lost because our identities are created by others - not by ourselves. The all-powerful externally created hegemony in this assumed-to-be-free society, and its internalised personal alienation, must be understood if self realisation can be achieved.
>
> (Cairns, 1976)

Another strong influence behind the festival established by Cairns was an ecological consciousness. Indeed, the group he founded behind the festivals is called "Down to Earth," and it put forth an "Earth friendly culture" that worked against what were seen as unsustainable patterns of consumption (St John, 2001). This political discourse led to what St John (2001) describes as a "Self-Earth nexus" wherein the needs of the individual are the same as those of the planet and that the first step towards healing the planet is to discover the self in mind, body, and spirit. This self-discovery will then flow on into the immediate social, cultural, and physical environments. A key part of this was to follow anti-consumption ethics.

A follow on effect of this ecological consciousness was the attraction of individuals who regard themselves as neo-pagans, eco-witches, shamans, and users of Magick who celebrate nature-oriented spirituality. Thus, there is a need to both defend and heal the Earth, otherwise referred to as Gaia, the ancient Greek Goddess of Earth. Subsequently, at ConFest, there are many villages (camps) titled "Pagan," "Forest," "Earth Sharing," "Nuclear Free," and "Green Connection" that run workshops on ecological awareness and various manifestations of the occult (e.g. chanting, trance dances), and they run alongside the Healing Village, where one finds the flower essences, reiki, and kundalini energising amongst a raft of others (St John, 2001).

However, due to the semi-regular nature of such events, the New Age never solidified as a concrete organised movement. Rather, in spite of there being many different groups that came together, they only formed loose networks that would once again disperse. This regular atomisation saw the New Age movement gradually fade during the 1980s and 1990s. In its place one would then find individual practitioners that ran small centres in cities that were often independent of each other, offering a variety of different services, such as meditation, reiki, and tarot reading (Jespers, 2014). In other words, the New Age milieu, with its countercultural bent, remained highly fragmented and on the fringes of mainstream society.

Then in the mid-1990s onwards, a big shift took place. Alternative religion, in particular the term spirituality, became popularised. However, in doing so it moved away from the counterculture, which decried the rampant consumerism that is seen as leading to the demise of the world as we know it, to becoming a constituent part of the capitalist consumerist order. As Carrette and King note, the 1990s was witness to an "explosion of literature on business and spirituality and a celebration of 'spirituality' as enhancing work performance" (Carrette and King, 2005: 128–129). In this explosion, books began to draw from the same Eastern mystical traditions that were a mainstay of the New Age in the same pick-and-mix fashion. For example, Georganne Lamont in her book *The Spirited Business* (2002) draws from a range of different religious sources, such as the Bhagavad Gita, Sufism, and Buddhism via the Dalai Lama. However, at the same time she never provides an effective definition of spirituality other than saying that it is what makes us alive and gives us purpose. In other words, the book is more of a guide to running a business wrapped with religious references detached from the tradition in which they are drawn (Carrette and King, 2005).

On this point, Sophia Rose Arjana (2020: 15) notes that we now see these "floating signifiers" – that is symbols that have been dislocated from their context – everywhere and represents a corporatised and generalised Eastern spirituality, that she refers to as the mystical marketplace born of "muddled Orientalism." Eastern imagery and concepts are replete in advertising, with Nike adorning its shoes with Arabic script that most would be unable to read, to being woven through television shows such as *Lost* (Arjana, 2020: 101, 197). The latter ends with the characters in a church-like setting that contains a stained glass window that contains the religious symbols representing Islam, Hinduism, Buddhism, Judaism, Christianity, and Taoism, suggesting that everyone is going through a universal mystical journey. Alongside this, Arjana also singles out the wellness industry, which has co-opted the "mind-body-spirit" mantra of the New Age, which can now be found in books, spa vacations, meditation retreats, and a wide array of online goods. In particular, she notes Gwyneth Paltrow's highly successful business *goop*, which sells products such as the Sun Potion "Transformational Foods" line that includes the Ashwagandha Ayurvedic Antioxidant that is billed as "wisdom in a jar," and is branded with the Faravahar symbol, the sign of Zoroastrianism – an incredible confluence of both Indian and Persian mystical power (Arjana, 2020: 97).

This commercialisation and effective secularisation of the New Age is the "new spirituality" that has emerged at the turn of the century that piqued the interest of Australian scholars like Tacey (2004) and Possamai (2005). However, as touched on above, it is something quite different to its forebears. There are less attempts to make a connection to the underlying religious discourses from which the various products, practices, and symbols are drawn. Rather, there are simply situations like yoga without chanting as expressed by an instructor:

> We don't do chanting because people are not comfortable with it … We never use the word 'God.' We talk about energy, we talk about peace, we talk about mindfulness. We use those New-Agey kind of words.
>
> (as cited in Arjana, 2020: 129)

In other words, this spirituality is now part of the cultural logic of late capitalism (Possamai 2003), as it is both eclectic and ephemeral, and this possibly explains why many of those who do engage in a range of so-called spiritual practices tend not to identify with a particular spiritual community.

The rise and fall of alternative spiritualities in Australia

At the turn of the millennium, there was a rise in the numbers of adherents to both NRMs and alternative spiritualities in Australia, in line with the speculation by scholars such as Heelas, Woodhead, and Tacey. For example, both the forerunners to the New Age and New Spirituality in Spiritualism and Theosophy saw around 14% growth in adherents between 1996 and 2001 (see Chapter 4). At the same time, there was phenomenal growth amongst alternative spiritual communities, particularly amongst the Wicca and pagans, with each group growing by 375.50% and 144.25%, respectively (see Table 8.1). Indeed, there were overall positive figures across the board, with a growth rate of more than 153% that saw the spiritual community swell from just 9,100 in 1996 to 23,032 in 2001. Therefore, in relative terms, there was a definite surge. However, as the numbers all started from a relatively low base, this jump can only be described as a mini revolution among these groups. Table 8.1 provides data from people who have claimed in the Australian census an affiliation to any nature religions, which are part of this spiritual movement, but does not provide more information to the wider spiritual movement. Some of them might have claimed to be non-religious, as seen in Chapter 7.

Interestingly, this surge coincides with what scholars have characterised as the popularisation of the spiritual (see Arjana, 2020; Carrette and King, 2005; Jespers, 2014). In particular, there was, as Arjana (2020) alludes to, a mystical/spiritual awakening on the small screen. The mid-1990s saw a raft of TV shows emerge that brought witchcraft and pagan practice into the mainstream, such as *Buffy the Vampire Slayer* and *Charmed.*[1] The former introduced viewers to the character Willow who goes on a journey of self-discovery as a witch. In doing so, viewers are introduced to the casting of spells and pagan rituals, such as chanting intertwined with messages about saving the environment. For example, in one episode, Willow meets a female group of Wiccans and is disappointed that they are effectively "hearth witches" more interested in working towards saving the environment through ritual

Table 8.1 Nature religions in Australia, 1996–2016

Nature Religions	*1996*	*2001 (% Growth)*	*2006 (% Growth)*	*2011 (% Growth)*	*2016 (% Growth)*
Animism	727	763 (+4.95)	873 (+14.42)	781 (−10.54)	883 (+13.06)
Druid	554	697 (+25.81)	1,022 (+46.63)	1,048 (+2.54)	829 (−20.90)
Nature religion (nec)	1,617	2,176 (+34.57)	2,225 (+2.25)	2,740 (+23.15)	3,075 (+12.23)
Paganism	4,353	10,632 (+144.25)	15,515 (+45.93)	16,851 (+8.61)	15,219 (−9.68)
Wicca	1,849	8,755 (+373.50)	8,206 (−6.27)	8,414 (+2.53)	6,616 (−21.37)
Total	**9,100**	**23,023 (+153.00)**	**27,841 (+20.93)**	**29,834 (+7.16)**	**26,622 (−10.77)**
Total population (%)	17,892,423 (0.05)	18,769,249 (0.12)	19,855,288 (0.14)	21,507,717 (0.14)	23,401,892 (0.11)

Source: Australian Bureau of Statistics.

dance that is directed towards worship of the Earth goddess Gaia, as opposed to doing real magic (Wilson, 2005). Alongside this, there are other witches in the show, such as the gypsy Jenny Calendar, a computer teacher and self-designated "techno pagan" who keeps her spells on a disk and does magic over the Internet (Winslade, 2001). Indeed, as Wilson (2005) notes, the show provides a fluid understanding of witchcraft and paganism, never really defining or anchoring the depictions in any historical or contemporary practice. Rather, it is the trendy teen pop-culture version that is designed to allow the individual to choose whichever version speaks to them.

Similarly, the show *Charmed* portrayed witches as individuals who are desirable as they were beautiful, successful women who were integrated into mainstream society (Berger and Ezzy, 2009). Further, Berger and Ezzy (2009) note that this approach, along with similar shows like *Buffy*, created what they called a "brand memory" akin to that of advertising and acted as surrogate for the Wicca community which has no formal centralised organisation. In other words, the shows with their inventory of "salient symbols" that are not anchored to any particular tradition helped draw teens, particularly young women, to explore Wicca for themselves.

This "brand memory" would no doubt have been enhanced by the phenomenon that was the *Harry Potter* series by J.K. Rowling, which first emerged on the young adult literary scene in 1997 and migrated to the silver screen in 2001 as an eight-film behemoth that concluded in 2011. The books, of which there are seven, have sold over 500 million copies in 80 different languages around the world, and the films grossed an incredible $7.73 billion globally (Foley, 2018; Mendelson, 2020). This is very different from the situation in the 1980s, where "most people learnt about witchcraft by finding other people who were witches" and where "information could [only] be found in a few specialised newsletters and in books from specialist occult bookstores" (Ezzy, 2019: 85). Further, Singleton et al. note that such works of fiction and media "might sustain interest in supernatural possibilities" (2021: 40) and, as we will present below, in hyper-real religions.

However, it would appear that the "brand memory" effect that has supported an increase in alternative spiritualities, such as Wicca and paganism, is starting to wear off. Indeed, we see a marked decline overall in both adherents of the NRMs listed in Chapter 4 and those in the wider alternative spirituality category, with 2011 representing a peak for both. Some of the NRMs listed from the census fared worse with an overall decline of 14.44%, while the nature religions declined by 10.77%. Interestingly, Wicca was the worst performer amongst the new spiritualities, with a 21.37% decline, which again speaks to a possible waning of interest from the generation brought in by popular culture. In contrast, paganism only fell 9.68%, bringing the community back to 2006 levels. As such, only time will tell if the community remains relatively stable as Ezzy (2019) has suggested.

Hyper-real religions

A recent trend has pushed this spiritual eclecticism even further. Some religions and spirituality mix elements from religious and philosophical traditions with a new source of inspiration for a religious syncretic work, namely that of global commodified popular culture. At a metaphorical level, these social actors are inspired by popular culture to express their spiritualities. At one end of the spectrum, we can find groups such as Jediism from the *Star Wars* movies, Matrixism from the *Matrix* trilogy, and neo-pagan groups inspired by stories from the *Lord of the Rings* and *Harry Potter*, who are actively using works of popular culture as part of their syncretic spiritualities. At the other end of the spectrum, we see members from mainstream religions, such as Christians, being influenced or inspired by, for example, the *Da Vinci Code.*

These hyper-real religions are a simulacrum (Baudrillard, 1994) of a religion partly created out of popular culture, which provides inspiration for believers/consumers. These contemporary expressions of religion are likely to be consumed and individualised, and thus have more relevance to the self than to a community and/or congregation (Possamai, 2012). For example, the birth of this phenomenon became observable in the 2001 Australian census, when close to 71,000 people claimed to be part of Jediism. Many of them recorded this for fun; however, it has been estimated by an insider that 5,000 individuals were serious about this. Furthermore, around the same time, approximately 53,000 people in New Zealand and close to 400,000 in the UK identified themselves as belonging to this hyper-real religion, but no figures are available on the "real" number of believers/practitioners. In the last census in Australia, the number went down to 48,000 (ABS, 2018).

Moving towards the Internet medium, a plethora of religious activities based on the *Star Wars Mythos* indicate that there is more to this phenomenon than just the census (see Possamai, 2012). In various sites, one can observe that the *Star Wars Mythos* is not based exclusively on the fiction written by movie director George Lucas, but shares many themes taken from Hinduism, Confucianism, Buddhism, Gnosticism, Catholicism, Taoism, and even the Knight's Code of Chivalry and that of the *Samurai Warriors.* This new medium is used by people to express their faith and discuss their activities; they view this religion as an old one re-mythologised for a contemporary public. Religious people and groups have been active on the Internet since the start, and the way religion is discussed and practised on the web has gone through recurrent transformations. It is, however, partly thanks to this new development of religious practices in the digital world that these new popular religions, such as hyper-real religion, have developed. It can easily be argued that the Internet is a new tool used for new religions to be practised and/or created by everyday people, and these people, in this context, are not illiterate or unlearned. They are quite active in the field of creation of popular religion, thanks to this new technology that allows one person to take part in these activities without leaving their house (see more on religion and social media in Chapter 10).

Religious groups can also attempt to stop people from being influenced by popular culture as a source of inspiration. When the *Da Vinci Code* was released in 2006, the Anglican Church in Sydney screened a trailer in 250 cinemas to tell cinema-goers about their website, which challenges the theories in the *Da Vinci Code*. Described as "Harry Potter for adults," this movie was banned in a cinema on the Central Coast of NSW because of the way it depicts the Catholic Church (Possamai, 2012). The Internet is also used by these groups and individuals where we can find sites that promote a Christian exegesis of popular culture. Some attacks against works of popular culture can be strong, such as those against Harry Potter and Marilyn Manson, and others softer, such as those against the *Star Wars* movies. A critique of the Force is that it is a flow of energy that has as opposites good and evil, and these would be "wrongly" equal. In this fictional worldview, the dynamic of opposing forces holds everything in harmony. Whereas the Force has a dark and light side, the Holy Spirit is for Christian good only, does not need to be balanced, and does not fit with the mythology of the Force (Possamai, 2009).

Conclusion

Here, it can be seen, that while scholars were right to note that there was an uptick in new spiritualities at the turn of the century, this was far from amounting to a revolution. Rather, as we have suggested, inspired by Heelas and Woodhead (2003), it can, at best, be described as a mini-revolution. Some categories, such as Wicca and paganism, certainly experienced a period of phenomenal growth in relative terms. This was particularly the case for the Wicca community, which almost quadrupled in size between 1996 and 2001. This surge was brought about by the popularisation of witches and spirituality more generally during the mid-1990s and early 2000s in both books and TV shows, which resulted in a new generation of youth becoming interested in the world of magic because of what Berger and Ezzy (2004) have likened as a marketing effect that subliminally drew in new adherents.

However, going forward, it would seem likely that there is another "betwixt and between" that is slightly different to that proposed by Heelas. Namely, that those who are now engaging in the consumptive alternative spirituality lite that is served up today are not committed enough to choose an identity and remain in what can be described as a liminal spiritual space, or a constant state of transition. As such, it is likely that the numbers will continue to decline and the spiritual milieu become less and less visible than it was at the end of the last century.

Note

1 *Buffy the Vampire Slayer* ran from 1996 to 2003, and *Charmed* began in 1998 and finished in 2006.

References

ABS. 2018. *Census reveals Australia's religious diversity on World Religion Day.* https://www.abs.gov.au/AUSSTATS/abs@.nsf/mediareleasesbyReleaseDate/8497F7A8E7DB5BEFCA25821800203DA4?OpenDocument

Amaral, L. 2015. New age spirituality. In Gooren, H. P. P. ed. *Encyclopedia of Latin American Religions.* Cham: Springer International Publishing. https://doi.org/10.1007/978-3-319-08956-0_51-1

Arjana, S.R. 2020. *Buying Buddha, selling Rumi: Orientalism and the mystical marketplace. Simon and Schuster.* London: Oneworld.

Baudrillard, J. 1994. *Simulacra and simulation.* Ann Arbor: The University of Michigan Press.

Berger, H., and Ezzy, D. 2004. The Internet as virtual spiritual community: Teen witches in the United States and Australia. In Dawson, L. L. and D. Cowan, E. eds. *Religion online: Finding faith on the Internet.* New York: Routledge, pp. 175–188.

Berger, H.A. and Ezzy, D. 2009. Mass media and religious identity: a case study of young witches. *Journal for the Scientific Study of Religion, 48*(3): 501–514.

Bruce, S. 2002. *God is dead: secularization in the West.* Oxford: Blackwell.

Cairns, J. 1976. Jim Cairns' invitation to the first ConFest. Retrieved from https://confest.org.au/index.php/about/history

Carrette, J.R., Carrette, J. and King, R. 2005. *Selling spirituality: The silent takeover of religion.* Abingdon, Oxfordshire: Routledge.

Ezzy, D. 2019. The ethics of Pagan Ritual. *Pomegranate, 21*(1): 76–99.

Foley, M. 2018. You won't believe how many people in the world actually own a copy of Harry Potter. *Bustle.* Retrieved from https://www.bustle.com/p/how-many-copies-of-harry-potter-have-been-sold-jk-rowlings-series-just-reached-a-huge-milestone-8088216

Gleig, A. 2014. New age movement. In Leeming, D. A. ed. *Encyclopedia of psychology and religion.* Boston, MA: Springer US, pp. 1204–1207.

Heelas, P. 2002. The spiritual revolution: From 'Religion' to 'Spirituality'. In Woodhead, L., Fletcher, P., Kawanami, H. and Smith, D. eds. *Religions in the modern world.* London: Routledge, pp. 412–436.

Heelas, P. and Woodhead, L. 2003. The Kendal project: testing the 'spiritual revolution' thesis: what is the state of religion and spirituality in Great Britain today? Is a spiritual revolution taking place? A research project was set up in Kendal in an attempt to find out. *Sociology Review,*

13, 18+. Retrieved from https://link.gale.com/apps/doc/A110221315/ITOF?u=deakin&sid=ITOF&xid=8b7e222a.

Humphreys, R. and Ward, R.S. 1995. *Religious bodies in Australia: a comprehensive guide.* Wantirna: New Melbourne Press.

Jespers, F. 2014. From New age to new spiritualities: secular sacralizations on the borders of religion. In Sutcliffe, S. and Gilhus, I. eds. *New age spirituality: rethinking religion.* Abingdon, Oxon: Routledge, pp. 197–211.

Mendelson, S. 2020. Every 'Harry Potter' movie ranked by worldwide box office. *Forbes.* Retrieved from https://www.forbes.com/sites/scottmendelson/2020/08/13/harry-potter-movies-ranked-box-office-jk-rowling-emma-watson-daniel-radcliffe/?sh=1ad8cbb952da

Possamai, A. 2003. Alternative Spiritualities and the Cultural Logic of Late Capitalism. *Culture and Religion,* 4 (1): 31-45.

Possamai, A. 2005. *In search of new age spirituality.* Aldershot: Ashgate.

Possamai, A. 2009. *Sociology of religion for generations X and Y.* London: Equinox.

Possamai, A. ed. 2012. *Handbook of hyper-real religion.* Leiden: Brill.

Possamai, A. 2019. New spiritualities in western society. In *Oxford research encyclopedia of religion.* DOI: 10.1093/acrefore/9780199340378.013.217

Singleton, A., Rasmussen, M.L., Halafoff, A. and Bouma, G. 2021. *Freedoms, faiths and futures: teenage Australians on religion, sexuality and diversity.* London: Bloomsbury Publishing.

St John, G. 1997. Going Feral: Authentica on the edge of Australian culture. *The Australian Journal of Anthropology, 8*(3): 167–189.

St John, G. 2001. 'Heal thy Self-thy Planet': confest, eco-spirituality and the self/earth nexus. *Australian Religion Studies Review, 14*(1): 97–112.

Tacey, D.J. 2004. *The spirituality revolution: the emergence of contemporary spirituality.* New York: Brunner-Routledge.

Wilson, D. 2005. Willow and Witch Craft? The Portrayal of Witchcraft in Joss Whedon's' Buffy the Vampire Slayer'. In Cusack, C. M. Hartney, C. and Lauro, F. D. eds. *The Buddha of suburbia: Proceedings of the Eighth Australian and International Religion, Literature and the Arts Conference 2004.* Sydney: RLA Press, pp. 146–158.

Winslade, J.L. 2001. Teen witches, wiccans, and "Wanna-Blessed-Be's": Pop-culture magic in buffy the Vampire Slayer. *Slayage: The Online International Journal of Buffy Studies,* 1. Retrieved from https://www.whedonstudies.tv/uploads/2/6/2/8/26288593/winslade_-_slayage_1.1.pdf.

9 Feminised religion and the patriarchy

Introduction

The three Abrahamic faiths are heavily patriarchal. Judaism, Christianity, and Islam all have a male God and contain scriptures that elevate men above their female counterparts. In particular, they all share the creation story outlined in the book of Genesis wherein Eve is portrayed as having derived from one of Adam's ribs ("This is now bone of my bones and flesh of my flesh; she shall be called "woman," for she was taken out of man," Genesis, 2:23). Therefore, she not only came after man but was also created from a small part of him, and is therefore inferior on both counts, and this hierarchical relationship is embellished with each retelling. For example, in the Christian tradition, the church fathers endorse this understanding with reference to 1 Corinthians 11:7–10, which states: "he [man] is the image and glory of God; but woman is the glory of man. For man did not come from woman, but woman from man; neither was man created for woman, but woman for man" (see Kvam et al., 1999).[1] Similarly, in the Islamic tradition, we find an affirmation of the Judeo-Christian understanding. Although neither Eve (Hawwa in Arabic) nor the rib story are directly mentioned in the Qur'an, we find the story reiterated in interpretations of verse 4:1, which alludes to the creation of Adam and Eve. For example, scholars like al-Zamakshari (1075–1144) use the biblical version of the rib story to explain that in verse 4:1, the *zawj* (mate) is drawn from the one *nafs* (soul) and that this extraction rendered in the form of *min* (from) means that although there was one soul, man was still primary and the woman secondary (Wadud, 1999):

> And *min* His ayat (is this:) that He created You (humankind) *min* a single *nafs*, and created *min* (that nafs) its *zawj*, and from these two He spread (through the earth) countless men and women. (4:1).
>
> (as cited in Wadud, 1999: 17)

DOI: 10.4324/9781003255338-9

Much of this understanding derives from the hadith literature where the Old Testament story has been incorporated. The retelling can be found in the most authoritative hadith compilations by al-Bukhari (810–870) and Muslim (817–875), which are regarded as secondary only to the Qur'an (Hassan, 1985). An often-cited example is a report on the authority of Abu Hurairah recorded in *Sahih al-Bukhari*:

> Treat women nicely, for a woman is created from a rib, and the most curved portion of the rib is its upper portion. So, if you should try to straighten it, it will break, but if you leave it as it is, it will remain crooked. So treat women nicely.
>
> (Al-Bukhari, 1997: 329)

Here the implication is that not only is woman inferior to man because she has come from his rib, but also that her nature is crooked. In other words, she is imperfect and fragile in contrast to man (Arpaguş, 2013), who, in the biblical tradition, as noted above, is made in the "image and glory of God." Indeed, both Hassan (1985) and Arpaguş (2013) note that the sources for these reports are certainly pre-Islamic, with the latter suggesting that the narratives go back as far as the time of Abraham.

Subsequently, with all three of the Abrahamic faiths exalting men above women, they have also historically excluded women from positions of authority. In all three traditions, only men could be rabbis, priests, and imams. More recently this has begun to change, but is still generally a minority practice that is not recognised by the orthodox within those traditions (see Calderini, 2021; Ferziger, 2018; Marx, 2012; Rue, 2008; Simon et al., 1993). Typically, it is movements, like Reform Judaism and the Protestant Christian denominations (Ferziger, 2018; Rue, 2008), which have led the way for female ordination. Similarly, there are challenges to androcentric understandings of religion within Islam and outside of the Abrahamic faiths. Susan Carland (2017), in her book *Fighting Hislam*, explores how Australian Muslim women, amongst others, are fighting to end sexism from within an Islamic paradigm that she calls a "faith positive feminism." Likewise, Halafoff et al. (2018) detail the "ultramodern" Buddhist movement in Australia, who have gender equality as a core principle, and their push for female ordination, which remains opposed by conservative groups in Australia and abroad.

However, as will be shown, whilst change has been taking place amongst some Christian denominations in Australia, the situation is far from straight forward, as they have become feminised. This means that female parishioners outnumber their male counterparts. Yet, this numerical superiority has not led to a marked shift in practice regarding leadership, particularly among Pentecostals. Rather, in a peculiar twist, it has resulted in what could be regarded as quasi-leadership roles for female pastors in Pentecostal churches. To highlight this development we provide a case study of Hillsong Church and their application of the practice of 'headship' that takes a complementarian view of the sexes. Though, before we move to Hillsong, we unpack how Christianity has become feminised in Australia.

The feminisation of religion in Australia

A somewhat ironic turn is that, while women have predominantly been shut out of taking leadership roles within their congregations, some religious communities have become increasingly feminised. This is particularly the case in relation to Christian contexts. It has been observed that since the 19th century, Christianity in both North America and European societies became a more female domain (Woodhead, 2012), and that this was the result of two developments. The first was the emergence of secular worldviews that competed with Christianity. The second factor was the view that the virtues being taught by the church, such as patience, compassion, and self-denial, were feminine traits. Subsequently, men either drifted or actively distanced themselves from the church. This increasing absence of men within church communities saw women become more important in church life and further reinforced the notion that attendance and worship were very much a female concern (Werner, 2009). Further, a secular/religious divide emerged between men and women that saw religion become a private matter. Men were immersed in the fields of work and politics that were deemed masculine realms ruled by reason and rationality, while the increased piety of women was welcomed as it was seen as curbing women's tendency towards excessive sexuality and preserved the family, the woman's domain, which was seen as the backbone of the national enterprise. In this way, the feminisation of religion became underpinned by a Judeo-Christian secularism (Scott, 2018).

In the case of Australia, Carey (1996) has noted that a similar process took place at the turn of the 20th century. As mentioned in Chapter 3, working men became increasingly disinterested in religion as Christianity was bound up with imperial ideology and was seen as both unmanly and un-Australian. Such was the distaste and lack of men in the pews that a Reverend Percy W. Wise lamented at the Melbourne Church Congress held in November 1906 that there was more desire to "play golf and tennis, to picnic in the country, or to lounge in…homes than…attend worship" (cited in Carey, 1996: 117). Because of these masculine pastimes in the form of sport – the opportunities for women to play sport were often limited (see Little, 2014) – church work became women's work, and by 1947, most Christian denominations had a sex ratio in favour of women (see Table 9.1). This reversed somewhat following WWII, particularly for Catholics, due to post-war migration that saw an influx of Roman Catholics from Italy (Carey, 1996; see also Chapter 4).

This trend outlined by Carey (1996) at the turn of the 20th century has continued with the most recent census and is in line with a consistent global gender gap with regard to Christianity (see Schnabel, 2018).[2] According to the 2016 census, women are more likely than men to report being Christian (55% to 50%, respectively), and this gap widened further when looking at church attendance (ABS, 2017). The 2016 National Church Life Survey (NCLS) found that 60% of church attenders, across all denominations, are female, and that this 3:2 ratio in favour of women has been constant since 2006. Further, while there was some slight variation, with Baptist, Churches of Christ, Pentecostal, and Lutheran Churches having marginally higher levels of male involvement at around 43–44%, the NCLS found that women outnumbered men in every age grouping across all denominations (Powell et al., 2018).

Thus, Christianity in Australia has become very much a woman's domain. However, in another ironic twist, despite this feminisation of Australian Christianity, a recent study on religion and values found that most Christian denominations had still relatively strong levels of patriarchy. All but one Christian group scored over 40 out of 100 on the patriarchal gender ideology index[3] developed by Perales and Bouma (2019), with some groups such as the Brethren and Jehovah's Witnesses scoring 69.70 and 54.43, respectively. Catholics, Anglicans, and the Uniting Church, the three largest groups, all had moderate scores of 40.11, 41.91, and 43.02, respectively. Pentecostals scored slightly higher at around 45. Comparatively, Islam ranked third with a score of 52.92, while Judaism was the most liberal religion with a score of 34.56,[4] and was closely followed by no religion and Buddhism with scores of 35.77 and 38.65, respectively. These scores have led Perales and Bouma to regard religions as the "remnant guardians of traditional gender relations" in Australia (2019: 338).

Table 9.1 Sex ratios of religions and total population for census years 1901–1991

	Census year	*1901*	*1911*	*1921*	*1933*	*1947*	*1954*	*1961*	*1971*	*1981*	*1991*
Christian											
	Anglican	109.70	107.12	104.53	102.37	100.27	100.56	100.03	99.55	93.85	92.88
	Baptist	91.40	88.81	87.06	88.32	88.18	89.10	90.27	88.22	88.51	90.21
	Brethren	59.77	81.61	84.09	81.22	80.71	84.46	88.30	90.36	90.34	89.98
	Catholic	104.16	102.82	99.99	99.91	97.71	103.68	103.55	99.69	96.77	95.65
	Churches of Christ	87.14	81.35	82.56	84.93	86.44	89.17	89.30	84.83	83.56	81.18
	Congregational	93.80	91.44	88.25	87.41	86.67	87.99	89.27	84.86	87.66	86.30
	Jehovah's Witnesses	NA	NA	NA	NA	NA	NA	NA	81.29	81.54	81.46
	Latter-Day Saints	104.76	92.41	98.52	92.31	92.57	NA	NA	NA	87.95	89.05
	Lutheran	136.72	130.54	122.15	115.35	108.79	107.94	106.08	99.78	95.27	95.01
	Methodist	99.65	96.94	94.15	94.09	95.53	95.85	96.28	92.37	94.23	NA
	Oriental Christian	NA	NA	NA	NA	NA	NA	NA	NA	NA	102.46
	Orthodox/Greek Catholic	449.79	458.23	88.18	NA	NA	146.17	121.45	109.93	105.1	104.66
	Other Protestant	126.58	134.84	125.19	107.82	100.40	103.55	105.06	94.95	90.93	91.53
	Pentecostal	NA	NA	NA	NA	NA	NA	NA	NA	88.03	87.80
	Presbyterian/reformed	108.36	107.76	102.28	100.07	97.41	98.03	97.63	93.78	91.65	95.40
	Quaker	131.38	123.33	107.65	93.69	80.04	NA	NA	NA	NA	73.38
	Salvation Army	90.83	86.04	85.76	84.54	87.58	90.10	91.19	88.05	85.52	81.76
	Seventh-day Adventist	73.45	73.45	69.63	75.15	73.81	78.84	82.64	81.44	82.78	83.69
	Unitarian	160.65	160.65	144.16	116.92	99.56	NA	NA	NA	NA	95.48
	Other Christian	138.52	88.26	101.03	87.93	92.01	89.73	92.19	97.77	84.92	85.77
	Total Christian	**106.12**	**104.58**	**101.21**	**99.72**	**98.02**	**100.27**	**100.19**	**96.75**	**97.26**	**90.09**
Non-Christian		510.79	301.98	208.49	136.37	122.93	116.16	110.50	113.80	126.58	104.07
No religion		396.27	463.65	354.31	334.04	253.84	236.80	204.20	152.92	118.27	115.50
Not stated		206.44	218.42	187.61	126.27	117.4	120.48	117.59	117.22	130.14	125.14
Total population		**110.14**	**107.99**	**103.37**	**103.20**	**100.41**	**102.38**	**102.24**	**101.10**	**99.42**	**98.53**

Source: Adapted from Carey (1996: 120).
Note: A number higher than 100 indicates that the religious group has more male adherents than female adherents.

Intriguingly, the scores by the Christian denominations line up closely with male participation in churches, while the higher scores by fundamentalist Christian and Pentecostal groups are driven by the practise of "headship." This is the doctrine where women are regarded as "equal but different," while men are "called to leadership" and women to "willing submission" (Perales and Bouma, 2019: 325). This is significant in relation to the Pentecostals as they are one of the fastest-growing Christian denominations in Australia, while the vast majority of all the other Christian groups are in decline (see Chapter 5). Indeed, only three defined denominations have grown their community between 1996 and 2016, and the Pentecostals are well out in front with +0.13%, followed by Oriental Christians and the Latter-Day Saints with +0.04% and +0.01%, respectively (see Table 9.2).

Given this growth in the Pentecostal community, which bucks the general decline in Christianity overall (−18.18%) between 1996 and 2016, this chapter explores the issue of gender and patriarchy within that community. In particular, we are focusing on Hillsong Church, the largest and most successful manifestation of Pentecostalism in Australia (see Chapter 10). Understanding these communities is important, for while they are small in relative terms, they have, as Lech Blaine (2020) outlined in *The Monthly*, an outsized influence within conservative political circles (see also Chapter 11).

Introducing Hillsong

Brian and Bobbie Houston founded Hillsong Church in 1983 in Sydney's Baulkham Hills at Norwest Business Park. This remains the original campus and hub of the church and has a series of auditoriums that range from 300 to 3,500 hundred seats, with film-recording, editing, and production facilities. Since then, Hillsong has expanded to 28 locations across Australia and has established 78 churches in 20 countries around the world.[5] Collectively, the local chapters minister to around 20,000, while altogether they service an average global attendance of around 150,000. Alongside this, the church uses its film facilities to beam into over 160 countries around the world via *Hillsong TV* (which is broadcast 24 hours a day, 7 days a week), while its record label, which has sold over 20 million albums, has 50 million Christians singing Hillsong songs worldwide every weekend. Finally, Hillsong's annual conference attracts in excess of 25,000 participants. All of this activity amounts to a global megachurch empire that saw the Australian

Table 9.2 Change in religious populations between 1996 and 2016

Religious denomination	*1996*	*% of population*	*2016*	*% of population*	*% Change*
Christian:					
Anglican	3,903,324	21.82	3,101,185	13.25	−8.57
Baptist	295,178	1.65	345,142	1.47	−0.18
Brethren	22,063	0.12	17,423	0.07	−0.05
Catholic	4,798,950	26.82	5,291,834	22.61	−4.21
Churches of Christ	75,023	0.42	39,621	0.17	−0.25
Jehovah's Witnesses	83,414	0.47	82,510	0.35	−0.12
Latter-day Saints	45,112	0.25	61,639	0.26	0.01
Lutheran	249,989	1.40	174,019	0.74	−0.66
Oriental Christian	31,342	0.18	51,013	0.22	0.04
Orthodox	497,015	2.78	502,801	2.15	−0.63
Pentecostal	174,720	0.98	260,558	1.11	0.13
Presbyterian and Reformed	675,534	3.78	526,689	2.25	−1.53
Salvation Army	74,145	0.41	48,939	0.21	−0.20
Seventh-Day Adventist	52,655	0.29	62,945	0.27	−0.02
Uniting Church	1,334,917	7.46	870,183	3.72	−3.74
Other Protestant	50,216	0.28	108,307	0.46	0.18
Other Christian	219,167	1.22	656,783[a]	2.81	1.59
Total	*12,582,764*	*70.32*	*12,201,591*	*52.14*	*−18.18*
Non-Christian:					
Buddhism	199,812	1.12	563,674	2.41	1.29
Hinduism	67,279	0.38	440,300	1.88	1.50
Islam	200,885	1.12	604,240	2.58	1.46
Judaism	79,805	0.45	91,022	0.39	−0.06
Other religions	68,647	0.38	221,590	0.95	0.57
Total	616,428	*3.45*	*1,920,826*	*8.21*	4.76
No religion	2,948,888	16.48	6,933,708	29.63	13.15
Inadequately described	54,164	0.30	107,008[b]	0.46	0.16
Not stated	1,550,585	8.67	2,238,735	9.57	0.90
Overseas visitor	139,594	0.78			
Total	4,693,231	*26.23*	*9,279,451*	*39.65*	*13.42*
Total Population	**17,892,423**	**100**	**23,401,868**	**100**	**30.79**

Source: Australian Bureau of Statistics.

[a] Other Christian includes Apostolic Assyrians, Other, and not further defined (nfd).

[b] Inadequately described includes the newer categories of secular beliefs and other spiritual beliefs.

arm alone take in a tax-free income of over $130 million in 2016 (Blaine, 2020; Evans, 2017; Hillsong Church, 2021a; Maddox, 2009).

Hillsong and headship

As touched on above, a core principle of Pentecostalism is the notion of headship which is drawn from discussions about 1 Corinthians 11: 2–16 (Bower, 2015). In particular, two portions. The first is verse 3 and the second are verses 7–10:

> [3] But I want you to realize that the head of every man is Christ, and the head of the woman is man, and the head of Christ is God.
>
> [7–10] A man ought not to cover his head, since he is the image and glory of God; but woman is the glory of man. For man did not come from woman, but woman from man; neither was man created for woman, but woman for man. It is for this reason that a woman ought to have authority over her own head, because of the angels.

From the first portion (11:3) it is understood that this grants man authority over women (Aune, 2006), while the second portion (11:7–10) is to be read as a metaphor in relation to women covering their heads while praying. That is, the unmarried women need to find a man, wherein the husband becomes the "covering" authority over her, and that it is often recommended that one find a pastor to perform this role (Bower, 2015). Subsequently, women are expected to submit to the authority of their men, and this is reflected in the notes in the New International Version (NIV) of the Bible. In relation to verse 11:3 where "the head of the woman is man," it outlines in a footnote: "Or of the wife is her husband." Similarly, the line "woman ought to have authority over her own head" has the footnote "Or have a sign of authority on her" which is read to mean that the woman keeps her modesty for her husband. However, it is suggested that such interpretations are a misreading of Paul's intent and that he was talking about women simply keeping a sense of decorum while praying in relation to men in general so as not to bring shame on themselves (see Brock and Wannenwetsch, 2018).

Given that the principle of headship is less than explicit in the Bible, it is perhaps not surprising then that there are no overt detailed theological attestations in Hillsong's services and conferences. Rather, scholarly accounts suggest that the principle is enacted through their various activities, while the church seeks to publicly downplay the concept. For example, Brian Houston stated in an interview with *Australian Story* that women are not required to submit to their husbands:

> Bobbie works alongside me. We're very much a team. In a sense, I've got a conservative, biblical idea that a man should take a role of leadership in his life, but I certainly don't adhere to the mentality that a woman must submit or that she should be pushed down. I absolutely believe that there's a sense of walking together in life.
>
> (Houston, 2005, as cited in Miller, 2016: 67)

Here, the notion of headship is glossed by the phrase "biblical idea," and the relationship is presented as egalitarian. Similarly, Tanya Riches, an insider researcher, emphasises the role that Bobbie Houston plays in the church, highlighting that her official title is Founder and Global Senior Pastor of Hillsong (2017: 91). However, the "About" page on Hillsong's website distinctly lists her as "Co-Global Senior Pastor," while Brian is listed as "Global Senior Pastor," and his photo is above, rather than beside hers (see Hillsong Church, 2021a). These small, but important, details suggest that Brian Houston is very much the primary leader and that Bobbie Houston is second in command.

Indeed, this is one of the key elements that observers note that speaks to an "aesthetic" of headship in Hillsong Church and the Pentecostal approach more broadly. Maddox outlines that the typical set-up of a Pentecostal Church is that they are run by a husband-and-wife team, whereby the wife derives authority "more from their husband's status than from any formal qualifications" (2013: 14). Further, she notes that Bobbie Houston is cognisant of this as she acknowledges "she never attended Bible College" and that because Brian is Senior Pastor and "she is married to him...[she is] respected as senior pastor with him also" (cited in Maddox, 2013: 14). This dynamic is also observable in the language used by the Pentecostal megachurch Planetshakers in relation to its Pastors Russell and Sam Evans. In their bios on the website, Russell Evan's story outlines his pedigree in that he was "Born on the mission field in Papua New Guinea and raised as a pastor's kid...[and] comes from a strong Christian lineage that is reflected in his depth of experience." In contrast, the opening line of Sam's bio is that she "has been standing alongside her husband...helping to champion the mandate of Planetshakers and implement the vision." Additionally, her journey towards Jesus was a solitary one following a "family breakdown" as a teenager (Planetshakers, 2021). In other words, Russell, with his long Christian lineage, is the authority, and Sam, like Bobbie, is accepted and respected as the wife-cum-pastor.

On this point, Miller (2016) suggests that the practice of using husband-and-wife teams allows Pentecostal Churches to sidestep issues around women being able to hold positions of authority in the church and avoid any explicit discussions of submission, for the female pastor's position is always implicitly subordinate to her husband. Miller also notes that this practice has a long lineage that dates back to the early days of the Pentecostal movement in the United States. In 1920, the American Assemblies of God (AOG) allowed women to be assistant pastors so that they minister to their husbands' congregations while the men were travelling. This was then extended in 1935 to allow women to become pastors in their own right, but with a restricted purview, namely, that they minister to other women and children. Thus, the female pastors do women's work, and this brings us to another key element of the "aesthetic" of headship in Hillsong in the women's Colour Conferences and the attendant "princess theology."

Colour Conference and princess theology

Alongside being the Co-Senior Global Pastor of Hillsong Church, Bobbie Houston is also the CEO of Colour Conference. "Colour," as it is colloquially known, is Hillsong's annual Christian women's conference, which first began in 1996 (Riches, 2017), and these types of segregated events are also a standard practice amongst other large Pentecostal Churches in Australia, such as Planetshakers, Influencers, and C3 (Miller, 2016). At the Colour Conferences, Bobbie Houston strongly emphasises complementarianism that essentialises the roles of men and women (Winter, 2020). In particular, Bobbie in her preaching advocates for a type of hyper-feminine womanhood:

> Femininity—the quality or nature of being a woman—is created and purposed by the Father to compliment [sic] the strength of masculinity . . . we need to value and celebrate Heaven-breathed womanhood in all its *beauty, softness, vulnerability and tenderness*. . . Godly femininity can be wonderfully disarming and significantly powerful in its contribution to the Body of Christ. It is no wonder that throughout the ages femininity has faced unrelenting attack, leaving many women ashamed and confused about this God-given gift.
>
> (as cited in Maddox, 2013: 16; emphasis added)

This call for women to be beautiful, soft, vulnerable, and tender manifests in a visual symbolic display at the conferences. Over the years, a recurring theme has been that of the princess. In 2005, the promotional material for Colour contained images of tiaras and flowers, and in 2008 and 2009, merchandise was sold with the slogans "Daughter of the King" and "Warrior Princess Daughter" (Maddox, 2013: 19), and this approach continues. In the promotional trailer for the Colour Conference Online for 2021, there are numerous shots of young women frolicking carefree in what can be described as childlike white lacy princess dresses (see Hillsong Church, 2021b) that also speak of purity and innocence. The video is also replete with images of natural floral scenes and a few small bursts of streamers and confetti that Winter argues also speak to "the centrality of heterosexual marriage within evangelical culture" and is a "representation of the bride of Christ," which Bobbie often refers to as "His girls" (2020: 155).

Maddox (2013: 19) also notes Bobbie Houston's tendency to address female members of the church as "girls" and regards it as infantilising, particularly in conjunction with the ubiquity of princess paraphernalia, as it paints a picture akin to the fairy tale princess waiting passively to be saved by a prince. Alternatively, this could be read as them waiting for a pastor to come and "cover" them with their authority as a husband.

Thus, while Hillsong has a female pastor in Bobbie Houston who is a prominent figure, and while the church is predominantly female and young (Riches, 2017), the role of women is circumscribed by adherence to the principle of headship. Although not explicit theologically, the practice is embodied in the symbolic actions of the leadership being a husband-and-wife team, wherein she undertakes gendered work. Moreover, a core part of this gendered work is to establish clearly delineated masculine and feminine roles, wherein women are directed by constant verbal and visual displays of idealised womanhood that is meant to culminate in marriage and submission to manly authority.

Conclusion

As outlined above, Australia, like Europe and North America, has experienced a feminisation of Christianity, driven by a Judeo-Christian secularism that has seen the majority of church pews across all denominations populated by women. However, despite this numerical dominance on the part of women, this has not led to a significant opening for widespread female ordination, nor has it seen patriarchal values thoroughly diminished. Rather, biblical understandings of the superiority of men continue to remain relatively strong, with all but one denomination falling under 40 points out of 100 on Perales and Bouma's (2019) patriarchal gender ideology index. Further, the Pentecostals, because of the practice of headship, scored even higher on the index. Yet, unlike their fellow Christians who are all in decline, the more patriarchal Pentecostals are growing in spite of feminisation. This begs the question: What is it about Hillsong's "princess theology" that is drawing young women to become, as Bobbie puts it, "His girls"?

We continue with our focus on Hillsong in the next chapter on new media. Many religions embrace new technologies, and Pentecostalism is among those leading the way.

Notes

1 All biblical excerpts in this chapter are drawn from the New International Version (NIV).

2 There is little difference in the proportion reporting amongst other religions in Australia (8.3% of men, 8.1% of women) (ABS, 2017). Schnabel (2018) found that the gender gap appeared to relate to predominantly Christian contexts and was similar in secular countries. However, in majority Muslim and Jewish contexts, the gender gap in favour of women was reversed, and the female gender gap was less pronounced in countries that had Eastern religions in the majority (e.g. Shinto, Taoism).

3 Perales and Bouma (2019: 328–329) utilised the HILDA Survey, which is a household panel study that collects annual information from individuals from the same households since 2001. They drew from waves (2005), 8 (2008), 11 (2011), and 15 (2015) of the survey and coded and reverse coded statements on gender division on a 7-point scale, ranging from strongly agree to strongly disagree (e.g. gender responsibility regarding childcare). In conjunction with this, they drew from waves 4 (2004), 7 (2007), 10 (2010), and 14 (2014), which collected data on self-reported levels of religiosity (e.g. attendance at worship, importance of religion) from the same cohort. This batch was brought forward a year to match the gender data on gender ideology that was collected. Regression models were then run controlling for variables known to affect gender attitudes (e.g. gender, ethno-migrant background, level of education). The survey follows 17,000 Australians every year. For more information visit https://melbourneinstitute.unimelb.edu.au/hilda.

4 A possible explanation for Judaism recording the lowest score on the patriarchal gender ideology index is that Jews from across different generations in Australia regard themselves as cultural Jews. In this formulation,

their cultural and ethnic identity is more important than the religious connection. In other words, being Jewish is part of a cultural legacy and their sense of community is connected to, but not defined by, religion (see von Mühlen, 2019).

5 The countries and number of locations are Indonesia (1); Argentina (1); Brazil (1); Canada (1); Denmark (1); France (4); Germany (4); Israel (1); Italy (1); Netherlands (2); Norway (8); Portugal (7); Russia (1); South Africa (9); Barcelona (3); Sweden (4); Switzerland (2); Ukraine (2); United Kingdom (8); and United States (12) (Hillsong Church, 2021a).

References

ABS. 2017. *2071.0– census of population and housing: reflecting Australia – stories from the Census, 2016* Retrieved from https://www.abs.gov.au/ausstats/abs@.nsf/Lookup/by%20Subject/2071.0~2016~Main%20Features~Religion%20Data%20Summary~70

Al–Bukhari. 1997. *The translation of the meanings of Sahih Al–Bukhari* (M. M. Khan, Trans. Vol. 4). Darussalam: Riyadh.

Arpaguş, H. K. 2013. The position of woman in the creation: a Qur'anic perspective. In Aslan, E., Hermansen, M. and Medeni, E. eds. *Muslima theology*. Peter Lang AG, pp. 115–132.

Aune, K. 2006. Marriage in a British evangelical congregation: practising postfeminist partnership? *The Sociological Review, 54*(4): 638–657.

Blaine, L. 2020. Hillsong's strange tides. *The Monthly*. Retrieved from https://www.themonthly.com.au/issue/2020/may/1588255200/lech–blaine/hillsong–s–strange–tides#mtr

Bower, S. A. 2015. *A woman's glory: a study exploring experiences of spiritual power and the gendered lives of women in two pentecostal communities in the USA and New Zealand* (PhD). University of Otago, Denedin, New Zealand.

Brock, B. and Wannenwetsch, B. 2018. *The therapy of the christian body: a theological exposition of Paul's first letter to the Corinthians, Volume 2*. Eugene, OR: Wipf and Stock.

Calderini, S. 2021. *Women as Imams: classical Islamic sources and modern debates on leading prayer*. London: Bloomsbury Publishing.

Carey, H. M. 1996. *Believing in Australia: a cultural history of religions*. St. Leonards, NSW: Allen & Unwin.

Carland, S. (2017). *Fighting Hislam: women, faith and sexism*. Carlton: Melbourne University Publishing.

Evans, M. 2017. Creating the Hillsong sound: how one church changed Australian christian music. In Riches, T. and Wagner, T. eds. *The Hillsong movement examined*. Cham, Switzerland: Springer, pp. 63–81.

Ferziger, A. S. 2018. Female clergy in male space: the sacralization of the Orthodox rabbinate. *The Journal of Religion, 98*(4): 490–516.

Halafoff, A., Garrod, J. and Gobey, L. 2018. Women and ultramodern buddhism in Australia. *Religions, 9*(5), 147. Retrieved from https://www.mdpi.com/2077-1444/9/5/147.

Hassan, R. 1985. Made from Adam's Rib?: The woman's creation question. *Al-Mushir, XXVII*(3): 125–155.

Hillsong Church. 2021a. *About Hillsong*. Retrieved from https://hillsong.com/about/

Hillsong Church. 2021b. *Colour Conference 2021 Online — Be Found In The Kiss* [YouTube]. Retrieved 1 June 2021 from https://www.youtube.com/watch?v=s10kvu0_Cjs

Kvam, K. E., Schearing, L. S. and Ziegler, V. H. eds. 1999. *Eve and Adam: Jewish, Christian, and Muslim readings on Genesis and gender*. Bloomington: Indiana University Press.

Little, C. 2014. Gender, class and sporting opportunity: working-class women and sport in early twentieth-century Australia. *The International Journal of the History of Sport, 31*(13): 1677–1693.

Maddox, M. 2009. Hillsong and the Mega-Churches. In Jupp, J. ed. *The Encyclopedia of Religion in Australia*. Melbourne, VIC: Cambridge University Press, pp. 325–329.

Maddox, M. 2013. "Rise Up Warrior Princess Daughters": Is Evangelical women's submission a Mere Fairy Tale? *Journal of Feminist Studies in Religion, 29*(1): 9–26.

Marx, D. 2012. Women rabbis in Israel. *CCAR Journal: The Reform Jewish Quarterly* (Fall), 182–190.

Miller, E. 2016. Women in Australian Pentecostalism: leadership, submission, and feminism in Hillsong Church. *Journal for the Academic Study of Religion, 29*(1): 52–76.

Perales, F. and Bouma, G. 2019. Religion, religiosity and patriarchal gender beliefs: Understanding the Australian experience. *Journal of Sociology, 55*(2): 323–341.

Planetshakers. 2021. *Russell & Sam: Global Senior Pastors of Planetshakers Church*. Retrieved from https://www.planetshakers.com/russell-sam/

Powell, R., Pepper, M. and Kerr, K. J. 2018. Gender mix in Australian churches. *NCLS Research*. Retrieved from http://www.ncls.org.au/news/gender

Riches, T. 2017. The Sisterhood: Hillsong in a feminine key. In Riches, T. and Wagner, T. eds. *The Hillsong movement examined*. Cham, Switzerland: Springer, pp. 85–105.

Rue, V. 2008. Crossroads: women priests in the Roman Catholic Church. *Feminist Theology, 17*(1): 11–20.

Schnabel, L. 2018. More religious, less dogmatic: toward a general framework for gender differences in religion. *Social Science Research, 75*: 58–72.

Scott, J. W. 2018. *Sex and secularism*. Princeton, NJ: Princeton University Press.

Simon, R. J., Scanlan, A. J. and Nadell, P. S. 1993. Rabbis and ministers: women of the book and the cloth. *Sociology of religion, 54*(1): 115–122.

von Mühlen, B. K. 2019. Women's lives: a study of different generations of Australian Jewish Women. *Australian Journal of Jewish Studies, 32:* 66–88.

Wadud, A. 1999. *Qur'an and woman: rereading the sacred text from a woman's perspective* (2nd ed.). New York: Oxford University Press.

Werner, Y. M. 2009. Religious feminisation, confessionalism and re–masculinisation in Western European Society 1800–1960. In Christensen, H. R. and Sjorup, L. eds. *Pieties and gender.* Leiden: Brill, pp. 143–166.

Winter, E. 2020. Appropriate, enigmatic, aspirational: the construction of femininity in online videos for evangelical women's conferences. In Page, S.J. and Pilcher, K. eds. *Embodying religion, gender and sexuality.* London: Routledge, pp. 145–161.

Woodhead, L. 2012. Gender differences in religious practice and significance. *Travail, genre et sociétés* 27(1): 33–54.

10 Religion and new media

Introduction

It is widely accepted now that religion has become highly mediatised. That is, what people predominantly read, see, and hear about religion is not provided directly through religious institutions, but rather through different forms of media. In particular, Hjarvard (2012) notes that there are three different forms of mediatised religion: *religious media*, *journalism on religion*, and *banal religion*. Of these three, both journalism and banal religion are seen as the dominant forms. Journalism is the most prominent and is largely a secular practice that is geared around factual reporting and public accountability, and for these reasons tends to bring religion into the political sphere. Further, as journalism is largely a secular practice, it does not seek to support any particular religious agenda. Rather, stories are typically judged on their newsworthiness and marketability, whereby outlets tend to prefer exposures, scandals, and moral evaluations that pander to popular sensibilities. As a result, coverage tends to be negative and focuses on stories, such as sex abuse scandals in the Catholic Church and issues pertaining to political Islam and Islamic extremism in the post-9/11 climate, and Australia is no exception in this regard (see Akbarzadeh and Smith, 2005; Weng and Halafoff, 2020). In relation to the Catholic Church, Barney Zwartz (2016), a former Religion Editor for *The Age*, captures this perfectly in an address reflecting on his career:

> The editor at the time, Michael Gawenda, was surprised that I applied for the religion round when it was advertised internally, because it was usually given to a junior reporter to test whether he or she was up to a "proper" round, like health or industrial relations. I argued that the paper typically only covered three religion stories: priests molesting children, the church in decline, and the

DOI: 10.4324/9781003255338-10

> troglodyte church holding back women and gays. Now these were all important stories, but if that was all we covered we were missing some of the most vital and revealing aspects of modern society.

Alongside journalism, the banal form brings religious symbols and motifs into the cultural sphere. This is done through magazines, novels, radio, television, films and computer games, and often the media in question has very little to do with explicit religion (Hjarvard, 2012). For example, shows like *Supernatural* are replete with religious story arcs from a variety of traditions and are not preaching a particular worldview. However, as Hjarvard notes, the motifs that are used tend to reinforce the dominant religion of the society in question, and this is very much the case with *Supernatural* ultimately favouring Christian (Catholic and Protestant) narratives through the use of angels and the Devil. In this way, the show came to reflect the normative religious orientation of the wider audience as part of a cultural circuit or feedback loop, effectively functioning as a backdrop that nominally reminds them of their heritage (Engstrom and Valenzano III, 2014). Similarly, *Harry Potter* – despite having been described by J.K. Rowling as a Christian resurrection narrative and decried by Christian leaders for "glamourizing Witchcraft" (Adler, 2007) and possibly contributing to a boom in the Australian Wicca community (see Chapter 8) – the books have largely been read as a secular tale (see Ostling, 2003). Again, the fantastical elements and Christian undertones are just part of the background cultural motifs that make for a rollicking and relatable story, as the readership are conversant with these well-worn tropes even when dislocated from their origins.

In contrast, religious broadcasting is seen as being the least mediatised, as much of the media is directly controlled by religious institutions and actors, and tends to have less reach. Alongside this, Hjavard regarded the Internet as a challenge to the authority of established churches as it fosters "more individualised and networked forms of religious communication" that ultimately leads to a pluralisation of voices (2012: 30). The first of these assertions is certainly true in relation to old media, such as the "free to air" and cable television. For example, the Anglican Church's airing of the Good Friday Liturgy, on the main ABC TV channel at 4 pm in 2020, garnered a paltry 60,000 viewers nationally (Eckersley, 2020) and is reflective of its decline over the years (see Chapter 4). Similarly, Hillsong's eponymous channel on the cable provider Foxtel failed to reach the top 20 list and was outgunned by Pawpatrol on Nick Jr, which came in 20th with 28,000 viewers (comparetv, 2021). This suggests that few are tuning in.

However, the second assertion is not entirely correct. While new media (e.g. Facebook, Twitter, Instagram, YouTube) certainly is allowing for a pluralisation of voices and contestation, it is not necessarily leading to an undermining of institutional authority or the inability to maintain or establish a brand. Rather, research has begun to show that there is a tendency for authority to be replicated in the cyber-religious realm and that the Web 2.0 has been a vehicle for growth in some communities, particularly the Pentecostal Churches – the only Christian denomination to grow in Australia (see Chapter 5). Further, a critique of mediatisation theory is that it tends to "overlook the agency of religious actors to adapt and resist" the way the media manipulates the meaning of religious symbols and the relations between religious organisations and the wider public (Lövheim and Hjarvard, 2019: 209). As such, this chapter explores how Christian actors in Australia, as a case study, are utilising social media to carve out their own digital space and push back against the impacts of religious journalism and the banal in both the political and cultural realms.

Christians and the Web 2.0

> These moving pictures are going to be the best teachers and the best preachers in the history of the world....Mark my words, there are two things coming; prohibition and moving pictures.
>
> (quoted in Murdock, 1997: 93)

Former journalist and corporate lawyer turned evangelist, Colonel Henry H. Hadley, uttered these words in 1897, just two years after the Lumière brothers' first cinema showing in Paris. He foresaw the incredible power and capacity of the medium to take the gospel to a much wider audience, and what this far-sightedness of Hadley highlights is that Christians have, for a long time, been early adopters of new technology (Lindvall, 2007; Murdock, 1997). Nearly 100 years later, a new media frontier emerged in the form of the Internet, and Christians once again happily partook in this development as a vehicle to spread the good word. Indeed, since its move from the old web to the Web 2.0 in the late 1990s, which saw the shift from relatively static websites (e.g. personal websites) to more dynamic applications that involve peer interaction (e.g. wikis, blogging, social networking), Christians have been writing books extolling its virtues. For example, in the year 2000, Walter Wilson published *The Internet Church*, which explains that Christians now have "the opportunity to reach every man, woman and child on the face of the Earth in the next decade" (as cited in Horsfield and Teusner, 2007: 278). Since then, there has been a slew of similar publications such as *The Blogging Church* (Bailey and Storch, 2007), *The Wired Church 2.0* (Wilson and Moore, 2008), and *The Reason Your Church Must Twitter* (Coppedge, 2009), and as a result Christians have become avid users of new media.

Christian blogging

Blogging obtained popularity in early 2000 as people began to grapple with Web 2.0 before being somewhat displaced by social networks that followed in the mid-2000s (Evolvi, 2018).[1] This is perhaps one of the simplest forms of online social media activity in that, as Horsefield and Teusner note, it effectively resembles a diary and allows for the ventilation of ideas that may have been "rejected, downplayed or ignored by mainstream media platforms" (2007: 289). Powered by free services such as Blogger and WordPress.com, which require limited knowledge of web design, it allows individuals to sidestep the need to have an intermediary and reach an audience that otherwise would not have been possible, and for this reason can be regarded as a democratic and liberatory space (Horsfield and Teusner, 2007). Indeed, the Internet is seen as a positive anarchic force that has facilitated the transfer of power away from big corporations and institutions back to the individual:

> The internet is the largest experiment involving anarchy in history. Hundreds of millions of people are, each minute, creating and consuming an untold amount of digital content in an online world that is not truly bound by terrestrial laws. This new capacity for free expression and free movement of information has generated the rich virtual landscape we know today… the world's largest ungoverned space.
>
> (Schmidt and Cohen, 2013: 9)

This autonomy granted by the Internet in the form of an alternative space free from the constraints of authority attracted many Christians to the platform. In particular, in a study of 200 blogs that were Christian in orientation, either explicitly or implicitly, Cheong, Halvais, and Kwon (2008) found that the two main (at times overlapping) motivations for writing were to document their personal experiences in relation to their understanding of faith (89 blogs; 44.5%) and for didactic purposes (78 blogs; 39%). Typically, in relation to the personal experience, people blogged about the meaning of the crucifixion and resurrection, participation in rituals (e.g. attending church), missionary work, pilgrimages, and so on, and tended to be geared towards justifying their faith. Those who fell into the didactic category tended to draw on authoritative texts such as the Bible, sermons and catechism reference texts that are generally supportive, rather than critical in nature. Indeed, it was found that criticism of the church, dogma, orthodoxies, and engagement with social issues such abortion and gay and lesbian issues were very much in the minority, with only a total of 26 and 19 postings taking up these issues, respectively, out of a total 789 posts that were analysed.

Alongside this, 49 follow-up email interviews also indicated that their blogs were very much personal vehicles, in that they were "cathartic" and helped individuals "to blow off steam," while for others it was very much about seeking to provide a "prophetic voice to give others inspiration" (Cheong et al., 2008: 122). In other words, their activities were very much independently driven in line with Hjarvard's (2012) surmising that the Internet would lead to a greater pluralisation of voices, wherein believers felt free to explore their faith in their own way, free from constraints. However, instead of this democratic participatory culture – that some have likened to a second Protestant Reformation – the first being linked to the printing press and having led to an erosion of authority and undermining of religious institutions (Possamai and Turner, 2014), what Cheong et al. (2008) found is that the offline religious landscape tended to be recreated online. For example, those engaging in blogging would routinely link to the blogs of religious authority figures from different denominations, such as Amy Wellborn (Catholic author),[2] Tim Challies (Baptist Church Elder and author),[3] and Jordan Cooper (Lutheran pastor, scholar),[4] as well as a blog titled the "Evangelical Outpost," which is run by a group called The Gospel Coalition.[5]

Thus, the Christian blogosphere in the US, to use Amy Welborn's own words, "is like looking at a big parish" (Grossman, 2007), and other studies have uncovered the same dynamic where offline authority has simply been transferred online. Teusner, looking at Christian blogging amongst those from the Protestant and Evangelical tradition in Australia, found from an examination of 20 blogs that, while some regarded themselves as "in exile from their denomination" or "churchless" (2012: 184) – and again speaks to a degree of freedom from institutions – the "emerging Church blogosphere emulates the authority structure of the offline religious world" (2012: 188). This was reflected in similar practices to those, outlined by Cheong et al. above, across two study periods. In the first period, 61 out of 103 hyperlinks to other blogs pointed to just six blogs, and all but one of these were run by offline religious professionals that worked either as pastors or in administrative positions within the church. In the second study period, 38 out of 68 hyperlinks to other blogs directed readers to just four sites that were again written by religious professionals (Teusner, 2012: 186–187).

Effectively what these studies show is that Christians, as they have been in the past, are early adopters of technology and have been able to recreate their offline social ecology in the online world of the blogosphere. Given this development, it is perhaps not surprising that this dynamic has since continued with the advent of social media and the practice of microblogging on platforms such as Facebook and Twitter.

Christian social media: from blogging to microblogging

As alluded to above, in the mid-2000s, the Internet underwent another shift with the emergence of new forms of social media. In 2004, Facebook emerged, and was followed quickly by YouTube in 2005 and Twitter in 2006. These social networking platforms, coupled with the emergence of smartphones, allowed people to use these applications on the move and created what has been described as the third wave with regard to religion and the Internet, wherein religion transitioned from being "in" cyberspace to becoming a "digital religion." What this means is that digital culture is the driving force that conditions religion and blurs the boundaries between the online and offline religious communities (Evolvi, 2021).

In relation to this, it has been observed that the Australian Pentecostal "megachurches" have been at the forefront of this shift to digital religion, drawing heavily on the new array of applications to amplify their message, while other churches have had to pivot hard in midst of the Covid-19 pandemic (Rocha et al., 2021). Indeed, just as Evangelicals were eager to blog, as outlined by Teusner, they have also been early uptakers of social media. A quick review of the online activity of three major Australian megachurches, Hillsong, Planetshakers, and C3, shows high levels of digital engagement by each of the churches and their respective founding pastors (see Table 10.1).

Here, it can be seen that all three of the megachurches have a strong social media footprint, with both the institution and their pastors being active across a range of different platforms. Intriguingly, all of the churches and their leaders were late adopters of Facebook as a means of outreach and community-building, despite being the first platform to emerge in the third wave. A possible explanation for this is that religious leaders are conservative when adopting new technologies and that they tend to stick to what they know (Farquhar, 2019). This would explain why YouTube (see Hillsong Church, 2021a) was the first social media platform to be adopted for the hosting of sermons following the conclusion of live-streaming on their website (see Hillsong Church Online, 2021). The video-sharing platform most closely resembles the Televangelism that predominated with the emergence of Bishop Fulton J. Sheen in the 1950s, who was regarded by *Time Magazine*, after winning an Emmy in 1952 for his show *Life Is Worth Living* (1951–1957), as "The First Televangelist" (Sleasman, 2016: 133–34).

This first foray into social media via YouTube proved an easy and effective transition. Since joining in April of 2007, Hillsong has amassed 413,000 subscribers and more than 34 million views (Hillsong Church, 2021f). Similarly, Planetshakers, after joining in September 2007, developed a following of over 1.18 million and an incredible 323 million views (Planetshakers, 2021), while C3, despite

Table 10.1 Social media uptake by Australian megachurches and their pastors

	Facebook	*YouTube*	*Twitter*	*Instagram*	*TikTok*
Founded	2004	2005	2006	2010	2016
Hillsong Church	2009	2007	2007	2011	2020[a]
Brian Houston	2010	2011	2009	2011	2019[a]
Bobbie Houston	2015		2009	2011	
Planetshakers	2008	2007	2009	2012	2019[b]
Sam Evans			2009	2011[a]	
Russel Evans				2012[a]	
C3	2011	2006	2010	2011[a]	
Phil Pringle	2010	2016	2009	2011[a]	
Chris Pringle	2017		2009	2011[a]	

Source: Publicly available profiles.

a Date of the first post, as the details of when the account was opened were not available.

b From a Facebook announcement.

having joined first in December 2006, has a more modest 8,000 subscribers and a touch over 1.8 million views (C3, 2021). Because of this increased outreach, the churches were relatively quick to take up the next social media offering in the form of Twitter. Hillsong was the trendsetter, having joined Twitter just a month after having launched its YouTube channel, and has since garnered close to 900,000 followers (Hillsong Church, 2021b) (see Table 10.2). Both Planetshakers and C3 would wait two and three years, respectively, before joining Twitter. This is perhaps another indication of the conservatism within church circles, insofar that there was a wait-and-see period before adopting a fundamentally new technology. Indeed, all of the pastors, with the exception of Russel Evans from Planetshakers, joined Twitter by 2009. This wait-and-see approach is also reflected in the uptake of Instagram and TikTok, with a gap of between one and two years before adoption of the new platform by both Planetshakers and Hillsong. That said, the uptake by the Pentecostals was still at a more rapid pace than some of their Catholic counterparts. The Vatican, for example, waited until 2012 to establish a Twitter account for Pope Francis (Evolvi, 2021).

What is also apparent is that not only is Hillsong a leader in relation to social media uptake, it also has the biggest social media footprint and the most extensive reach in terms of followers. This is due to, as Wagner has noted, the fact that social media has become a core part of the church's branding strategy:

> an important part of Hillsong's brand ecosystem is its online infrastructure of both official and unofficial websites and *social media.* These platforms are connected by mutually reinforcing sonic, textual, or visual references.
>
> (Wagner, 2017: 259; emphasis added)

Indeed, all of their sites (websites included) operate in accordance with the practice of transmedia storytelling. That is, the story is told through the navigation of multiple platforms to tell a much deeper story, that allows for both the connecting of the community to the transcendental and the bridging of both the offline and online worlds (Burroughs, 2013). For example, Hillsong's primary Twitter account @Hillsong provides followers with snippets of scripture, such as "Jesus answered, 'I am the way and the truth and the life. No one comes to the Father except through me.' John 14:6 (NIV)" (Hillsong Church, 2021c) and directs followers to both sonic and visual material, such as part of

Table 10.2 Followers by platform for each church and their pastors, 2021

Church	*Facebook followers*	*YouTube followers*	*Twitter followers*	*Instagram followers*	*TikTok followers*	*Total*
Hillsong Church	1,983,671	413,000	886,928	2,868,957	102,500	**6,255,056**
Brian Houston	352,000	38,500	601,960	724,716	759	**1,717,935**
Bobbie Houston	52,000		175,662	301,671		**529,333**
Planetshakers	1,644,852	1,180,000	178,992	597,590	5240	**3,606,674**
Sam Evans			9,321	36,651		**45,972**
Russel Evans				52,431		**52,431**
C3[a]	5,831	8,600	2,153	11,145		**27,729**
Phil Pringle	22,000	583	38,600	29,735		**90,918**
Chris Pringle	504		7,760	13,760		**22,024**

Notes: Figures have been rounded up where only an approximation is given. In addition, there is likely overlap amongst those that follow the respective churches across the different platforms. Therefore, the total figures are simply an indication of reach, and not an accurate account of the number of adherents (figures compiled 26 April 2021).

[a] Used the founding church in Sydney account or the global account depending on which was established first.

a live-streamed concert by the church's band Hillsong UNITED at Madison Square Gardens that can be viewed at their YouTube channel, and an in-home worship experience on Instagram (see Hillsong Church, 2020a, 2021e).

All of this allows followers to feel connected to the church despite not being there physically. The music, which is predominantly recorded live – an important aspect of the genre – lets parishioners vicariously engage in "co-performance by the congregation," thereby enabling a sense of emotional uplift that takes individuals outside of themselves (Thornton, 2020: 112–113). Similarly, the short daily devotional with different pastors creates a sense of intimacy and provides an opportunity for individuals, despite their being apart, to momentarily engage in collective affirmations (see Burroughs, 2013) of the religious message through posting comments like "Amen" and "SO GOOD!" with the praying hands emoji (see Hillsong Church, 2020b).

Both C3 and Planetshakers employ similar social media strategies, with the latter itself starting in 1997 as a Pentecostal youth-revival style concert before becoming a church in 2004 (see Shanahan, 2020). An attendant outgrowth of this move to "digital religion" is that the pastors themselves become a key part of the branding and marketing strategy, and it is here that a similar dynamic in relation to religious authority versus the laity is created.

Branding has indeed become normalised among religious groups. According to Einstein (2008), religions can no longer rely on "brand loyalty." Religions must compete to attract new members and keep existing ones. According to Einstein's (2008) research, in an increasingly competitive market, religious groups have taken on names, logos, and slogans to make their voices heard. As "religion is increasingly moving from pew to pixel" (Einstein 2008: 8), less and less people might attend a religious service, but that does not mean that they are not likely to read books on religion, watch religious movies, check religious sites on the Internet, follow religious social media accounts, and so on.

Reifying authority via social media

As touched on above, all of the pastors are also active on at least one or more social media platform, and have become what are now regarded "pastor-preneurs," brand ambassadors, and effectively religious celebrities, as they minister to "megachurches" with more than 2,000 at each service, and have over the years continued to grow in numbers and influence (Cheong, 2016; Twitchell, 2007: 229). To give a sense of the quantum increase in reach afforded by social media, Brian Houston, from January 2017 to the end of March 2021, has increased his following on Twitter by almost 100,000. He began on 507,418 followers and rose to 601,853 (see Figure 10.1). This is an increase of over 20,000 followers a year, ten times the level to be regarded as a "megachurch." Subsequently, a pattern of behaviour has emerged in their online activities that serves to amplify their position as religious authorities and as distinct from the laity. Authority in that space is devolved, dispersed, and dissipated (Turner 2007), but it still exists. As the educated and elite carriers of religion are now challenged by a global spiritual marketplace, especially on the Internet and in social media, these forms of religious authority are being redefined through the digital world.

Sircar and Rowley (2016), in an examination of Hillsong's social media presence across Facebook, Twitter, Instagram, and YouTube, found that their activity can be described as sales, promotion, events, and giving. Facebook was largely used to support media-based worship through promoting events, particularly their conferences and associated ticket sales. Twitter was used by lead Pastor Brian Houston to put out Christian messages and promote his books, while his wife and fellow Pastor Bobbie Houston would update the sisterhood community (see Hillsong Church, 2021d). Similarly, Instagram was used for promotion

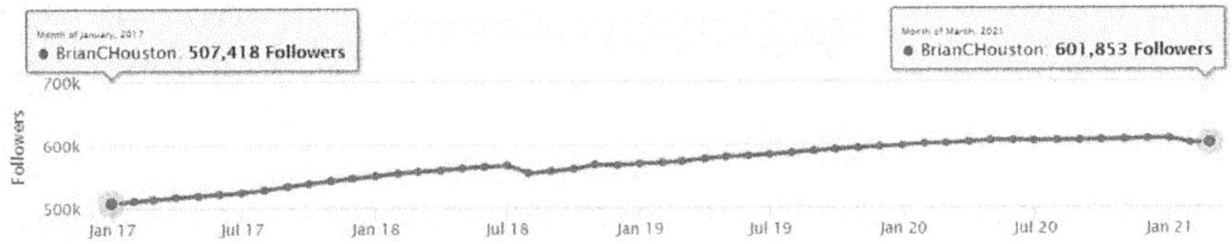

Figure 10.1 Pastor Brian Houston's Twitter following, January 2017–March 2021.
Source: Adapted from Social Blade (2021).

and sales, while YouTube was used to broadcast sermons, music videos, and past events such as conferences. Further, they found that across all the platforms there was no two-way communication from the leadership of the church with its members and that this appeared to be a distinct social media strategy across the institutions in many locations. That is, leaders, such as Brian and Bobby, will post material but not respond to the comments made by members.

On this point, Cheong makes a similar reflection in relation to the social media practice of pastor-preneurs more broadly. Not only are they not responding to the parishioners, but they also routinely engage in cross-promotion with other clergy. This is done as a means of maintaining their "power differential between the priest and laity" and further establishes their authority "by publicly demonstrating their relationship with, endorsement of, and inspired affiliation to other clergy celebrities" (2016: 93), and this is readily observable amongst pastors of megachurches in Australia. Indeed, Sam Evans from Planetshakers, Phil Pringle from C3, and Brian Houston all utilise this strategy.

For example, Planetshakers founding Pastor Sam Evans posted a picture of herself on Instagram, reading the book *Stay*, along with the caption: "Look what I'm doing @sophia_barret. And Loving it!" (see Evans, 2016). The way this is phrased, and given that Evans has tagged the author Sophia Barrett along with the playful "Winking face with Tongue" emoji, she is engaging in direct conversation with Sophia, rather than speaking to her followers on Instagram. Further, Sophia Barrett is herself a founding pastor of the Evangelical Audacious Church based in Manchester, and *Stay* is her first book (see Barrett, 2021). In this way, the post functions as an exclusive conversation between peers, wherein Sam is endorsing the work of a colleague.

Likewise, Pastor Phil Pringle from C3 in a tweet gave a shout out to another Evangelical pastor in Carey Nieuwhof (see Nieuwhof, 2021) who founded the Connexus Church in Ontario, Canada, by endorsing his blog post "5 Reasons Why Engagement is the New Church Attendance" with the tagline "Jesus did't say 'Attend me'.' He said 'Follow me'" which appears to be a play on the act of following on social media platforms (see Pringle, 2021). Similarly, founding Pastor Brian Houston of Hillsong was observed responding to a character endorsement from his friend Rick Godwin, who is the founding pastor of Summit Christian Centre in San Antonio, Texas (see Christian Summit Center, 2021). Godwin tweeted: "Brian Houston has been a best friend over 30yrs. He's one of the most generous, compassionate, + ethical leaders in ministry. God has blessed churches around the world through his ministry. Honored to be his friend. Lyu mate!" Houston then retweeted Godwin with the response: "Thank you Ricardo…it's so good to have friends like you who are so vocally supportive. You're not a fair weather friend" (see Houston, 2021).

Thus, through this practice of only engaging in online interactions with fellow clergy and simply basking in the adoration of their followers, the pastor-preneurs are reformulating their offline status online by creating elite circles of communication that show that they are apart from the laity. As those that they are linking to are very much pastor-preneurs in their own right, with their own substantial presence on social media. For example, both Rick Godwin and Carey Nieuhoff have substantial flocks of their own on Twitter, with over 44,000 and 38,000 followers, respectively, at the time of writing. In short, the relationships are mutually constitutive and reinforcing and serve to amplify their influence.

Conclusion

Given the developments related above, it would seem that the prediction by Hjarvard (2012), amongst others, that churches and their brands would be undermined by the pluralising forces of the untameable Internet was misplaced in a similar vein to those who declared inexorable ascent of secularism. Indeed, the so-called anarchic Internet has not led to a second Protestant Reformation, wherein there is an ever-increasing cacophony of voices that has seen the dissolution of the church. Rather, in each iteration of the web, Christian seekers have routinely gravitated back towards religious professionals for guidance. In the age of the blogosphere, this led to a crystallisation of a handful of blogs, both in the US and the Australian contexts, that became what Cheong et al. (2008) have referred to as the A-list who all worked within churches in one capacity or another, thereby bridging offline and online worlds. Similarly, with the shift to Web 2.0 and the attendant move from cyber-religion – religion on the Internet – to "digital religion," the boundaries between the offline and online became fundamentally blurred and new means of asserting authority developed. However, in contrast to the seemingly organic development in the blogosphere where readers are perhaps inadvertently reconstructing the power-dynamics from the offline world, pastor-preneurs, through their willingness to adapt to the social media reality, have become active agents of building and developing branded online churches and new techniques of establishing, maintaining and amplifying their authority. Through aggressively marketing themselves both individually and through cross-promotion of clergy as an elite class, pastor-preneurs have managed again to set themselves apart from the laity as the stewards of salvation. Thus, it seems, in the age that Zygmunt Bauman (2000) has dubbed as "liquid modernity", on account of the "software universe" that has unsettled both time and space, the holy water always finds its level.

Notes

1. Reflective of this decline in the practice of blogging is the decision of Technorati, the largest search engine and ranker of blogs, to decommission its database in 2014 in favour of pursuing an advertising platform (Finn, 2014).
2. See Amy Welborn's blog (2021).
3. See Tim Challies blog (2021).
4. See Jordon Cooper (2021).
5. The Gospel Coalition has a wide variety of authors that are religious scholars, pastors, or work for a religious institution (see Evangelical Outpost, 2021).

References

Adler, S. 2007. Harry Potter author J. K. Rowling opens up about books' Christian imagery. *MTV News*. Retrieved from http://www.mtv.com/news/1572107/harry-potter-author-jk-rowling-opens-up-about-books-christian-imagery/

Akbarzadeh, S. and Smith, B. 2005. *The representation of Islam and Muslims in the media (the age and herald sun newspapers)*. Melbourne: School of Political and Social Inquiry, Monash University.

Bailey, B. and Storch, T. 2007. *The Blogging Church*. San Francisco: Jossey-Bass.

Barrett, S. 2021. *About me*. Retrieved from https://sophiabarrett.co.uk/about-me/

Bauman, Z. 2000. *Liquid modernity*. Cambridge: Polity Press.

Burroughs, B. 2013. 10.'And I'm a (Social Media) Mormon: digital ritual, techno-faith, and religious transmedia. *Qwerty-Open and Interdisciplinary Journal of Technology, Culture and Education, 8*(2): 71–81.

C3. 2021. *C3 SYD: About*. Retrieved from https://www.youtube.com/c/C3SYD/about

Challies, T. 2021. *Challies*. Retrieved from https://www.challies.com/

Cheong, P. H. 2016. Religious authority and social media branding in a culture of religious celebrification. In Hoover, S. M. ed. *The media and religious authority*. University Park, PA: Penn State University Press, pp. 81–104.

Cheong, P. H., Halavais, A. and Kwon, K. 2008. The chronicles of me: Understanding blogging as a religious practice. *Journal of Media and Religion*, 7(3): 107–131.

Christian Summit Center. 2021. *About*. Retrieved from https://summitsa.com/about/

comparetv. 2021. *Top 20 programs: all subscription channels*. Retrieved from https://www.comparetv.com.au/australia-tv-ratings/top-20-pay-tv-programs/

Cooper, J. 2021. *Just and sinner*. Retrieved from https://www.patheos.com/blogs/justandsinner/author/jcooper/

Coppedge, A. D. 2009. *The reason your church must Twitter*. Retrieved from https://www.southernohiosynod.org/aws/sos/asset_manager/get_file/20639

Eckersley, I. 2020. Cathedral Good Friday service broadcast on ABC TV Australia-wide. *Anglican Focus*. Retrieved from https://anglicanfocus.org.au/2020/04/09/cathedral-good-friday-service-broadcast-on-abc-tv-australia-wide/

Einstein, M. 2008. *Brands of faith: marketing religion in a commercial age*. New York: Routledge.

Engstrom, E. and Valenzano III, J. M. 2014. *Television, religion, and supernatural: hunting monsters, finding Gods*. Lanham, Maryland: Lexington Books.

Evangelical Outpost. 2021. Retrieved from https://www.thegospelcoalition.org/blogs/

Evans, S. [s_a_m_e_v_a_n_s]. 2016, 29 September. *Look what I'm doing @ sophia_barrett*. Retrieved 22 April 2021 from https://www.instagram.com/p/BK6Rz_TDJJR/

Evolvi, G. 2018. *Blogging my religion: secular, Muslim, and Catholic media spaces in Europe*. London: Routledge.

Evolvi, G. 2021. Religion, new media, and digital culture. *Oxford Research Encyclopedia of Religion*. Retrieved from https://oxfordre.com/religion/view/10.1093/acrefore/9780199340378.001.0001/acrefore-9780199340378-e-917

Farquhar, L. 2019. From Facebook to Instagram: the role of social media in religious communities. In Grant, A.E., Daniel, A., Stout, Chen C.H. and Sturgill, A. F. C. eds. *Religion online: how digital technology is changing the way we worship and pray* (Vol. 1). Santa Barbara, California: ABC-CLIO, pp. 27–46.

Finn, G. 2014. RIP Technorati blog search & rankings: the once popular blog tools have been sunset. *Search Engine Land*. Retrieved from https://

searchengineland.com/rip-technorati-blog-search-rankings-popular-blog-tools-sunset-195186

Grossman, C. L. 2007. Bloggers keep the faith, contentiously. *USA Today*. Retrieved from https://usatoday30.usatoday.com/news/religion/2007-11-26-faith-bloggers_N.htm

Hillsong Church [@HIllsong]. 2020a, 12 May. *Join us everyday on our Instagram account for a new...[Tweet]*. Retrieved 27 April 2021 from https://twitter.com/Hillsong/status/1260015987534868481

Hillsong Church [Hillsong]. 2020b, 12 May. *Join us everyday right here on Instagram for a new...[Instagram Post]*. Retrieved 27 April 2021 from https://www.instagram.com/tv/CAEXPNCHwkp/?hl=en

Hillsong Church. 2021a. *About*. Retrieved from https://www.youtube.com/c/hillsong/about

Hillsong Church. 2021b. *@Hillsong*. Retrieved from https://twitter.com/Hillsong

Hillsong Church [@Hillsong]. 2021c, 22 March. *"Jesus answered, "I am the way and the truth and...[Tweet]*. Retrieved 27 April 2021 from https://twitter.com/Hillsong/status/1373763078400057344

Hillsong Church. 2021d. *The Sisterhood Australia*. Retrieved from https://hillsong.com/australia/sisterhood/

Hillsong Church [@Hillsong]. 2021e, 2 March. *Your grace abounds in deepest waters...[Tweet]*. Retrieved 26 April 2021 from https://twitter.com/hillsongunited/status/1366551332052680704

Hillsong Church. 2021f. *YouTube channel: about*. Retrieved from https://www.youtube.com/c/hillsong/about

Hillsong Church Online. 2021. *Join a service*. Retrieved from https://hillsong.com/online/

Hjarvard, S. 2012. Three forms of mediatized religion: changing the public face of religion. In Hjarvard, S. and Lövheim, M. eds. *Mediatization and religion: nordic perspectives*. Göteborg: Nordicom, pp. 21–44.

Horsfield, P. and Teusner, P. 2007. A mediated religion: historical perspectives on Christianity and the internet. *Studies in World Christianity, 13*(3): 278–295.

Houston, B. [@BrianCHouston]. 2021, 11 February. *Thank you Ricardo. In a very difficult season it's so good...[Tweet]*. Retrieved 23 March 2021 from https://twitter.com/BrianCHouston/status/1359825456766226433

Lindvall, T. 2007. *Sanctuary cinema: origins of the christian film industry*. New York: NYU Press.

Lövheim, M. and Hjarvard, S. 2019. The mediatized conditions of contemporary religion: Critical status and future directions. *Journal of Religion, Media and Digital Culture, 8*(2): 206–225.

Murdock, G. 1997. The re-enactment of the world: religion and the transformations of modernity. In Hoover, S. M. and Lundby, K. eds. *Rethinking media, religion, and culture.* Thousand Oaks, CA: Sage Publications, pp. 85–101.

Nieuwhof, C. 2021. *About me.* Retrieved from https://careynieuwhof.com/about-me/

Ostling, M. 2003. Harry Potter and the disenchantment of the world. *Journal of Contemporary Religion, 18*(1): 3–23.

Planethsakers. 2021. *planetshakerstv: about.* Retrieved from https://www.youtube.com/user/planetshakerstv/about

Possamai, A. and Turner, B. 2014. Authority and liquid religion in cyber-space: the new territories of religious communication. *International Social Science Journal, 63*(209–210): 197–206.

Pringle, P. [@philpringle]. 2021, 25 January. *Jesus didn't say 'Attend me.' He said 'Follow me.'...[Tweet]* Retrieved 29 April 2021 from https://twitter.com/philpringle/status/1353441404567969793

Rocha, C., Vokes, R. and Openshaw, K. 2021, 6 April. Can the Holy Spirit be livestreamed? *Sapiens.* Retrieved from https://www.sapiens.org/culture/worshipping-online-covid-19/

Schmidt, E. and Cohen, J. 2013. *The new digital age: reshaping the future of people, nations and business* (First edition). New York: Alfred A. Knopf.

Shanahan, M. 2020. Marketing and branding practices in australian pentecostal suburban megachurches for supporting international growth. In Rocha, C., Hutchinson, M. P. and Openshaw, K. eds. *Australian pentecostal and charismatic movements.* Leiden: Brill, pp. 126–147.

Sircar, A. and Rowley, J. 2016. *Social media and megachurches.* Paper presented at the Social Media: The Good, the Bad, and the Ugly: 15th IFIP WG 6.11 Conference on e-Business, e-Services, and e-Society, Swansea, UK, Springer.

Sleasman, B. C. 2016. The Medium is the ministry: televangelism and the electronic age church. In Ward Sr, M. ed. *The Electronic church in the digital age: cultural impacts of evangelical mass media* (Vol. 1). Santa Barbara, California: Praeger, pp. 127–149.

Social Blade. 2021. *Brian Houston [@BrianCHouston].* Retrieved from https://socialblade.com/twitter/user/brianchouston/monthly

Teusner, P. E. 2012. Formation of a religious Technorati: negotiations of authority among Australian emerging church blogs. In Campbell, H. A. ed. *Digital religion: understanding religious practice in new media worlds.* London: Routledge, pp. 182–189.

Thornton, D. 2020. A match made in heaven: why popular music is central to the growth in Pentecostal Charismatic Christianities. In Rocha, C., Hutchinson, M. P. and Openshaw, K. eds. *Australian Pentecostal and charismatic movements.* Leiden: Brill, pp. 109–125.

Turner, B. 2007. Religious authority and the new media. *Theory, Culture and Society, 24*(2): 117–34.

Twitchell, J. B. 2007. *Shopping for God: how Christianity went from in your heart to in your face.* New York: Simon & Schuster.

Wagner, T. 2017. The "Powerful" Hillsong Brand. In Wagner, T. R. T. ed. *The Hillsong movement examined.* Cham: Palgrave Macmillan, pp. 253–269.

Welborn, A. 2021. *Charlotte was both.* Retrieved from https://amywelborn.wordpress.com/

Weng, E. and Halafoff, A. 2020. Media representations of religion, spirituality and non-religion in Australia. *Religions, 11*(7): 332.

Wilson, L. and Moore, J. 2008. *The Wired Church 2.0.* Nashville: Abingdon Press.

Zwartz, B. 2016. Religion in the media: how has it changed, where is it going, why does it matter? *ABC Religion & Ethics.* Retrieved from https://www.abc.net.au/religion/religion-in-the-media-how-has-it-changed-where-is-it-going-why-d/10096622

11 Politics and religion

The use and abuse of faith

Introduction

Prime Minister Scott Morrison uttered these words, alongside his wife and two daughters, as he claimed victory over Labor in the federal election held on Saturday, 18 May 2019 (The Guardian, 2019). These openly religious sentiments by the Prime Minister come as no surprise as he, in the lead up to the election, allowed the media into his Pentecostal Church for Easter service. His church is the evangelical Horizon Church that offers concert-like ceremonies, where people sing, dance, and engage in ecstatic practices such as speaking in tongues, and, indeed, the Prime Minister was photographed enthusiastically singing along and dancing with the 1,000 strong congregation (Mazzoni, 2019). However, what may surprise is that this outward religiosity of the Prime Minister is the continuation of an ongoing trend that stems from the Howard era. Although Howard was not himself overtly religious, over the course of his tenure as prime minister, he deftly manoeuvred a right-wing cross-denominational religious clique within the Liberal Party, known as the Lyons Forum, in an attempt to return Australia to an imagined 1950s born of childhood nostalgia (Maddox, 2005).

So effective was the Lyons Forum that it helped Howard to capture the Catholic vote that was historically aligned with the Labor Party, and propelled the Liberal-National Coalition to successive electoral victories. This shift effectively saw the Coalition become the de facto Christian party. As a result, Labor, under Kevin Rudd, sought to negate this advantage by also turning to religion, and due to this now bipartisan approach has seen faith regularly take centre stage in political debate. Further, this turn to religion by both sides of politics has seen the somewhat paradoxical development of religious representation remaining strong within the parliament, whilst profession of faith

DOI: 10.4324/9781003255338-11

has declined across Australia (see Chapter 5). For example, between 1993 and 2010, the proportion of Liberal Party candidates identifying as Catholic more than doubled, moving from around 19% to over 40%. During the same period, the proportion of Labor candidates identifying as Catholic remained above 30% despite a decline from a peak of around 40% in 2001 (Donovan, 2014), and it was speculated, as of 2017, that more than 40% of the Coalition and about 30% of the Labor Party identified as Christian (James, 2017). Yet, between the 2011 and the 2016 census, those professing to be Christians dropped by 9% to constitute only a slight majority of Australians (52%), whilst those professing no religion increased by a staggering 48% to constitute almost one-third (30%) of the population (ABS, 2018).

This chapter charts this development and explores how religion has been instrumentalised across a range of key issues in same-sex marriage, abortion, euthanasia, and freedom of religion. Alongside this, we also unpack the rise in rhetoric around Australia's Judeo-Christian heritage and how this, since the advent of 9/11 in 2001, has seen the Muslim diaspora community ensnared in an imagined "clash of civilisations" and sacrificed for political point scoring in the name of national security. This, as we will come back to in Chapter 12, seems to contrast with an Australian population that is becoming less Christian and more multicultural.

Howard and the Lyons Forum

Established in 1992, the Lyons Forum was a crypto-Christian faction within the Liberal Party formed by Senators John Herron and John Tierney, along with Alan Cadman, John Bradford, Chris Miles, Kevin Andrews and John Forrest from the Lower House. The agenda of the group was likened to that of America's religious right and was couched in the language of "family values" that set forth a series of policy prescriptions that sought to entrench the heterosexual nuclear family and stop abortion. However, unlike their American counterparts, the Lyons Forum often eschewed overtly religious language and regularly demurred when questioned about its Christian underpinnings. The aim of this strategy was to create ambiguity about the nature of the Lyons Forum, so as not to alienate the wider secular public (Maddox, 2001, 2005). In other words, the aim of the group was to introduce Christian values by stealth in what has been described as a "culture war" (see Davis, 2014).

Howard was a regular attendee of the Forum in its early days, and it is credited with both turning around his electoral fortunes in 1996 and having a significant hand in formulating much of his policy agenda, which Maddox (2005: 25–26) powerfully describes:

> 'Family values' and 'individual responsibility' turn out to be pious appeals to the old God behind which the Market God disguises its chaotic theophanies. At its most extreme, this God undermines democratic traditions while justifying hatreds: vilification of homosexuals, punishing the unemployed, cruel border protection and illegal war.

Effectively, Howard was happy to exploit the God of the Lyons Forum as a means of prosecuting his neoliberal social-right agenda. One of his first acts of solidarity with the Forum was to sign their petition against Dr Hewson – the then leader of the Coalition – for his support of the 1994 Gay and Lesbian Mardi Gras to be aired on the ABC during prime time. The issue for Howard was not solely the prospect of gays on television in the family viewing timeslot. Rather, it was about the Liberal Party having moved towards recognising minority rights, whereas Howard was keen to reinstate a socially conservative agenda wherein the Liberal Party would "govern for everyone," and not be captured by what he saw as special interest groups (Maddox, 2005). To this end, the Lyons Forum was the perfect vehicle as they sought to emphasise the popular appeal of social conservatism and align it with the mainstream (Maddox, 2001), thereby creating an 'us and them' dichotomy, and this would become his modus operandi.

In the 1996 election victory, the Liberal Party had reversed a long-standing trend between the two major parties. They turned a 9% deficit amongst Catholic voters into an 11% lead, and this lead was maintained in subsequent elections (Warhurst, 2007). Coalition with this shift in the Catholic vote, the composition of the Coalition saw a change in its religious complexion, with a rise in the number of Catholic MPs. Indeed, by 2002, there was a "Catholicisation" of the conservative parties, with 13 of Howard's 43 frontbenchers professing a connection to the church (The Sydney Morning Herald, 2002).

With this change in the composition of the Coalition, the Lyons Forum was able to incrementally shift the culture and the climate of public debate and pursue a range of issues that were consonant with their Christian values. For example, following the initial victory in

1996, Kevin Andrews introduced the Euthanasia Laws Bill as a private member, after an open invitation from Howard for members to follow their conscience on the matter. The Bill quickly came to be known as the Andrews Bill, which was passed in 1997 and overturned the Northern Territory's *Rights of the Terminally Ill Act 1995*, and would become the template for a raft of other issues. That is, Howard would allow for others to step forward and pursue carefully selected wedge issues giving him a degree of distance, despite the fact that they were effectively government policies.

Howard's evangelical turn

By the turn of the millennium, the Lyons Forum had begun to go quiet, and this was largely because they felt they had won the culture war. As Liberal Senator Alan Ferguson put it:

> The Forum has served its purpose. It was formed in opposition to make sure that all policy was assessed for its impact on families. But once we're in government, the party doesn't have as much input into policy, the executive does. But we keep the structure alive, in case we ever need to revive it.
>
> (as cited in Maddox, 2005: 102)

As a result of this quietism, Howard began to turn to the religiosity of high-profile government figures and also began a shift towards courting the evangelical community. Key figures in this regards were the then Treasurer Peter Costello (a Baptist) and the then health minister Tony Abbott, who considered becoming a Catholic priest in his youth but did not complete his studies at the seminary and would later come to be known as the "Mad Monk." The former began making overtures to the megachurch Hillsong by giving an address in July of 2004 at the SuperDome conference where he exclaimed to the some 21,600 registered delegates that the nation needs more religion: "We need a return to faith and the values which have made our country strong" (Brissenden, 2004). In the lead up to this, Abbott gave an address in March to the Adelaide University Democratic Club, where he put abortion back on the federal agenda, an issue that had been quarantined by both parties since 1979. Abbott argued that teenage promiscuity was leading to a high abortion rate, despite the fact that the levels had remained stable since the late 1970s (Gleeson, 2011; Maddox, 2005).

Enter Rudd and Labor's (re)turn to religion

Following the 2004 election defeat, the then shadow minister for foreign affairs Kevin Rudd heard this clarion call and formed a discussion group on religion with a view to educating Labor colleagues about the perils of allowing the Coalition to exploit the religious vote (Warhurst, 2007). Following this, he emphasised the point in a wide-ranging interview, in which he also comes out as a Christian, on *Compass* in 2005 when asked if he is on a crusade:

> No I'm not on a crusade. I'm doing what I think at this time in Australia's political history is right. And that is to engage this debate about faith, values and politics and not to vacate the ground for the other mob. For those on the political right who believe that faith is their natural preserve. I don't intend to stand around or let that happen. I've got a responsibility for the tradition of Christian politics that I come from.
>
> (Compass, 2005)

Both Rudd and Julia Gillard (who was also featured and would later identify as an atheist) recognised where they felt the election was lost and where they needed to go. Gillard noted that it was impossible to overlook the importance of the abortion debate reignited by Tony Abbott. Whilst Rudd flagged both the rise of Family First, which has its roots in the Assemblies of God movement and helped the Coalition win at least four marginal seats through a preference deal, and the need to move away from mainstream churches towards the Pentecostals (Compass, 2005). This indicates that Rudd was of the view that he needed to mirror the tactics of Howard.

Emblematic of this shift was the fact that in the 2007 election campaign, in what was an Australian first, both Howard and Rudd addressed 100,000 Christians across the country in a live-streamed webcast. Organised by the Australia Christian Lobby (ACL), they spoke to members from over 700 churches, whilst around 200 Christian leaders were on hand at the National Press Club to pose questions. Front and centre at the event were members of Hillsong who led the congregation in prayer before the debate got underway. During the course of the webcast, both Howard and Rudd affirmed that marriage should only be between a man and a woman and both appealed to family values. Howard announced a $189 million package to provide a free Internet filter to families to fight against pornography, and to counter this, Rudd stated that a Labor government would prepare a family impact statement for every submission to cabinet (Donald and Iggulden, 2007; The Sydney Morning Herald, 2007).

Gillard, Rudd 2.0, and Abbott

Interestingly, when Gillard deposed Rudd in late June 2010, she was very quick to distance herself from the outward religiosity of her predecessor. In an interview with Jon Faine, she stated: "I am not going to pretend a faith I don't feel." However, whilst openly declaring her atheism she was also keen to not alienate the Christian bloc that Howard and Rudd had so carefully sought to construct. To this end, like those before her, she was also mindful of outlining her Christian deposit, emphasising that she "grew up in the Christian Church," that she "won prizes for catechism, for being able to remember Bible verses," and that "she is steeped in that [Christian] tradition" (ABC News, 2010). In other words, Gillard was willing to maintain Labor's perceived electoral gains amongst Christian voters.

Shortly before the 2013 federal election, Rudd was reinstated after a campaign of internal destabilisation and a string of poor polls under Gillard that threatened electoral annihilation for Labor. This created a tantalising dynamic, as it meant that the election would be contested by two of nation's arguably most religious political leaders, and early on in the campaign the persistent issue of same-sex marriage arose as a potential wedge issue. Rudd had a change of heart on the matter, and at the end of the first leaders' debate, held on the 11th of August, he promised to move a bill to legalise gay marriage in the first 100 days if elected. The rationale for change was that the "state is secular," and that it was simply a "mark of decency" to afford same-sex couples equality under the law (Young and Farr, 2013).

Whilst Abbott was successful in transforming his public image from one of a religious zealot to an individual that now sees "shades of grey" (Taylor, 2013), his religiosity was by no means a thing of the past. Rather, as Katharine Murphy (2013) perceptively notes, Abbott kept his faith and quietly put the message out to the Christian faithful, as he realised, like Rudd before him, that elections are won from the secular centre.

Abbott, after winning the 2013 election, assembled one of the most religious frontbenches in the history of the Australian parliament, with almost half of his cabinet practising Catholics. This included both liberal and conservative religious members. Those counted in the more liberal category included Malcolm Turnbull (whom Abbott supplanted as leader in 2009), Christopher Pyne, George Brandis, and Joe Hockey, whilst the latter consisted of Kevin Andrews, Barnaby Joyce, Andrew Robb, and Mathias Cormann. In addition to the Catholic contingent, the ministry also included non-Catholics in Eric Abetz, who is from the Christian Reformed Churches of Australia, and Scott Morrison who is aligned with the Pentecostal Australian Christian Churches group formerly known as Assemblies of God,[1] of which Horizon Church is a member (Seccombe, 2015).

The return of Turnbull and the persistent "Freedom of Religion" problem

When Turnbull was reinstated as leader and prime minister after a leadership spill on 14 September 2015, he was held hostage by the Christian right in the party that was instrumental in having him replaced by Abbott back in 2009, and the matter would dog him for his stint as prime minister. In order to get the numbers to regain the leadership, Turnbull made a deal with conservatives in the party that he would hold a plebiscite on same-sex marriage following the next election.

The logic behind the drive to hold a plebiscite on gay marriage, led by Senator George Brandis, was to delay a vote on the matter in the parliament, as the Electoral Commission explained it would need several months to prepare a vote, and as many as 29 weeks if the vote was held in conjunction with an election. An additional benefit of holding a plebiscite is the fact that they are non-binding and simply test whether the public opposes or supports a proposal. The hope was that the matter could then be overtaken by other issues, as polling since 2007 had shown the public was consistently in favour of same-sex marriage. The matter also threatened the unity of the Liberal Party, as the conservative minority that helped to reinstall Turnbull were directly at odds with his pro-marriage equality stance. Reflective of this was Turnbull's decision to attend the 2016 Gay and Lesbian Mardi Gras, the first sitting prime minister to do so (Hutchens and Hasham, 2016; Smyth, 2017).

However, the strategy again failed to make a significant impact. Although Turnbull's authenticity was eroded on account of his being held hostage by conservatives within the party, his personal positions on issues such as same-sex marriage and climate change allowed him to capture voters who were regarded as "soft-Labor" and helped to afford him a narrow single-seat majority in the House of Representatives (Strangio and Walter, 2018).

Following the Coalition victory, Turnbull sought to keep his election promise and legislate for a compulsory plebiscite on same-sex marriage, but this was twice rejected in the Senate by an alliance of Labor, the Greens, and the Xenophon Team. As a result, the government turned to its Plan B, which was to hold a non-compulsory postal ballot to be conducted by the Australian Bureau of Statistics. This development, in turn, saw Abbott immediately move into campaign mode and seek to move the debate to religious freedom:

> And I say to you if you don't like same-sex marriage, vote no. If you're worried about religious freedom and freedom of speech, vote no, and if you don't like political correctness, vote no because voting no will help to stop political correctness in its tracks.
>
> (Karp, 2017e)

Fellow conservative Scott Morrison was more circumspect, simply putting the message out to the community in an interview on ABC's *7:30* that it is "OK to say no" and that was how he was going to vote (News.com.au, 2017). Others were less so, with the debate becoming toxic. For example, The Coalition for Marriage put out a series of ads authorised by Marriage Alliance spokeswoman Sophie York that suggested same-sex marriage could lead children to be forced to question their sexual orientation and gender identity. In particular, mothers in the 30-second ads linked marriage equality to the Safe Schools anti-bullying programme that teaches acceptance of sexual diversity, claiming that schools will tell boys they can wear a dress and will make them role-play being in a same-sex relationship (Karp, 2017a).

Indeed, the "No" campaign would go on to outspend the yes vote by a ratio of around 2:1, with the Coalition of Marriage spending almost \$1 million compared to the Equality campaigns spending \$494,000 on television ads (Bickers, 2017). Nevertheless, when the postal vote was completed on 15 November 2017, the yes vote achieved a resounding victory. Nearly 80% of eligible voters participated; of those, 61.6% chose marriage equality. Particularly in Tony Abbott's seat of Warringah, where the yes vote achieved 75% – a thorough repudiation of his religious convictions (ABC News, 2017; Koziol, 2017). It led to the passing of the marriage equality bill on 7 December 2017.

Yet, whilst marriage equality carried the day, it was not a total loss for the religious minority within the Coalition. Rather, the holding of postal vote itself was a victory. The conservatives, as was the case during the attempts to amend the *Sex Discrimination Act* under Howard, had once again set the parameters of the debate, wherein both religion and demonisation of the LGBTQI community was placed front and centre and normalised in the political discourse. In other words, whilst they had lost this battle in the "culture war," the war was by no means over. Rather, Morrison, just a handful of days following the result, was already manoeuvring to keep the quest for religious freedom alive. In another interview on ABC's *7:30*, the then treasurer argued that as many, or probably more, want protections of religious freedoms than want same-sex marriage legalised, despite when pressed on the fact that less than 40% voted no:

> I don't accept for a second that just because only 40% of people, or just under that, voted not to proceed with same-sex marriage, that's not the only people who care about religious freedoms and freedom of speech in this country... I say that figure is well over half the population and about probably the same level or greater than voted for same-sex marriage.
>
> (Karp, 2017d)

Alongside this, Peter Dutton and Matthias Cormann put forward the idea of a separate religious freedom bill to be considered the following year that would allow individuals to express their views about what constituted marriage and allow for parental protections, such as enabling the withdrawal of students from the anti-bullying programme Safe Schools (Karp, 2017b, 2017d).

The never-ending quest for religious freedom

Interestingly, when Scott Morrison stepped into the limelight following the conclusion of the same-sex marriage postal vote and explained on ABC's *7:30* that there now needed to be consideration of religious freedom bill, he was explicit in stating that he was "acting on his own personal convictions" (Karp, 2017d). This was in stark contrast to earlier comments made by Turnbull that the bill to legalise same-sex marriage did not "impose any restrictions on religious freedom at all" (Karp, 2017c), and was designed, as host Leigh Sales noted, to "burnish his [Morrison's] leadership credentials" (Karp, 2017d). It also indicated that Turnbull was increasingly at odds with a number of his senior team in Morrison, Dutton, and Cormann, who all felt that the bill put forward by Liberal Senator Dean Smith did not provide the requisite protections for people of faith. Indeed, several government members tried to pass amendments to the bill that legalised same-sex marriage that would have provided more safeguards, such as the right for civil celebrants to also be allowed to object to gay weddings (Karp, 2017b).

As result of these ructions within the party, Turnbull moved quickly to dispel the disquiet by appointing former Howard Minister Phillip Ruddock to head an expert panel, which included Jesuit Priest Father Frank Brennan,[2] that would undertake a review of Australian law in the wake of marriage equality to see if religious freedoms are adequately protected. This was a deft move as the report was not to be completed until 31 March 2018, thereby potentially allowing for the issue to go cold. Turnbull was largely against action on freedom of religion, stating that the government needed to proceed carefully in order to avoid "unintended consequences" (Hutchens, 2017). Thus, when the report was eventually submitted in May, after having been granted an extension on account of the volume of submissions, Turnbull refused to publicly release the report. He argued that government needed time to consider its response (Elton-Pym, 2018).

However, time was not on Turnbull's side. Not long after the delaying of the Ruddock report, members of the religious right in the party, namely Tony Abbott, Kevin Andrews, and Eric Abetz, would lead an insurrection. Abbott, in particular, had been scheming since being ousted in 2015, and he and his accomplices attached themselves to Peter Dutton and urged him to challenge for the leadership. However, the plan was not to install Dutton as prime minister. Rather, it was meant to mortally wound Turnbull's leadership and cause the Coalition to lose at the next election, thereby creating an opening for a possible Abbott return to the leadership. The rationale behind this scheme was that Turnbull was "Labor-lite" and had betrayed the true conservative values of the party, especially on the issues of same-sex marriage and the subsequent freedom of religion debate. For much of the right of the party, energy policy was simply a proxy for this sense of betrayal (Maley, 2018; Savva, 2019b).

By this stage, Turnbull realised that his position as leader could not be salvaged and chose Morrison as his successor, and through a second round of petition within the party, Morrison would go on to win 45-40 to become Australia's 30th prime minister (Hartcher, 2018; Savva, 2019b).

Morrison and the renewed push for religious freedom

Following the battle there was some rear-guard action from Turnbull's camp with strategic leaks from the Ruddock Review on religious freedom that was designed to hurt the Liberal candidate Dave Sharma ahead of the by-election in the seat of Wentworth scheduled for 20 October 2018 (see Savva, 2019b). The leaks highlighted that the review recommended that the federal government amend the *Sex Discrimination Act* so "that religious schools may discriminate in relation to students on the basis of sexual orientation, gender identity or relationship status." This would be allowed, provided that the schools had a policy that clearly declared their position and gave notice to parents, students, and prospective students that was founded in the precepts of the religion in question. The review also recommended that teachers, staff, and contractors could be discriminated against on the basis of sexual orientation as long as it was clearly advertised (Karp, 2018).

These disclosures were particularly damaging as the seat of Wentworth returned the third highest yes vote of 80.8% in the postal plebiscite on same-sex marriage. Further to this, the main challenger to Sharma was independent candidate Dr Kerryn Phelps who is a prominent member of the LGBTQI community and actively campaigned for the yes vote by appearing in one of their ads. In response, the government would hastily explained that they would amend discrimination laws to prevent any possibility of students being expelled from religious schools on the basis of their sexual orientation. But such reassurances were not enough, and the Coalition would go on to lose the seat to Phelps who secured a 19% swing (Holman, 2017; Karp and Davies, 2018; The Sydney Morning Herald, 2018) – another clear illustration of the disjuncture between the religious posturing of many in the Coalition government and the wider public.

Effectively, Morrison, like Abbott before him, sought to avoid making his religious convictions a political liability and kept the issue of religious freedom largely out of the debate. This was achieved, in part, by failing to produce either legislation to protect LGTBQI students in religious schools or a draft Religious Discrimination Bill ahead of the election as promised (see Croome, 2019), and this trend continued following the Coalition's "miracle" victory. It would not be until 29 August 2019 that the first iteration of the Religious Discrimination Bill would be released.

The Exposure Bill seeks to protect against discrimination on the grounds of religious belief, both directly and indirectly, and applies across the areas of employment, education, and government services. Here, *direct discrimination* is when the discriminator treats a person with a protected attribute less favourably than someone without that attribute, whilst *indirect discrimination* takes place when a discriminator imposes an obligation which disadvantages persons that have protected attributes in situations where the obligation is not reasonable. Interestingly, this applies equally to both religious and non-religious people. This means that this bill, without further provision, would prevent religious schools or employers from discriminating on the basis of religion or lack thereof. However, this is overcome by Clause 10 of the bill which states that it is not discrimination if a "religious body" conducts itself in a way that could reasonably be considered in "accordance with the doctrines of the religion" (Aroney, 2019). In short, the proposed bill effectively grants a positive right to religious organisations to discriminate on the basis of religion with a view to protecting their ethos.

Alongside this the Exposure Bill also includes an Israel Folau (see Chapter 12) clause in Subsections 8(3) and 8(4), wherein the employer, with a value of $50 million or more, can only impose a restriction on religious belief if it can prove that it is necessary as a protection against unjustifiable financial hardship (Aroney, 2019). Thus, it potentially paves the way for individuals like Folau to be able to publicly declare that gays are going to hell without any ramifications. Or, as the Law Council noted, the bill could effectively legalise hate speech (Karp, 2019a).

However, the bill was savaged by Christian groups who argued that it did not go far enough and had some perverse unintended consequences. For example, the Anglican diocese of Sydney complained that the exemptions for religious bodies did not apply to bodies engaged in "solely commercial activities," meaning that both *Anglicare* and *Anglican Youthworks* would not be able to hire only Christian workers and volunteers. Anglican groups also raised concerns about the Folau clause, with the possibility of financial hardship being imposed by third-party sponsors, as was the case with Qantas in relation to Rugby Australia (see Brook, 2019b). Further, a coalition of religious leaders from Christian, Muslim, and Jewish communities signed a letter that said it would be better to have no bill at all rather than what was on offer (Karp, 2019b; Savva, 2019a).[3]

Subsequently, the bill has been redrafted as of 10 December 2019 to include religious hospitals, aged care facilities, accommodations, camp sites, and conferences sites and, at the time of writing this book, has received a second round of consultation (Karp, 2019c; see Chapter 12).

Australia and its Judeo-Christian heritage

Concomitant with this increasing religiosity within the Australian parliament has been the tendency to invoke Australia's Judeo-Christian heritage, and this has often been at the expense of the nation's other religious communities, particularly Muslims. As noted earlier, this trend also began with Howard following the advent of 9/11. Howard happened to be in Washington on the day of the attack; he was profoundly affected and declared that it was an "attack upon the way of life we hold dear in common with the Americans" (Siracusa, 2005: 42) and would see him join the "coalition of the willing" in the war on terror in Afghanistan and later Iraq. In this moment, Howard understood the events to be a manifestation of Huntington's (1993, 1996) "clash of civilisations" theory where the fault lines between societies would be religion and the dominant battle would be between the Christian West and Islam (see Crabb, 2009; Stratton, 2016).

Howard would go on to describe the decision to invoke the Australia, New Zealand, and United States (ANZUS) treaty as an instinctive move that "just emerged" and "made sense" at the time, and this instinct yielded significant benefits (Howard, 2001). The hard-line approach on terror, in conjunction with border protection, resonated with the public and yielded a 2% swing to the Coalition at the 2001 election held on 10 November. This was the biggest swing to a presiding government since 1966, and he would acknowledge that the issues of security and border protection were integral to his re-election (Siracusa, 2005). As a result, he would step up the rhetoric in the years to come and routinely reference the importance of the nation's Judeo-Christian heritage as the foundation stone for Australian society. For example, a week ahead of the election in 2004 in an interview with Geraldine Doogue, Howard stated:

> I am of the Christian tradition myself, and respect it in a very traditional way, and regard the Judeo-Christian influence on Australia as the single greatest influence for good in the Australian community.
>
> (as quoted in, Compass, 2004)

Further, it is important to note here that Judeo-Christian for Howard is not an abstract category that simply includes all from those traditions. Rather, his application of the phrase is much narrower in its orientation and is defined by Australia's history. As Jayasuriya (2006) notes, for Howard, Judeo-Christian is very much an ethnic category that is anchored in Australia's Anglo-Celtic colonial origins. That is, to be Australian is to be European, Christian, and white, and this is reflected in his "natural" decision to join the "coalition of the willing" in response to an attack on a shared way of life and effectively become an anglophone outpost and deputy sheriff of the region that belies both its geography and multicultural melting pot. Certainly, this understanding of "white" was more elastic than during the time of the White Australia policy, as it includes those who were previously regarded as not white, such as the Italians, Greeks, Maltese, and other previously non-white categories who came to be accepted as part of the wider Christian community following waves of migration in the 1960s and 1970s (see Chapters 3 and 4). Thus, Howard's use of Judeo-Christian evokes a re-imagined White Australia that is united by a universalised Christianity that has a set of common values at its core (Stratton, 2016).

This myopic view of Australia would ultimately culminate in the *Australian Citizenship Act 2007* that introduced a new citizenship test that was designed to stress the core values of the country. As such, in the accompanying booklet, it was explicitly outlined that Australia's values (e.g. freedom of speech, equal worth of men and women, rule of law, democracy, freedom of religion) were Anglo-Saxon/Celtic and drawn from the Judeo-Christian ethic:

> These values and principles reflect strong influences on Australia's history and culture. These include Judeo-Christian ethics, a British political heritage and the spirit of the European Enlightenment. Distinct Irish and non-conformist attitudes and sentiments have also been important.
>
> (as cited in Fozdar and Spittles, 2009, pp. 505–506)

Thus, over time, through this routine characterisation, Howard and his government discursively created a dichotomy between what constituted true Australians and those who were a threat to our way of life, and more often than not the target was Muslims. Indeed, the citizenship test, alongside the harsh border protection policies instigated by the Tampa affair in 2001, were specifically designed to stigmatise asylum seekers, refugees, and immigrants, many of whom were from Afghanistan and Iraq – two countries that Australia wilfully helped to destabilise in the "war on terror."

Here, it is important to note that Howard was not alone in this regard. Rather, just as he brought Labor along with the courting of the Christian vote during his tenure, many within the Labor camp were also complicit in the construction of Australia as a Judeo-Christian nation. For example, through an analysis of speeches between 2000 and 2006, Crabb (2009) found that there was minimal difference between the two parties with regard to invoking Christianity, with Coalition and Labor leaders doing so 22.7% and 21.1% of the time, respectively. Further, and perhaps unsurprisingly, the most prominent categories in which Christian terms were used were "foreign relations" (predominantly in relation to terrorism) and speeches coded as "fabric of society."

Since then, as noted above, leaders have continued to emphasise the importance of the nation's Judeo-Christian heritage, as did Tony Abbot with his ill-feted exhortation for Muslims to join "Team Australia" when announcing a raft of new counterterrorism measures. Similarly, Morrison, in a more subtle way, has put out the same message. Whilst he appears to avoid using the phrase Judeo-Christian, he continues to propagate the notion of shared values with the West and the idea that our shared way of life is under threat:

> Knowing who we are and what we stand for is as true today as it ever was. We will continue to bring clear objectives and enduring values to our international engagement. Freedom of thought and expression … *of spirit and faith* … of our humanity, including inalienable human rights. Freedom of exchange, free and open markets, free flow of capital and ideas. Freedom from oppression and coercion, freedom of choice. These have never been more important. And they *are under threat*, not just from the direct challenge of *competing worldviews*, but the complacency of western liberal democratic societies that owe their liberty and prosperity to these values.
> (Morrison, 2019b; emphasis added)

Indeed, in Morrison's (2008) maiden speech to parliament, he explained that he does not subscribe to the black-armband view of history and lauds James Cook as a man before his time who "embodied the true spirit of the enlightenment age." Further to this, he explains that we should revere him and respect his achievements rather than focus on any historical guilt for the brutality shown towards the indigenous community. In doing so, Morrison exhorts us to remember our "white" British roots and enlightenment values, that we are part of the West, and that this needs to be protected. In other words, Morrison is singing from the same hymn book as his mentor John Howard.

Conclusion

Here it can be seen that Howard from 1992 onwards skilfully utilised the Lyons Forum to prosecute a conservative social agenda, wherein he selected key wedge issues like LGBTQI rights and was able to entice a small contingent of Catholic voters that had historically been attached to Labor to come across to the Coalition. Following this, he then turned to the evangelical community to further press his religious advantage and pursued the fast-growing Pentecostal Hillsong Church. This move along with another electoral victory in 2004 would cause consternation within the Labor camp, which would see them, under the leadership of Rudd, attempt to negate these gains. Subsequently, with both major parties courting the Christian vote, religion well and truly moved from the periphery to the mainstream, with the pinnacle being the online webcast to 100,000 Christians in the 2007 election.

However, this bipartisan turn to religion would lead to something of a paradox as there was no real cohesive Christian vote to court. Rather, the real result of these religious turns would be to increase the appeal of politics to those of faith, through members of evangelical churches, such as Louise Markus in 2004, who was elected to parliament. As a result, whilst the wider public continues to decline in attachment to religion, the parliament has remained considerably more religious and out of step. This disjuncture was clearly illustrated by the marriage equality vote in 2017 that saw Tony Abbott's electorate return a "Yes" vote of 75%.

Alongside this, the persistent pursuit of the religious vote by Labor, particularly by the avowed atheist in Julia Gillard, helped to further normalise the place of religion in political discourse and paved the way for more outwardly religious leaders such as Abbott and Morrison, who previously would have been seen as being beyond the pale for a largely secular polity. As a result they have been able to pursue a religious agenda, such as the fight for religious freedom, despite the fact that neither the public nor the religious communities themselves are actively seeking it.

Finally, just as Howard manufactured a bipartisan religious turn, he also successfully crafted a narrative of Australian identity that is European, white, and Christian and which functions at the expense of other religious communities in Australia, particularly Muslims. This too has been taken up across the floor of parliament, with both major parties often invoking Christianity in relation to terrorism and the Australian way of life, and with Scott Morrison returned to Kirribilli House at the 2019 election, this narrative looks set to remain firmly entrenched.

Notes

1 The Assemblies of God in Australia changed their name to Australian Christian Churches in 2007 (Australian Christian Churches, 2021).

2 The other members of the panel were Australian Human Rights Commission President Rosalind Croucher, retired Federal Court Judge Annabelle Bennett, and academic Nicholas Aroney.

3 The letter was co-signed by the Catholic Archdiocese of Sydney, the Anglican Diocese of Sydney, the Executive Council of Australian Jewry, the Australian National Imams Council, and the Greek Orthodox Church in Australia (Ireland, 2019).

References

ABC News. 2010. Gillard won't play religion card. Retrieved from https://www.abc.net.au/news/2010-06-29/gillard-wont-play-religion-card/885142

ABC News. 2017. Results: same-sex marriage postal survey. Retrieved from https://www.abc.net.au/news/2017-11-15/same-sex-marriage-results-ssm/9145636

ABS. 2018. Census reveals Australia's religious diversity on World Religion Day. *Media Release*. Retrieved from https://www.abs.gov.au/AUSSTATS/abs@.nsf/mediareleasesbyReleaseDate/8497F7A8E7DB-5BEFCA25821800203DA4?OpenDocument

Aroney, N. 2019. *Religious Freedom and Religious Discrimination*. Paper presented at the Freedom for Faith Conference, NSW Parliament House, 4 September. Abstract retrieved from https://papers.ssrn.com/sol3/papers.cfm?abstract_id=3455089

Australian Christian Churches. (2021). About us. Retrieved from https://www.acc.org.au/about-us/

Bickers, C. 2017. Yes side outspent in gay marriage postal vote campaign, advertising analysis shows. *News.com.au*. Retrieved from https://www.news.com.au/lifestyle/gay-marriage/yes-side-outspent-in-gay-marriage-postal-vote-campaign-advertising-analysis-shows/news-story/08664ebc71081f69f6aa94e7202515ee

Brissenden, M. 2004. Politicians eye religious powerhouse. *ABC News*. Retrieved from https://www.abc.net.au/news/2004-07-15/politicians-eye-religious-powerhouse/2009790

Brook, B. 2019b. Sponsors in line of fire over Folau sacking. *News.com.au*. Retrieved from https://www.news.com.au/sport/sports-life/sponsors-in-line-of-fire-over-folau-sacking/news-story/fff0082ae8e7ea2756adb7e1f4173a2b

Compass. 2004. What our leaders believe. Retrieved from https://www.abc.net.au/religion/watch/compass/what-our-leaders-believe/10142928

Compass. 2005. Kevin Rudd: The God factor. Retrieved from https://www.abc.net.au/religion/watch/compass/kevin-rudd-the-god-factor/10140636

Crabb, A. 2009. Invoking religion in Australian politics. *Australian Journal of Political Science*, *44*(2): 259–279. doi: 10.1080/10361140902862784

Croome, R. 2019. Why 2019 was not a religious freedom election. *ABC Religion & Ethics*. Retrieved from https://www.abc.net.au/religion/why-2019-was-not-a-religious-freedom-election/11139472

Davis, M. 2014. Neoliberalism, the culture wars and public policy. In Miller, C. and Orchard, L. eds. *Australian public policy: progressive ideas in the neoliberal ascendancy*. Bristol: Bristol University Press, pp. 27–42.

Donald, P. and Iggulden, T. 2007. Howard, Rudd woo Christians online. *ABC News*. Retrieved from https://www.abc.net.au/news/2007-08-10/howard-rudd-woo-christians-online/636110

Donovan, T. 2014. The irrelevance and (new) relevance of religion in Australian elections. *Australian Journal of Political Science*, *49*(4): 626–646.

Elton-Pym, J. 2018. Ruddock's religious freedom report handed to Malcolm Turnbull. *SBS News*. Retrieved from https://www.sbs.com.au/news/ruddock-s-religious-freedom-report-handed-to-malcolm-turnbull

Fozdar, F. and Spittles, B. 2009. The Australian citizenship test: process and rhetoric. *Australian Journal of Politics & History*, *55*(4): 496–512.

Gleeson, K. 2011. Tony Abbott and abortion: Miscalculating the strength of the religious right. *Australian Journal of Political Science*, *46*(3): 473–488.

Hartcher, P. 2018. He was in it right up to his neck': How Scott Morrison deposed a prime minister. *The Sydney Morning Herald*. Retrieved from https://www.smh.com.au/politics/federal/he-was-in-it-right-up-to-his-neck-how-scott-morrison-deposed-a-prime-minister-20190312-p513jl.html

Holman, J. 2017. Same-sex marriage campaigners hit back with Yes advertisement. *ABC News*. Retrieved from https://www.abc.net.au/news/2017-08-30/same-sex-marriage-yes-campaign-advertisement/8857438

Howard, J. 2001. Press Conference 14 September. *Transcript*. Retrieved from https://pmtranscripts.pmc.gov.au/release/transcript-12308

Huntington, S.P. 1993. The clash of civilisations? *Foreign Affairs*, *72*(3): 22–49.

Huntington, S.P. 1996. *The clash of civilizations and the remarking of world order*. New York: Simon & Schuster.

Hutchens, G. 2017. Philip Ruddock to examine if Australian law protects religious freedom. *The Guardian*. Retrieved from https://www.theguardian.com/australia-news/2017/nov/22/philip-ruddock-to-examine-if-australian-law-protects-religious-freedom

Hutchens, G. and Hasham, N. 2016. Prime Minister Malcolm Turnbull refuses to endorse same-sex marriage pledge. *The Sydney Morning Herald*. Retrieved from https://www.smh.com.au/politics/federal/same-sex-marriage-plebiscite-promised-this-year-if-coalition-wins-election-20160306-gnbma9.html

Ireland, J. 2019. Church groups threaten to withdraw support for religious discrimination bill. *The Sydney Morning Herald*. Retrieved from https://www.smh.com.au/politics/federal/serious-unintended-consequences-church-groups-threaten-to-withdraw-support-for-religious-discrimination-bill-20191129-p53fbj.html

James, J.D. 2017. As Australia becomes less religious, our parliament becomes more so. *The Conversation*. Retrieved from https://theconversation.com/as-australia-becomes-less-religious-our-parliament-becomes-more-so-80456

Jayasuriya, L. 2006. The Australian-Asian connection: from Alfred Deakin to John Howard. *AQ: Journal of Contemporary Analysis:* 12–40.

Karp, P. 2017a. Coalition for marriage ad blitz links marriage equality to gender education. *The Guardian*, p.*29*. Retrieved from https://www.theguardian.com/australia-news/2017/aug/29/coalition-for-marriage-ad-blitz-links-marriage-equality-to-gender-education

Karp, P. 2017b. Peter Dutton says religious freedom could be protected after marriage equality. *The Guardian*. Retrieved from https://www.theguardian.com/australia-news/2017/nov/16/peter-dutton-says-religious-freedom-could-be-protected-after-marriage-equality

Karp, P. 2017c. Same-sex marriage bill does not hinder religious freedom, says Turnbull. *The Guardian*. Retrieved from https://www.theguardian.com/australia-news/2017/nov/17/same-sex-marriage-bill-does-not-hinder-religious-freedom-says-turnbull

Karp, P. 2017d. Scott Morrison: at least as many voters want religious freedom as marriage equality. *The Guardian*. Retrieved from https://www.theguardian.com/australia-news/2017/nov/20/scott-morrison-at-least-as-many-want-religious-freedom-as-marriage-equality

Karp, P. 2017e. Senate blocks government attempt to restore compulsory plebiscite for marriage equality. *The Guardian*. Retrieved from https://www.theguardian.com/australia-news/2017/aug/09/abbott-says-vote-no-to-marriage-equality-and-stop-political-correctness-in-its-tracks

Karp, P. 2018. Ruddock religious freedom review: what is it and what do we know so far?. *The Guardian*, p.*12*. Retrieved from https://www.theguardian.com/australia-news/2018/oct/11/ruddock-religious-freedom-review-what-is-it-and-what-do-we-know-so-far

Karp, P. 2019a. Religious discrimination bill could legalise race hate speech, Law Council warns. *The Guardian*. Retrieved from https://www.theguardian.com/law/2019/sep/04/religious-discrimination-bill-could-legalise-race-hate-speech-law-council-warns

Karp, P. 2019b. Religious discrimination bill so flawed it cannot be supported, Anglicans say. *The Guardian*. Retrieved from https://www.theguardian.com/world/2019/oct/01/religious-discrimination-bill-so-flawed-it-cannot-be-supported-anglicans-say

Karp, P. 2019c. Religious discrimination bill, what will Australians be allowed to say and do if it passes?. *The Guardian*. Retrieved from https://www.theguardian.com/world/2019/dec/14/religious-discrimination-bill-what-will-australians-be-allowed-to-say-and-do-if-it-passes

Karp, P. and Davies, A. 2018. Kerryn Phelps zeroes in on climate change and Peter Dutton's eligibility. *The Guardian*. Retrieved from https://www.theguardian.com/australia-news/2018/nov/05/kerryn-phelps-seeks-urgent-briefing-on-peter-duttons-eligibility

Koziol, M. 2017. Same-sex marriage postal survey: 'Love has had a landslide victory' as 'yes' wins. *The Sydney Morning Herald*. Retrieved from https://www.smh.com.au/politics/federal/samesex-marriage-postal-survey-love-has-had-a-landslide-victory-as-yes-wins-20171113-gzkk7f.html

Maddox, M. 2001. *For God and country: religious dynamics in Australian federal politics*. Canberra: Department of the Parliamentary Library.

Maddox, M. 2005. *God under Howard: the rise of the religious right in Australian politics*. Sydney: Allen & Unwin.

Maley, J. 2018. The rise and spectacular fall of Malcolm: what did Turnbull get so wrong? *The Sydney Morning Herald*. Retrieved from https://www.smh.com.au/politics/federal/the-rise-and-spectacular-fall-of-malcolm-what-did-turnbull-get-so-wrong-20180823-p4zze5.html

Mazzoni, A. 2019. Scott Morrison allows cameras inside his Hillsong-style mega-church for a VERY animated Easter service with his wife and kids. *Daily Mail*. Retrieved from https://www.dailymail.co.uk/news/article-6943821/Scott-Morrison-claps-sings-enjoys-Easter-Sunday-church-service-family.html

Morrison, S. 2008. Maiden speech. *Hansard*. Retrieved from https://parlinfo.aph.gov.au/parlInfo/search/display/display.w3p;query=Id:%22chamber/hansardr/2008-02-14/0045%22

Morrison, S. 2019b. Lowy Lecture: "In our Interest". Retrieved from https://www.pm.gov.au/media/speech-lowy-lecture-our-interest

Murphy, K. 2013. Tony Abbott keeps the Catholic faith, quietly. *The Guardian*. Retrieved from https://www.theguardian.com/world/2013/jun/11/tony-abbott-conservative-catholic-election

News.com.au. 2017. Federal Treasurer Scott Morrison reveals he is voting 'no' in same-sex marriage plebiscite. Retrieved from https://www.news.com.au/national/politics/federal-treasurer-scott-morrison-reveals-he-is-voting-no-in-samesex-marriage-plebiscite/news-story/d7be152a9ef873e777dcb653af478a20

Savva, N. 2019a. Faith in PM weakens with religious freedom debacle. *The Australian.* Retrieved from https://www.theaustralian.com.au/commentary/faith-in-pm-weakens-with-religious-freedom-debacle/news-story/56d2e7d85f07d4117e1fc46507f2429b

Savva, N. 2019b. *Plots and prayers: Malcolm Turnbull's demise and Scott Morrison's ascension.* Scribe Publications.

Seccombe, M. 2015. Prime Minister Tony Abbott and the Christian right. *The Saturday Paper.* Retrieved from https://www.thesaturdaypaper.com.au/news/politics/2015/08/29/prime-minister-tony-abbott-and-the-christian-right/14407704002308

Siracusa, J. M. (2005). John Howard, Australia, and the coalition of the willing. *Yale Journal of International Affairs, 1*, 39.

Smyth, J. 2017. Same-sex marriage reignites Australia's culture wars. *Financial Times.* Retrieved from https://www.ft.com/content/f793f132-96f8-11e7-b83c-9588e51488a0

Strangio, P. and Walter, J. 2018. Turnbull versus shorten: The major party leadership contest. In Guaja, A., Chen, P., Curtin, J. and Pietsch, J. eds. *Double dissolution: The 2016 Australian federal election.* Canberra: ANU Press, pp. 81–105.

Stratton, J. 2016. Whiteness, morality and Christianity in Australia. *Journal of Intercultural Studies, 37*(1): 17–32.

The Sydney Morning Herald. 2007. Howard, Rudd court Christian vote. Retrieved from https://www.smh.com.au/national/howard-rudd-court-christian-vote-20070810-gdqtsa.html

Taylor, L. 2013. Tony Abbott: the journey from rank outsider to Australia's new leader'. *Guardian Australia*, p.*8*. Retrieved from https://www.theguardian.com/world/2013/sep/08/tony-abbott-australias-new-prime-minister

The Guardian. 2019. 'I've always believed in miracles': Scott Morrison claims victory for the Coalition – video. Retrieved from https://www.theguardian.com/global/video/2019/may/19/ive-always-believed-in-miracles-scott-morrison-claims-victory-for-the-coalition-video

The Sydney Morning Herald. 2002. Howard has faith in the God squad. Retrieved from https://www.smh.com.au/national/howard-has-faith-in-the-god-squad-20020816-gdfjnh.html

The Sydney Morning Herald. 2018. Wentworth voters beware religious freedom con. Retrieved from https://www.smh.com.au/national/nsw/wentworth-voters-beware-religious-freedom-con-20181010-p508tg.html

Warhurst, J. 2007. Religion and politics in the Howard decade. *Australian Journal of Political Science, 42*(1): 19–32.

Young, M. and Farr, M. 2013. Rudd pops the question on gay marriage during election debate. *News.com.au.* Retrieved from https://www.news.com.au/national/rudd-pops-the-question-on-gay-marriage-during-election-debate/news-story/766ba9f896ba47144e172d1f1d6a2d1b

12 Conclusion

Australia as a post-secular society?

Introduction

Australia is among the most successful societies when it comes to religious diversity. Religious groups are able to speak to one another and to atheist groups, in the public sphere and in a constructive way. While Australia can thus be argued to be a post-secular society because of this freedom to speak, some sticky issues, however, such as Shari'a (Possamai, 2017 and Chapter 5), same-sex marriage (Possamai-Inesedy and Turner, 2016 and Chapter 11), and the current freedom of religion debate (Possamai and Possamai-Inesedy, 2021 and below), have not always met these standards of constructive argumentation, as the philosopher Habermas envisioned (see Chapter 2). But these processes of de-secularisation, in the sense that religion is becoming part of public life, take on different intensities at different levels in a society. For the purpose of this chapter, and as a conclusion to this book, we summarise the recent changes that have taken place in Australia, informed by the nuanced analysis of the de-secularisation process by the Belgian sociologist Dobbelaere (2002). However, before taking that turn, we need to contextualise this development a little more with David Martin's (2005) important observation that the transition from religion to secularisation, and vice versa, is a far from linear process.

If social evolutionists from the late 19th and early 20th centuries were expecting religion to fully disappear with the advent of science, the reality is far more than simply a comeback in post-secularism (see Chapter 2). Religion never disappears. It might go into hiding or come back in a non-visible way, but it is always present. As seen in Chapter 3 on the creation of Clause 116 in the Australian constitution about the secular protection of religion, this was meant for a religious purpose; namely, preventing any religion from being able to dominate any other, rather than trying to shut religion out.

DOI: 10.4324/9781003255338-12

To illustrate this paradigm, we draw on David Martin's (2005) work which underlines the different dynamics of secularisation, rather than simply assuming that there is only one type, as has been the case in many previous social scientific studies, such as that of Durkheim explored in Chapter 6. The fundamental argument of Martin's work is that secularisation is not a clear-cut process, as already noted in Chapter 2. The move from religion to secularisation, and vice versa, is not a homogenous and unilateral process, as this chapter will show.

Three levels of secularisation/de-secularisation

The multiple modernisation thesis (see Chapter 2) provides a backdrop to understanding the different types of de-secularisation processes in the world that started in the late 20th century. What needs to be done now is to be able to characterise the specific de-secularisation process in Australia using an analytical method of analysis. For this, Dobbelaere's (2002, 2015) theories of secularisation is of help here. He does not work on the different dynamics of secularisation (horizontal process) like Martin, but on its different levels (vertical process). For Dobbelaere (2002), there are three levels. The first one is Societal Secularisation (also called in his terms "laïcisation" for the societal or macro level). It deals with the change of structure, which has occurred with the industrialisation of Western societies, and refers to a functional differentiation process. Through this process many subsystems are developed which perform different functions that are structurally different. Religion, as an institution, is thus no longer an overarching institution, but one of many. The second dimension is Organisational Secularisation (also called in his terms "religious change" for the organisation or meso level) and reflects changes at the level of religious organisations, such as churches, denominations, sects, and new religious movements. At this level, the study of the decline and emergence of certain types of religious groups can be conducted. The last dimension, Individual Secularisation (also called "religious involvement" for the individual or micro level), refers to the individual level and deals with the way an individual believes in a specific religion and how this person is integrated into a religious group.

As there are multiple processes of secularisations, there will thus be multiple processes of de-secularisations such as the political reentering of the public sphere by certain religious groups, the cultural transaction operated by religious and spiritual groups and individuals via consumer culture and popular culture, and the growth of a type of religious social capital generated by the transnational networks of new immigrant and ethnic communities. This chapter now attempts to pinpoint the processes of de-secularisation in Australia through each of these levels.

Societal de-secularisation

Government

As seen in Chapter 11, since the election of a conservative federal government in 1996 in Australia, preference for religious provision of services has become a policy priority. Senior church people have increasingly become influential with senior political operatives. The rise of the Pentecostal Hillsong Church (Sydney) has drawn politicians to their gatherings, and in 2004, the Pentecostal Steven Fielding won a senate seat for his Christian aligned Family First Party. Over the last 25 years, religion, it can be argued, has progressively moved back into the mainstream of the political flow. While past politicians have kept their faith to the private sphere, public displays of religiosity became prominent during the Howard government's third term, but it is still far from the US type of presidential races in which faith-based politics is of high importance (Maddox, 2005). The overt appeal to the Gospel and to Christian values is more common in the discourse of American presidents than in Australian prime ministers.

Jakubowicz (2003) uses the expression "the new Australian conservative modernity" to make reference to the country's resurgent social values of Christian conservatism (see Chapter 11), the active governmental priorities of disengagement, and a rapidly expanding culture of surveillance and obedience. In contemporary Australian society, we find a moral concern (if not panic) over Muslims and a process of the delegitimation of diversity (see Chapter 5 on Islamophobia). Delegitimation "does not deny diversity, but rather seeks to reassert a traditional hierarchy of cultural power within which diversity is only acceptable within the dominant moral order" (Jakubowicz, 2003: 344). In this process, Fozdar (2011) detects a retreat from multiculturalism that is in part a consequence of the conservative values of the Howard government (1996–2007). In this new Australian modernity, political leaders portray "Christianity as the norm, as a non-migrant religion, and as the taken-for-granted foundation for the nation's values and laws" (Fozdar, 2011: 632).

Randell-Moon (2009) and Maddox (2009) demonstrate that in the Australian case (a secular liberal society where a strong division between church and state is supposedly definitive), religion still has a part to play in politics. In this "secular" liberal culture, religion is often actually a significant factor in voting decisions and is intruding more and more into the public sphere since the beginning of the 21st century. If Christianity was for many years a silent backdrop to Australian national identity, Fozdar (2011) observes that there is now an even stronger sense of legitimacy for the public place of Christianity, and one of illegitimacy for other religious traditions.

We can thus argue that by having religion coming back to the public sphere of politics, we are faced with a process of de-secularisation at the societal level. However, as seen in Chapter 11, this re-emergence of religion in political life has taken a new step with the, Religious Discrimination Bill, as explored in the next section.

Legislation

Australia has had a series of national inquiries into freedom of religion and belief over more than 20 years, and religious groups have been invited to take part in this process in the public sphere (see, e.g., Joint Standing Committee in Foreign Affairs, Defence and Trade, 2000; Ruddock et al., 2018; Bouma et al., 2011). Poulos (2019) and Possamai and Possamai-Inesedy (2021) qualitatively analysed all these reports and have highlighted a significant change in the way "the problem" with religious freedom is addressed. Until 2011, the main concern in Australia was mainly on how to deal with religious diversity and on how to protect the freedom of minority religions. The 2011 Bouma et al. report highlighted the beginning of a shift. A major Christian grouping expressed their sense of being under "threat" from the support provided to the rights of minority groups, not just minority religions. Strong voices from these submissions emerged around that time and progressively found their place in the public sphere to express religious freedom, shifting from simply asking for the right not to be discriminated against because of one's religion, to requesting a "right" for freedom of expression to be able to discriminate in the name of religion.

Because of the postal plebiscite in Australia on same-sex marriage, and its subsequent legalisation in December 2017 (see Chapter 11), two interim reports from the parliament and an expert panel report (Ruddock et al., 2018) – which received 15,620 submissions and held 90 meetings with 152 organisations and 32 individuals – were released in 2017–2019. These reports led to a partial endorsement of the government and the release of the exposure draft, Religious Discrimination Bill in 2019, which has not yet been voted on at the time of writing.[1] The second interim report in 2019 (Joint Standing Committee on Foreign Affairs Defence and Trade, 2019) from the House of Representatives followed the comprehensive Ruddock et al. (2018) report and acknowledges that laws in Australia need to be harmonised to ensure stronger protection for religion. As with its first report (Joint Standing Committee on Foreign Affairs Defence and Trade, 2017), it underlines the difficulty of striking the right balance of "conflicting rights," that is "between the right to freedom of religion and belief and the rights to freedom of speech and to non-discriminatory treatment" (Joint Standing Committee on Foreign Affairs Defence and Trade, 2019: 71). One of its sections is specific to Christianity, and while the report does not homogenise all Christian groups, it does raise at length the strong concern from some religious people to be able to express freely their religious views. As Christianity, still the dominant religion, is declining in Australia (from 61% of the population in the 2011 census to 52% in 2016), some of them express a concern for religious liberty, almost fearing that they will become a minority group under threat.

For some of these submissions and accounts, religious rights are above other human rights, and some of these Christian groups want to be able to express this freely in the public sphere. Because of the increase of anti-discrimination laws in Australia over the years, some Christian groups are asking to be able to speak about their religious views without being charged with bigotry and discrimination. These reports came out not only during the time of the same-sex marriage legislation, but also at a time that an Australian leading rugby league player, Israel Folau, was the subject of a controversy when he claimed in April 2018 on social media that God's plan for gay people is "Hell." He explained afterwards that he was not homophobic or bigoted, but that he simply provided his understanding of his Bible teachings. His contract with Rugby Australia was consequently terminated.

However, while the Folau case was certainly a lightning rod for the religious freedoms debate, it is important to note some earlier cases that are still part of the social memory. Behind these reports are the Catch the Fire case (Joint Standing Committee on Foreign Affairs Defence and Trade, 2017: 58) in which two pastors of a Christian organisation were brought to court by the Islamic Council of Victoria for criticising Islam (Deen, 2008). This case highlighted the difficulty in distinguishing criticisms of the doctrines of Islam and incitement of hatred towards followers of Islam. Another key case is Christian Youth

Camps Limited v Cobaw Community Health Service Limited (Joint Standing Committee on Foreign Affairs Defence and Trade, 2017: 60) in which a Christian Brethren youth camp refused to accept a booking for a programme run for same-sex attracted youth. The Christian youth camp was sued for discrimination on the basis of sexual orientation. Similarly, Burker v Tralanggan (Joint Standing Committee on Foreign Affairs Defence and Trade, 2017: 64) was a case in which a Christian couple refused, on religious grounds, to rent their flat to a same-sex couple. In this context, some religious people in Australia are requesting for greater freedom of expression to be able to ventilate their religious view (and thus enhancing religious freedom in the way they conceive it) outside of their church and community and in the public sphere without fear of retribution.

Although religion has never fully disappeared from within the public sphere in Australia, it is now coming back strongly. Even if the number of Christians has gone down in the census, those who are left can be more vocal than before and are able to influence the government and legislation towards their interest. In this sense, the macro level of Australia has certainly become more religious since the Howard government. With this renewed Christianisation at the macro level, are we observing a push further away from post-secularism in which all religions, including the non-religious, are in dialogue? Is this showing that, at this level, Australia is moving towards a post-post-secularist phase, where one religion becomes more dominant?

Organisation de-secularisation

New religious movements (NRMs) and groups

During the move to multiculturalism in the 1970s, new religious groups developed in Australia as communities and/or organisations (see Chapter 4). Increased diverse immigration corresponded with a rise in non-Christian religions and in NRMs around the same time (Bouma, 2008), while at the same time attendance at mainstream churches in Australia had decreased. Such changes have meant that Australia has moved from a culture of "obligation" towards a culture of "consumption/choice."

Australia is one of the most religiously diverse countries in the world (Bouma, 2006), and, apart from the way Australian Aboriginal peoples have been treated since the first colony, this has happened largely peacefully and without major clashes between religious groups. With regard to NRMs, and according to, for example, Bouma (1999), Sheen (1996) and Possamai and Possamai-Inesedy (2009), there have nevertheless been incidents of discrimination, vilification, harassment, and conflict in Australia. With Islam, especially after 9/11, there have been negative media portrayals, together with discriminatory rhetoric, policy, and practices at the level of the state against Muslims (see Poynting and Perry, 2007; see also Chapter 5). However, according to Bouma (1999), and taking into consideration other countries, Australia appears to have an enviably low rate in the occurrence of religious intergroup hostility. Richardson (1999) believes that Australia has its share of controversy, but not as much as in Western Europe.

Nevertheless, there are now many more religious groups offering their "product" in a religious market which are tried out by many consumers. Indeed, this country is home to many ideas and practices found in alternative spiritualities and NRMs, and is currently hosting many New Age spiritual practices and ideas (see Chapter 8).

Faith Based Organisations (FBOs)

Maddox (2005) studied how, in Australia, the former neoliberal Howard government saw the potential for welfare to be delivered "cheaper" by the churches than by the government, thereby positioning religious institutions and organisations as available to fill the gaps that the shrinking Australian welfare state could not fill. The Howard government shifted sectors of the public social welfare services to a coalition of community organisations, including churches, which have longstanding experience in philanthropic activities. Maddox also suggests that this government claimed to believe that welfare was best delivered by agents other than the government, and especially by Christian agencies, as opposed to other faith groups. The logic of neoliberalism has clearly extended its market competition ideology to civil society in the delivery of health care and public services (Hall and Lamont, 2013). This, as Maddox (2014) claims, makes these services dependent on the benevolence of charitable organisations, rather than on a fair and predictable source of revenue generated by government taxes.

Howe and Howe (2012) have already traced the long history of these FBOs in Australia, especially the changes brought by neoliberalism since the 1990s. They attempted to address the economic impact of these organisations, but at the time of writing their article, they only had ad-hoc figures to present. Harding et al. (2011) acknowledge that the process of tax exemption for not-for-profit organisations has not always been transparent and that charities are not always held accountable. Tax concessions tend to favour older organisations and religious charities with higher economic capital. Contrary to the discourse that these charities are relieving the financial burden of governments, governments are arguably losing important revenue via large tax deductions, which may or may not be fully warranted or properly acquitted. But the study by Harding et al. found in the literature a dominant stance that governments might lose even more revenue if they were to provide the services themselves, than they do while relying on religious groups to provide them.

As the concessions allowed to religions do not tend to have either transparency or strong oversight (which is not the case for other types of government expenditure), there are issues with regard to both the accountancy and the accountability of charity work. Calculating the value and the economics of tax concessions and of social welfare effectiveness is complex, confusing, and administratively costly, and thus in economic terms the current concessions may not be effective. This has led Australia to recently push for a statutory definition of charity, and for endorsements of tax concessions to be administered by a centralised authority.

In December 2012, any Australian not-for-profits that wanted tax exemption for their charity work had to register with the new Australian Charities and Not-for-profits Commission and had to provide information about their work. The charities that were previously deemed eligible to receive tax concessions were automatically included in the register. In the first report on the outcomes of the Commission, Penny Knight and David Gilchrist (2014) presented an analysis of the 40,000 registered charities that provided information. They found that these charities' combined 2012–2013 income was close to AUD100 billion, and that they employed around 8% of the Australian workforce. Of these charities, 10% account for 90% of the total income and 90% of the jobs, and this 10% included a large proportion of hospitals and higher education providers. Out of all the surveyed charities, 12,253 (32%) listed the advancement of religion as their purpose, and 9,808 (26%) self-described simply as "Basic Religious Charities."

> Religious activities were the main activity for a quarter of charities, making this by far the largest area of charity work—more than four times higher than any other single activity.
>
> (Knight and Gilchrist 2014: 28)

Basic Religious Charities are currently exempt from reporting on financial issues.

In the Productivity Commission Research Report (2010) on the contribution of the not-for-profit sector, one can discover that the charity sector has grown rapidly over the last decade. This sector represents 4% of GDP (close to AUD43 billion) and comprises close to 5 million volunteers (representing AUD14.6 billion in unpaid work). It is estimated that in 2008–2009, at least AUD4 billion was given in tax relief (2010: 155). In 2007, of the 58,779 not-for-profits that had an "active tax role," 12,174 (21%) were religious. However, of the total share of donations, 36% was for religious organisations (2010: 77). In 2005, 30% of the Australian population donated an average of 529 dollars to FBOs. In 2006–2007, the value of deductible gifts was over AUD1.8 billion, and the estimated cost of this in tax revenue was AUD860 million (2010: 155).

Schools

Since the Howard Coalition government (1996–2007), Australia has witnessed the proliferation of religious schools due to the introduction of a federal non-government school funding system. If towards the end of the 1970s there were just above 20% of students in Australian non-government schools, the proportion has gone up to just over 34% in 2009 (Buckingham, 2010). These new schools have been filled by families who could not previously afford this type of schooling for their children. The ABS (2013) observed that even if some children reported to have no religion in Catholic and other non-government schools, they were more likely to attend a secular and government school (75%). Religious schools have thus lower proportions of children from a non-religious background. On top of this, the ABS (2013) reveals that the rates of attending government schools decrease as the level of income of the parents increases.

In 2006, the Howard government established the National School Chaplaincy Program to facilitate the work of chaplains offering pastoral care and informal support for students in government primary and secondary schools. Such chaplaincy services were said to be different from, and complementary to, those offered by existing youth workers and school counsellors, who usually had qualifications in psychology. The funding was $20,000 per school, per year. This scheme continued to be funded through the former Labor government (2007–2013). In August 2010, when the atheist Julia Gillard was the prime minister, it announced funding of $222 million for school chaplaincy services from 2012 to 2014 (Stephens, 2010), and the current coalition government continues to fund the program at a similar level with an injection of $245.7 million over four years from 2019, which amounts to $61.4 million a year (Crowe, 2021).

In researching chaplains in government schools, Hughes and Sims (2009) discovered, among many factors, that these professionals are willing to be underpaid while following their vocation. The same research mentions school principals who stated that they could not replace these chaplains with anyone else doing the same job at the same level of payment. It could be inferred from their statements that there is a perception that the religious vocation of these spiritual labourers justifies this underpayment. Further to this debate, on 1 July 2010, the Australian Psychological Society (APS) made a submission to the consultation process for the National School Chaplaincy Program, claiming that chaplains sometimes go beyond their role as providers of religious guidance and informal student support, purporting to serve as counsellors. The APS contended that "Chaplains should not be employed to counsel students, especially on issues related to mental health and other complex personal problems" (Thielking and Stokes, 2010: 8). In the same submission, the APS queried the expenditure of substantial government funds on the chaplaincy programme, arguing that early intervention services for students with mental health needs should be provided by professionals who are both qualified and registered to do the job properly (Thielking and Stokes, 2010).

While the macro level in Australia is being de-secularised as seen above, there is a flow on effect at the meso level. Resources from the federal government are helping FBOs and religious schools to flourish. The multicultural system in Australia is also welcoming of non-Christian and new religions to establish themselves as groups and have some influence at the meso level, but they are not reaching out at the macro one. At the meso level, Australia can be regarded as post-secular, religious groups and non-religious ones usually interact cooperatively at an organisational level. But what of the micro sphere?

Individual de-secularisation

As in many other Western countries, Australians appear to no longer need to belong to a specific religious group in order to "believe." The "spiritual" revolution outside of an organised religion has not really happened in Australia, but it has led to some cultural changes (Bouma, 2006; Possamai, 2005; Tacey, 2000; see also Chapter 8). Cases in point are the New Age and neo-pagan network, hyper-real religions (i.e. religions such as Jediism and Matrixism created from popular culture by individuals), Western appropriation of forms of Buddhism, or even traditional religions lived outside of their institutions, such as believing without belonging (Davie, 2002). Although churches are noting declines in attendance, it does not mean that people are less religious/spiritual.

Part of this growth of spirituality in Australia is not happening just outside of religious groups but inside as well. As Wuthnow (2001: 307) claims, "many people who practice spirituality in their own ways still go to church or synagogue." Indeed, social scientists find (see Hughes et al., 2004; Marler and Hadaway, 2002) that the large majority of the people surveyed claim to be religious and spiritual at the same time. This claim might reflect a stronger engagement in religious practices and beliefs than, for example, a non-practising Catholic who still claims to be of that religion in the census.

At this individual level, it can be observed that Australia is also being de-secularised through the growth of spirituality.

As showed in Chapter 10, we also see religious people somewhat influenced by social media and popular culture instead of, or on top of, attending the bricks and mortar of religious institutions. The decline in church attendance is not always an indication that people are less religious as some find their religious messages and information through other ways.

There is indeed a religious vitality happening at the micro level in Australia which is beyond the remit of any institution.

The theory on post-secularism is based on the notion that religions are part of the public sphere and this religious vitality at the ground level is not restricted to the private sphere. Popular culture, social media, festivals, religious groupings, and religious consumption are part of the Australian public sphere and, as for the meso level, are also part of post-secularism.

Conclusion

In the beginning Australia saw religion being used as a tool of social control to help build a modern secular society. It was used by the state to "civilise" the prisoner in penal colonies, the free settlers, and the Indigenous inhabitants of the land. Although Australia was also born as a modern secular state, religion was used in conjunction with the state for this modernisation process. Overall, the colonisation process of Australia itself might explain its hybridity between the US (started modernisation without any established church) and Europe (had tension with established church during the modernisation process).

With the case of the religious freedom debate in Australia, we are witnessing a significant move towards Christian sanctification (Martin, 2005). While the government is pushing a Christian agenda, and the religious freedom debate is aiming at changing laws in favour of a conservative view, we have a strong de-secularisation process at the macro level which does not match the trend among the overall populations at the meso and micro levels. Australia is also quite particular with regard to religion in the public sphere as it is the only OECD country without a Bill of Rights and with the largest tranche of anti-terrorism laws that disproportionately target Muslims (Richardson, 2013; Tittensor et al., 2020).

At the meso level, while we have an increase of non-Christian movements, we see, however, an impact from the state through the provision of advantages to Christian schools, such as chaplaincy programme, and the redistributing welfare resources to FBOs that largely benefit those of a Christian orientation. At the individual level, we observed an increase of non-Christian religions, alternative spirituality, and non-religion, but none of these non-Christian groups and movements are properly structured and organised to have deep impact at the macro level.

If we come back to the notion of social memory, Australia started being a land for people who would later be called Australian Aboriginal peoples. This land was taken to make place for a new Christian social memory that attempted, willingly or unwillingly, to change their ways of being and knowing. With Federation, the separation of church and state was not a secular move but a religious one (see Chapter 3). Even if the state was secular, it continued to promote a strong Christian social memory. After WWII, the growth of non-Christian religion, of spirituality, and of the religious nones has been reflected in population trends. This means that Australia is currently a multifaith society (Cahill, 2015) and post-secular (Possamai, 2017). However, since the Howard government, the state has continued to put forward a Christian agenda so its social memory does not dwindle, even if the number of Christians is declining (see Chapter 5). Further, while not all Christians are conservative, the traditionalists tend to align with conservative governments and are pushing for religious rights to be above that of others (Bouma and Halafoff, 2017).

More specifically, it has been observed that Australia is going through a de-secularisation process at three levels. There has been a growth of spirituality at the micro level at the end of the last century, which seems to have reached its apex (see Chapter 8). At that level, many people are influenced by popular culture and social media (see Chapters 8 and 10), and they can experience faith outside of a religious institution. It is also at that level that more and more people are living their non-Christian faith, which is impacting on the meso level. Many of these religious groups have sought within the rubric of multiculturalism to organise and represent their community with a view to helping their believers at the micro level. However, the influence of these non-Christian groups does not seem to have much reach at the macro level. Rather, as explored in Chapter 11, the macro sphere is more Christian and monocultural than any of the other levels. As, such, all three realms experience a de-secularisation process, but in different ways and intensities. While the micro and meso levels are more diverse, the macro is more Christian.

Finally, while Australia is at the intersection of four social memories in being Christian, Australian Aboriginal, post-Christian, and non-religious, there are attempts to promote one preference over others, and although it is acknowledged that Australia, especially compared to European countries, is a successful multicultural society not riven by intergroup conflict (Bouma, 2016), this preference for one group over others at the macro level does not make Australia as much of a multi-faith or post-secular country as one would think.

Note

1 Indeed, the bill as of November 2021, is in the process of being redrafted for a third time (Martin, 2021).

References

ABS 2013. *4102.0 Australian social trends, Nov 2013*. Canberra: Australian Bureau of Statistics.

Bouma, G. 1999. Social justice issues in the management of religious diversity in Australia. *Social Justice Research*, *12*(4): 283–295.

Bouma, G. 2006. *Australian soul: religion and spirituality in the 21st century*. Port Melbourne: Cambridge University Press.

Bouma, G. D. 2008. The challenge of religious revitalisation to multicultural and multifaith Australia. *International Journal of Diversity in Organisations, Communities & Nations, 8*(1): 1–4.

Bouma, G. 2016. The role of demographic and socio-cultural factors in Australia's successful multicultural society: How Australia is not Europe. *Journal of Sociology, 52*(4): 759–771.

Bouma, G., Cahill, D., Dellal, H. and Zwartz, A. 2011. *Freedom of religion and belief in 21st century Australia: A research report prepared for the Australian Human Rights Commission.* Sydney: Australian Human Rights Commission.

Bouma, G. and Halafoff, A. 2017. Australia's changing religious profile—rising Nones and Pentecostals, declining British Protestants in superdiversity: views from the 2016 census. *Journal for the Academic Study of Religion, 30*(2): 129–143.

Buckingham, J. and Buckingham, J., 2010. *The rise of religious schools.* Australia: Centre for Independent Studies.

Cahill, D. 2015. From secularist to pluralist: post-World War II Australia. In Davies, D. and Powell, A. eds. *Sacred selves, sacred settings.* Farnham: Ashgate, pp. 123–144.

Crowe, D. 2021. Calls to extend school chaplaincy program to help deal with pandemic. *The Sydney Morning Herald.* Retrieved from https://www.smh.com.au/politics/federal/calls-to-extend-school-chaplaincy-program-to-help-deal-with-pandemic-20210831-p58nlk.html

Davie, G. 2002. *Europe: the exceptional case: parameters of faith in the modern world.* Darton: Longman & Todd.

Deen, H. 2008. *The Jihād Seminar.* Perth: University of Western Australia Press.

Dobbelaere, K. 2002. *Secularization: an analysis at three levels* (Vol. 1). Bruxelles, Bern, Berlin, Frankfurt am Main, New York, Oxford, Wien: Peter Lang.

Dobbelaere, K. 2015. The secularization of the sanctity of life and death. In Douglas, D. and Powell A. eds. *Sacred selves, sacred settings: reflecting Hans Mol.* Farnham: Ashgate, pp. 67–86.

Fozdar, F. 2011. The 'Choirboy' and the 'Mad Monk': Christianity, Islam, Australia's political landscape and prospects for multiculturalism. *Journal of Intercultural Studies, 32*(6): 621–636.

Hall, P.A. and Lamont, M. eds. 2013. *Social resilience in the neoliberal era.* New York: Cambridge University Press.

Harding, M., O'Connell, A., Stewart, M. and Chia, J. 2011. Taxing Not-for-profits. Research Report for the Not-for-profit Project, *Melbourne Law School.* Retrieved November 17, 2021, https://law.unimelb.edu.au/__data/assets/word_doc/0006/1977270/2.-TaxingCharitiesFINAL2.doc

Howe, B. and Howe, R. 2012. The influence of faith-based organisations on Australian social policy. *Australian Journal of Social Issues, 47*(3): 319–333.

Hughes, P., Black, A., Bellamy, J. and Kaldor, P. 2004. Identity and religion in contemporary Australia. *Australian Religion Studies Review, 17*(1).

Hughes, P. and Sims, M. 2009. The effectiveness of chaplaincy in government schools in Australia: Report to the National School Chaplaincy Association. Retrieved from https://schoolchaplaincy.org.au/wp-content/uploads/2012/09/chaplaincyeffectiveness.pdf

Jakubowicz, A. 2003. Hard shell and soft centre: Australia as a truly modern nation. *International Journal of Diversity in Organisations, Communities and Nations, 3*: 337–50.

Joint Standing Committee on Foreign Affairs Defence and Trade. 2000. *Conviction with compassion: a report on freedom of religion and belief.* Canberra: Parliament of Australia.

Joint Standing Committee on Foreign Affairs Defence and Trade. 2017. *Interim report: legal foundations of religion and belief.* Canberra: Parliament of Australia.

Joint Standing Committee on Foreign Affairs Defence and Trade. 2019. *Second interim report: legal foundations of religion and belief.* Canberra: Parliament of Australia.

Knight, P. and Gilchrist, D. 2014. *Australian Charities 2013: The first report on charities registered with the Australian Charities and Not-for-profits Commission.* Perth: Curtin University, https://business.curtin.edu.au/local/docs/Curtin-Australian-Charities-Report-2013.pdf, date accessed 4 October 2015.

Maddox, M. 2005. *God under Howard: The rise of the religious right in Australian politics.* Sydney: Allen & Unwin.

Maddox, M. 2009. An argument for more, not less, religion in Australian politics. *Australian Religion Studies Review, 22*(3): 345–367.

Maddox, M. 2014. *Taking God to school: the end of Australia's egalitarian education*? Sydney: Allen and Unwin.

Marler, P.L. and Hadaway, C.K. 2002. Being religious" or "being spiritual" in America: a zero-sum proposition? *Journal for the Scientific Study of Religion, 41*(2): 289–300.

Martin, D. 2005. *On secularization-towards a general revised theory.* Aldershot: Ashgate.

Martin, S. 2021. Coalition split over religious discrimination bill with MPs having 'serious concerns' over Folau clause. *The Guardian.* Retrieved from https://www.theguardian.com/australia-news/2021/nov/03/coalition-split-over-religious-discrimination-bill-with-one-mp-having-serious-concerns-over-folau-clause

Possamai, A. 2005. *In search of new age spirituality.* Aldershot: Ashgate.

Possamai, A. 2017. Post-secularism in multiple modernities. *Journal of Sociology,* 53(4): 822–835.

Possamai, A. and Possamai-Inesedy, A. 2009. Scientology down under. In Lewis, J. ed. *Scientology.* New York: Oxford University Press, pp. 345–361.

Possamai, A. and Possamai-Inesedy A. 2021. Freedom for and from religions in Australia. Beyond post-secularism? *Social Compass, 68*(3): 359–374.

Possamai-Inesedy, A. and Turner, B.S. 2016. Same Sex marriage and the Christian conservative reaction. In Goulet, J. G. ed. *Understanding and experiencing religious diversity in today's world.* Santa Barbara: Praeger, pp. 203–228.

Poulos, E. 2019. Constructing the problem of religious freedom: an analysis of Australian government inquiries into religious freedom. *Religions, 10*(10): 583.

Poynting, S. and Perry, B. 2007. Climates of hate: Media and state inspired victimisation of Muslims in Canada and Australia since 9/11. *Current Issues in Criminal Justice, 19*(2): 151–171.

Productivity Commission Research Report. 2010. *Contribution of the not-for-profit sector.* Canberra: Commonwealth of Australia.

Randell-Moon, H. 2009. Tolerating religious' others': some thoughts on secular neutrality and religious tolerance in Australia. *Australian Religion Studies Review, 22*(3): 324.

Richardson, J. 1999. New religions in Australia: Public menace or societal salvation? *Nova Religio: The Journal of Alternative and Emergent Religions,* 4(2): 258–265.

Richardson, J.T., 2013. Managing minority religious and ethnic groups in Australia: Implications for social cohesion. *Social Compass, 60*(4): 579–590.

Ruddock, P., Croucher, R., Bennett, A., Brennan, F. and Aroney, N. 2018. *Religious freedom review: report of the expert panel.* Canberra: Australian Government – Department of Prime Minister and Cabinet.

Sheen, J. 1996. Living within the tensions of plurality: religious discrimination and human rights law and policy. In Bouma, G. ed. *Many religions, all Australians: religious settlement, identity and cultural diversity.* Melbourne: Christian Research Association, pp. 163–180.

Stephens, S. (2010). The Prime Minister puts her faith in chaplaincy. *ABC News.* Retrieved from https://www.abc.net.au/news/2010-08-10/the-prime-minister-puts-her-faith-in-chaplaincy/938248

Tacey, D.J. 2000. *Reenchantment: the new Australian spirituality.* Sydney: Harper Collins.

Thielking, M. and Stokes, D. 2010. *Submission to the consultation process for the National School Chaplaincy Program.* Australian Psychological Society.

Tittensor, D., Hoffstaedter, G. and Possamai, A. 2020. Hyper-securitisation and belonging: understanding the plight of young Muslims in Melbourne, Australia. *Journal of Muslim Minority Affairs, 40*(3): 480–496.

Wuthnow, R. 2001. Spirituality and spiritual practice. In Fenn, R. ed. *The Blackwell companion to sociology of religion.* Oxford: Blackwell Publishing, pp. 306–320.

Index

Note: **bold** page numbers refer to tables.

CPSIA information can be obtained
at www.ICGtesting.com
Printed in the USA
LVHW081221130522
718653LV00005B/109

9 781032 186030